The New Acceleration

Artificial Intelligence and the Technologies Making Life Faster

by David Kerrigan

Preface

In 1999, Bill Gates, the world's richest man for most of the last 25 years, wrote a book called Business @ the Speed of Thought. For a long time, I thought that was probably as fast as you could aspire to, and way faster than most businesses were capable of. Yet just a decade and a half later, the speed of thought is no longer fast enough. Technology is pushing us to go much faster. The oft-quoted 1990s ambition of a computer on every desk and in every home has been totally usurped by the advent of a computer in every hand - truly information at your fingertips. But that paradigm too is about to be displaced.

What we have thus far called computers are changing, transforming both before our eyes and away from our gaze. They are evolving into pervasive tools that no longer remain siloed as our servants - now they can take over from us in many spheres. And as they change, we will be forced to change. Many people will struggle to keep up, and there are going to be many casualties along the way, both businesses and people left behind or swept aside. The new, faster world is not just about the speed of business. Faster technology is being driven by consumers and even Governments. Nobody will escape it.

When Business @ the Speed of Thought was published, Google was barely a year old, Amazon was 5 and Microsoft had saved Apple just two years earlier with a $150m investment. Now Amazon, Alphabet (Google's parent) and Apple are the 3 most valuable companies in the world and leading the next revolution - The New Acceleration.

Acknowledgements

My thanks firstly to family, and my friends - especially Marie, Sudha, Karolina, Louise, Johanna, Peter, Aideen, David, Caroline, Lorraine, Susan, Sylvia, Fergal, Ken, Roisin, Phelim, Sinead, Trish and Rob.

All extracts, figures and illustrations used are copyright their original creators.

Also by The Author

Your Phone Can Save Your Life (2015)
Life as a Passenger (2017)

Visit the Web Site

Colour versions of all illustrations, as well as links to all references and recommended resources are available at http://david-kerrigan.com

Contents

Acronym Guide

Lots of acronyms are used in the field of Artificial Intelligence....but thankfully you don't need to understand them to make sense of this book! Here's a list of them and there's also a short Glossary at the end of the book with brief definitions of key terms.

AI - Artificial Intelligence
AGI - Artificial General Intelligence
AMP - Accelerated Mobile Pages
ANI - Artificial Narrow Intelligence
ANPR - Automatic Number Plate Recognition
API - Application Programming Interface
ASR - Automatic Speech Recognition
AR - Augmented Reality
AV - Autonomous Vehicle
CNN - Convolutional Neural Networks
CPU - Central Processing Unit
CTC - Connectionist Temporal Classification
CV - Computer Vision
DARPA - Defense Advanced Research Projects Agency
DL - Deep Learning
DRS - Dash Replenishment Service
FPGA - Field Programmable Gate Array
GAN - Generative Adversarial Networks
GPU - Graphics Processing Unit
LDA - Latent Dirichlet Allocation
LSTM - Long Short Term Memory
ML - Machine Learning
MLP - Multilayer Perceptron
NLG - Natural Language Generation
NLP - Natural Language Processing
NLU - Natural Language Understanding
PWA - Progressive Web Apps
RL - Reinforcement Learning
RNN - Recurrent Neural Networks
TPU - Tensor Processing Unit
TTS - Text To Speech
UI - User Interface
VR - Virtual Reality

Chapter 1: The Next Wave of Technology - Hard & Fast

"If everything seems under control, you're not going fast enough."

Mario Andretti

Our relationship with technology has changed a lot in the last 25 years but it will change dramatically more in the next 25, and it may not all be for the better. Countless new technologies have already delivered a lot of benefits to society, but we're rapidly reaching a point where many people are beginning to wonder if it's time to reconsider our easy acceptance of technology in all walks of life. Whether viewed as invited or invading, technology is undeniably becoming pervasive. You may already think it could hardly become yet more commonplace but that's exactly what's happening. And your ability to regulate or determine the amount of technology you want in your life may be diminishing.

With the emergence of developments such as Artificial Intelligence (AI), the pace of change is accelerating and the reach of technology is broadening. Technology is rapidly achieving capabilities that just a few years ago were solidly in the realm of science fiction. As you'll see in this book, while we are probably still decades away from so-called artificial general intelligence, we are firmly already in the presence of highly capable artificial narrow intelligence, whether we realise it or not. Anyone with a smartphone has access to it, and anyone in a developed country has a Government already using it.

The Hard Wave

The history of technological developments has seen an increasing number of tasks becoming automated; human inputs being reduced as processes become mechanised or computerised. So far, this has largely related to repetitive tasks that have little variation and take place in controlled environments; e.g. robots on assembly lines in factories, or trains on closed circuits. To date, implementing these technologies as fast as possible when they become available has been the default and obvious response due to the clear benefits they offered in terms of productivity, reliability and/or cost reduction. Thus far, most technology deployment decisions have actually been fairly easy. Replacing back-breaking work in fields with mechanisation and intensification of agriculture may have destroyed direct jobs but it is clearly more efficient, and arguably required in order to meet growing demand for food. Over time we managed to create new jobs to replace those lost in agriculture even if there was hardship along the way; the greater good prevailed.

That easy era is rapidly coming to an end as technology encroaches into new realms. The coming decades will see repeated examples posing one of the most fundamental questions facing societies around the globe...how much of our lives and traditional activities do we delegate to technology as automation readies a move from a supporting role to a leading role? Technology has largely been quite consumer friendly, innocuously growing into our lives in a gradual way. But the scope of change now ahead requires awareness and active management - we need both new public policy decisions and new personal decisions as the range and capabilities of technology fundamentally shift, changing the equilibrium of society forever. Technology is approaching (or may already have reached) a point where laissez-faire and "hope it works out" is no longer enough. We now have, or are about to have, capabilities that challenge fundamental assumptions across society, not just those in distinct industrial silos. Make no mistake, it's going to be hard for many people to recognise, respond to and survive in this new era.

Objective

The aim of this book is to provide a look at what's changing as well as explain how we'll see these technologies move from the labs into our lives. What is making our lives ever faster and who is in control? I also want to pose questions about the implications of new technologies - from the obvious questions about the impact on jobs to the less apparent challenges facing civil liberties and social order. The next 9 chapters will hopefully provide a useful primer and equip you to critically assess what's happening and enable more informed decisions about what technologies you want or need to embrace and make you aware of technologies being adopted which could impact you, even without your active participation.

While I am overall positive about the current and impending developments, for example in areas such as healthcare as well as the general conveniences, we have to think about both the benefits and the consequences; we need to be aware of the trade-offs ahead. It may seem cliched but it's true and more apt than ever that technology itself is rarely inherently good or bad - how it's applied and by whom, with what motivation and oversight are the critical factors. I'm not advocating that you should necessarily always embrace new technologies - if you spend a couple of hours reading this book and simply reflect in an informed way on what role you want technology to play in your life and in society, then I'll consider the book to have served its purpose.

Avoiding Complexity

Many of the technologies under discussion here are complex and at the cutting edge of current human knowledge. They involve a lot of acronyms and concepts that are fully understood only by a limited number of experts. But understanding the potential impacts on individuals, corporations and society thankfully doesn't require you to be an engineer with a deep knowledge of software. I'll provide a high-level overview of the key technologies and concepts with some tangible real-world examples, but my aim is to provide an introduction and awareness rather than a complete explanation. I'll refer you to further materials for those keen to dig deeper.

Outline of Chapters

This chapter sets the scene and establishes the importance of taking time to consider what sort of future we want to shape with the amazing new tools that are emerging. Then, Chapter 2 looks at our existing relationship with technology - how we typically assess and embrace innovations - and highlights the dramatic developments that have accelerated the pace of life. We'll have a look at where we are today, how we got here and at some of the things we may not realise about our current relationship with technology. When seen laid out with timelines, it quickly becomes apparent that without even realising it, we are in the midst of accelerating change. Things are really speeding up, both the underlying speed of the technology itself and the experiences it enables. By assessing adoption in the last 10-20 years, we'll see how we got to now.

Chapter 3 looks at the importance of speed and how computing and connectivity advances have created a world hungry for more speed, an acceleration that is possible only with the next revolution in technology. Understanding the trajectory we're on will give context to the emergence of new developments and outline the exponential nature of progress.

Chapter 4 introduces the biggest technological advance in decades. The family of technologies known as AI underpins virtually all of the major technological challenges we face, promising radical breakthroughs or apocalyptic disaster depending on whom you believe. Without either boundless optimism or presumptions of doom, I want to take a measured look at this fascinating discipline. With a particular focus on the area of AI known as Machine Learning (ML), I want to guide you through a summary of this much talked about topic, to help you reach an informed opinion as we start to think about the areas that AI will revolutionise.

Chapter 5 explores the area of computer vision and the breakthrough capabilities in this sphere powered by recent ML advances. The implications of computers that can "see" are among the most significant you can imagine.

Chapter 6 continues to look at another area of computing that has long eluded engineers - computers that can listen, understand and speak; Voice Computing. Again, thanks to advances in ML, voice computing is now firmly in the realm of the possible after decades confined to the world of science fiction.

Taken together, Chapters 5 and 6 frame the question about how our relationship changes with computers when they can see, hear, talk and think. In a human analogy, computers are learning to understand the world around them, to listen to us, and talk to us, just like a growing child. Consider how different our relationship is with a toddler compared to a teenager - how we interact with them and what we expect of them is totally different, though separated only by about 10 years. Computers are no longer in their toddler years - just like humans, computers are growing up and putting years of learning into practice as they find their new place in the world - our world.

Having looked at the technologies of AI, Computer Vision and Voice Computing, we'll continue in Chapter 7 to look in depth at how these technologies are coming to life in one specific domain - Retail, and I'll also highlight other sectors facing seismic change.

In Chapter 8, we'll look at some more examples of AI in action and then explore the physical and virtual manifestations of the "new computers" by examining how the new technologies are driving changes in automation across industries.

Chapter 9 pauses to look at issues around ethics and equality. What will it mean as we face autonomy, not just automation - machines making decisions not just following our lead. While technology has brought many benefits, we have in recent years undoubtedly started to notice some negative impacts of it - overuse of devices, fake news, etc. The policies adopted by corporations as well as Governments, combined with how people respond, will determine whether we harness the power of these technologies more for the greater good or for the benefit of the few.

Chapter 10 concludes the discussion with a summary and some final questions to consider.

If you come away from reading the book with a desire to try some AI for yourself, I've listed some resources in Appendix A that let you download and experiment with Machine Learning Tools. Many powerful tools are available for free and are surprisingly accessible for those interested in gaining a rudimentary understanding of the technologies.

What's Not Included

There are of course plenty of other concomitant technologies to consider - as you'll see from the diagram in Chapter 2 about the innovation curve, at any time there are myriad technologies at various stages of development that may or may not become important. Either on their own or combined with another technology in some not-yet-obvious way, any of these technologies, even ones that don't yet attract much attention, may surprise us. But in order to keep the scope of this volume manageable, we will largely ignore other hot topics of the moment like Augmented Reality (AR), Virtual Reality (VR), Blockchain and Internet of Things (IOT). That's not to say these aren't important but I don't believe their impact will be as dramatic as that of AI technologies, though in many cases, so-called AI technologies will be used in combination with other emerging technologies to create innovative advances and experiences.

It's also worth pointing out that many of the topics raised in this book could easily fill an entire volume of their own and still not be comprehensive - this is very much intended as an overview and introduction to get you up to speed by creating an awareness and suggesting areas to think about.

What's It To You?

As I've said, we are on the cusp of a new "harder" era as technology is moving into new areas. Our relationship with technology will change and our relationships with each other may change too. As a society, we're not well equipped for this - we have little in the way of precedent to draw on, we have little experience of such concentrations of power in the hands of a few large corporations and face a very real risk of disenfranchisement of many. If that sounds dramatic, it is meant to. If you choose not to pause and consider your attitude to technology, you risk seeing a future where technology is no longer beholden to us and it becomes a force for oppression rather than good.

Words like revolutionary, disruptive and game-changing are thrown around all too frequently as new technologies emerge. And while the glut of new technologies in recent decades undoubtedly includes many interesting ones, in general most are evolutionary or incremental rather than being truly epoch-defining. That's not the case with AI. It genuinely merits the use of the terms like revolutionary. It's important when examining this level of change to reset expectations and to focus on the big picture - thinking with a timeframe measured in years or even a decade rather than the more immediate, more certain challenges we're used to considering. It's simpler to deal with shorter, more certain time frames that make for easier understanding, analysis and commentary but this approach doesn't serve us well when facing change of this magnitude. Judging AI based on where it is today might lead you to conclude you've nothing to worry about - but as you'll see in Chapter 3, the exponential nature of progress means what we'll see in just a few years will be far more potent that what we have today.

Change on this scale is bound to be highly complex and contentious, even if it doesn't seem massively urgent. Such has been the pace of change in recent decades that we can be slightly blasé about it all - putting us at risk of missing a truly significant change. When you're in the midst of daily life, this may all seem abstract, hypothetical or irrelevant (for now at least). But if you just dropped your kids to school driving your own car and then continued to your workplace in your car before parking it for the rest of the day, remember that according to the World Economic Forum in 2016[1] some 65 percent of those kids will leave school to a job that doesn't yet exist. Even if technologies like self-driving cars don't arrive and change your daily routine, that may not be the whole story: instead of facing their classmates or offshore facilities competing for jobs, your kids may find a robot or an algorithm where they expected to sit.

Busy people living busy lives don't tend to think much about big issues they perceive to be far in the future. But the kinds of issues we face in the coming decades really need thought and debate on a wider societal level, or we may end up with a result we don't much like. Is technology creating the kind of future you want? Have you thought about it? Technology is almost always double-edged. The day stone tools were invented we could chop wood but axe murder also became possible. There is often a sense that as an individual you have no influence on the future of these technologies and related

---

[1] http://www3.weforum.org/docs/Media/WEF_FutureofJobs.pdf

policies. But of course, if everyone thinks that way it very quickly becomes a self-fulfilling prophecy. There is still time to influence the shape of regulation and policy, but as discussed in Chapter 9, regulations are being considered right now that will have a long-term impact.

In a world of sound bites, quick wins and instant gratification, we rarely stop to consider complex issues in any depth. Although at first glance, AI may seem like just another cool technology, it may in fact be one of the most profound change-enablers in human history, with far-reaching implications. Modern politics has created a culture of short termism that's ill-equipped to tackle big issues proactively. And on an international scale, challenges like peace, health, poverty and global warming may seem of more immediate import than AI but I think it's important to urgently extend the debate to a wide audience. AI may hold the key to tackling many of the world's largest, most intractable challenges.

Much of the commentary on this topic to date has been quite extreme - from advocates saying it's nearly ready, to doubters claiming it's more like 30 years away, to opponents saying it'll never work or shouldn't be allowed. I believe it's important to look rationally at the challenges and opportunities facing us - there aren't yet always simple facts to base our decisions on, with much ignorance, speculation or extrapolation muddying the debate. But if we don't at least start to think about it, start to ask questions and consider consequences, we risk either delaying benefits or arriving unaware at undesirable outcomes.

The issues in this book raise larger questions about how we as a society deal with massive change. Who are the leaders - the politicians, the technologists, the regulators? Who is involved or even aware? Who sets the agenda? Can regulators keep up? Who are the lobby groups and how transparent is lobbying activity? Will there be a disconnect between consumers and governments? Will governments push for AI in the search for efficiency and greater law and order, or will they be too wary of the potential for unpopular job losses and accusations of invasion of privacy? This book aims to suggest a wider and more thoughtful assessment of the issues that will shape the world for us and for our children.

Somewhat predictably, the negative response to AI developments from commentators, both amateur and professional, has been swift and scathing. There seems to be an ever-increasing number of people who revel in criticising the efforts of others, believing that pointing out flaws somehow makes them seem clever. Is it a significant new technology or another pointless Silicon Valley indulgence tackling first world problems created in a bubble, coming hot on the heels of the Juicero[2] debacle, while there are real world problems left untackled? Is Silicon Valley more interested in revenues or ethics?

History tells us that to criticise a brand-new technology in its first iteration is naive if not outright stupid. If nothing else, this for me emphasizes how we urgently need to re-look at how we evaluate innovation in the hard wave. We need to reset our expectations around the timelines to develop new technologies, the pivots along the way, the setbacks and the dead ends. We also need to start debating the impacts of technology in a pragmatic manner; knee-jerk negativity as a default position does nobody any favours, while blind technophiles would do well to consider toning down their hyperbolic claims and set aside their focus on progress at any price. Let's not mistake mere change for progress.

Finding Their Fit

As you think about how technologies may be applied, remember to think in broad terms - inventions do not always find success related to their originally intended purpose. AI will likely end up delivering solutions we haven't imagined. Viagra was intended to treat heart and blood pressure issues, just as Slinky and Play-Doh were never intended as toys. Inventors are often not the ones who successfully bring a technology to market - they are frequently too focused on fitting the technology to their original vision and profit goals, regardless of its actual suitability. Sometimes they just don't see the potential for their own creations: the pioneer of wireless technology, Martin Cooper, predicted that wireless communications would not replace wired. There's the infamous IBM quote about there being a worldwide market for about 5 computers. The high-end video cards

---

[2] https://www.theverge.com/2017/9/1/16243356/juicero-shut-down-lay-off-refund

developed by the likes of NVidia for gaming turn out to be ideally suited to Machine Learning tasks. They are now hugely in demand and being deployed in their thousands in data centres.

In the Hard Wave, innovation is expensive. Spending on R&D is the new arms race among the world's largest companies. Alphabet, Amazon and Microsoft each spent over $12bn on R&D in 2016. Each has created special divisions focused on "secret" projects: Google has both ATAP (for projects with a 2-year timeline) and X (for moonshot projects that may take many years to tackle big problems), Amazon's Lab126 employs over 3,000 people and Microsoft has seven Research sites around the world. Although the payback for a successful breakthrough may be huge, investment in innovation is not always about immediate or even near-term commercial success - it may be used to attract top quality researchers to a company or simply to make a brand statement.

Even in what's seen as a fast-moving space such as technology, it can sometimes take a decade before a major technological breakthrough starts to show results in terms of impacts and revenues. Commentator Om Malik cites Amazon's launch of Amazon Web Services (its cloud computing operation) in 2006: Back then, he says, *"there weren't very many of us who had an idea that it would one day become the key component of an economic engine that would jump-start entrepreneurial activity across the planet."*[3]

Constructive Criticism

Proponents of some of the more way-out technologies can hide behind Einstein's adage that *"For an idea that does not first seem insane, there is no hope."* Though there is some element of truth to it, it can be abused to rationalise truly dumb innovations. While failure may be worn as a badge of honour in Silicon Valley, I'm not advocating investing in obviously silly ideas just for the sake of it. But it seems inevitable that we will continue to see massive investments in AI and related fields and these will take place under intense scrutiny.

---

[3] https://www.theguardian.com/technology/2014/jan/05/lost-year-new-technology-2013-gadgets

Yet so much media commentary about – and public perceptions of – technology tends to miss the point. Much of the time what matters is not the gadget in question but the underlying technology that makes it possible. Be wary of seemingly considered-looking criticism that may well be born of a subtly-lobbying vested interest, threatened by the technological direction.

As you consider the rise of AI, it can be hard to get a true sense of what's going on. It's a complex technology, replete with seemingly endless acronyms, and it's emerging at a time of tension between the media and reporting on companies the same media see as killing them. This and the desire to simplify or sensationalise developments means that it's hard to have a balanced debate on the true merits of the technologies. To be clear, I'm not advocating that people don't point out flaws or gaps where they exist, nor that we aren't entitled to hold companies to account when they ask us to invest in their offerings. Innovators should be expecting a challenging conversation when they try to find a place in the world for their creations - but they should be granted a dialog, not an instant put-down. It is easy for commentators, be they professional or amateur, to deride. In the face of some of the ludicrous claims, a degree of cynical reaction is often justified. But revelling in (or anticipating) failure from a position of safety does not make you look smart, nor does judging a new technology too harshly in its first iteration.

Silicon Valley commentator Ben Evans has written extensively about the perception of Innovation[4]. As he puts it, much commentary can resemble a sort of Schrodinger's Startup - simultaneously labelling a development as trivial nonsense that'll never work and an evil threat to civilisation: *"For as long as people have been creating technology, people have been saying it'll never amount to anything. As we create more and more...the urge to dismiss seems only to get stronger, and so does the urge to defend".*

Who Knows Best?

As we develop these powerful new capabilities, there will be much

---

[4] http://ben-evans.com/benedictevans/2017/5/24/not-even-wrong-ways-to-dismiss-technology

change, and many questions about how best to proceed. This will create considerable tension as established orders are challenged and significant reskilling is required. It's a bigger shift than previously experienced and a challenge to government, business, individuals and society. Such is its importance that we can't leave it solely to the proponents of technology, nor can we risk the naysayers preventing progress.

Already parents aren't in a position to advise children on career choices - many of the jobs which parents would have considered attractive for themselves are fading into obsolescence but they don't understand what skills will likely best serve the next generation. Business leaders too may not understand what steps to take - many think they've relevant experience and have "seen it before" but this shift is happening fast and touches the untouchables. Although the IT industry may have cried wolf too many times, AI is not wearing sheep's clothing. The biggest mistake we can make in assessing AI is applying assumptions from the last generation of computing to plan for the next one.

Perils of Predicting

"Your intuition about things you don't know much about isn't very good. I don't think we're doing a good job as a society deciding what things are really important to do."

Larry Page, co-founder Google

Nothing in society beyond the most trivial can be precisely predicted. Technology is at a point of sophistication where its impacts on society are significantly beyond isolated improvements or even predictable improvements. On the other hand, it is not the case that it is hopeless to try to anticipate things to come. Intuition, research and debate can help to identify possible and likely futures. Even though the future cannot be predicted (and certainly no prediction of the future, no matter how eminent the source, should be uncritically "believed"), there are theories and methods that futurists have developed, tested, and applied in recent years which have proven useful. "Preferred futures" can and should be envisioned, invented, implemented, continuously evaluated, revised, and re-envisioned. It is also important to remember that any radical idea about the future may appear at first to be ridiculous, but it's important not to let that initial response become our definite opinion. Because new technologies permit new behaviours and values, challenging old beliefs and values which are based on prior technologies, much that will be characteristic of the future is initially novel and challenging. It can typically seem at first impossible, stupid, "science fiction", or ridiculous. And then it becomes familiar and, eventually, "normal."

Here's a sample of some of the very bad predictions regarding technology that have been made over the years[5]:

Year	Prediction
1800	High Speed Rail Travel is not possible because passengers, unable to breathe, would die of asphyxia
1902	Flight by machines heavier than air is unpractical and insignificant, if not utterly impossible
1903	The horse is here to stay, but the automobile is only a novelty, a fad
1927	"Who the hell wants to hear actors talk"?
1946	Television won't last because people will soon get tired of staring at a plywood box
1977	There is no reason for any individual to have a computer in his home
1995	The truth is no online database will replace your daily newspaper

Figure 1: Bad Predictions

A Complex Future

Regardless of how exactly and when AI impacts the world, we know for sure we won't continue to exist for long in the "normality" we know today. Two of the biggest dangers of trying to imagine the future are 1. assuming linear progression and 2. assuming too much too soon or too little too long. In researching the topic, I found a perhaps predictable amount of debate and disagreement among experts and

---

[5] https://twitter.com/galka_max/status/965092080883261440?s=09

13

commentators. Assessing things only against what we know in a world built on current capabilities, we may miss something important. Using existing thinking to assess new developments is notoriously fallible. Technology is once again posing questions that challenge both society and individuals to make difficult decisions that weigh potentially very sizeable benefits against lifestyle and political/socio-economic upheaval. I for one believe it would be a shame not to try to find the best way to harness the potential of AI, but to miss out on its benefits through ignorance would be a tragedy, just as failing to understand and plan for the negative consequences would be too.

Deciding What We Want

"Nobody knows the future. The future is not set. There is no fate but what we make for ourselves"

John Connor, Terminator T2

Just because we can automate something, should we? So far, it's been fairly easy to decide but as the value of the activity being replaced increases, it needs more consideration. People will need time to get used to AI - just like any technology, it will face a hype curve and an adoption curve as it matures. It will face incident, accident and attack from vested interests as it tries to find its place in our world. As Henry Ford once said, *"if you'd asked people what they wanted, they would have asked for faster horses"*. You can't reliably predict reaction to a completely different technology than what you're familiar with. Asking people their views about AI in simplistic surveys at this point does a disservice to the complexity of the issue, and sidesteps the fact that much remains to be determined to make the technology practical, let alone viable.

As you'll see in the coming chapters, we may need to rethink our understanding of the word computer in order to have a meaningful debate about the future. We'll need to understand the strengths and weaknesses of the technology, its dependence on data, its potential for abuse and the ethical questions about how might it be used and how would we like it to be used. Let's look next at how we've tackled technology to date and how we might prepare for the next revolution.

Chapter 2: How We Got to Now (and what you may have missed on the way)

If you fell into a coma in 1988 and awoke in 2018, you'd notice immediately that those 30 years would have brought huge technology-driven change. Though some areas probably would appear very familiar, the proliferation of the Internet, and Mobile technology would amaze. You'd be hard pressed to find businesses that didn't have an email address or a web site. There'd be electric Tesla cars creeping past with an eerie silence and TVs that hang on walls. Laptop computers thinner than a pen but boasting more power than a supercomputer. You'd never have seen a Kindle, a laptop, an iPad, a smartphone, an Amazon Echo, a Fitbit, a Bluetooth headset, a Wi-Fi connection, contactless payments, a digital camera, let alone virtual reality, Netflix or Spotify. Some commentators have christened this rise of technology as the fourth industrial revolution. But without the benefit of a 30-year perspective, it may be a more helpful approach to remember that we can't always see the forest for the trees, and for all the visible technological changes in our lives, there are also unseen ones powering the progress - advances in databases, servers, networking and countless others that we depend on without realising.

Less Visible

The visible year on year changes between phones have now slowed from the earlier specifications race with a plateau in things like the number of megapixels. But in fact, the pace of change is accelerating with the race to imbue the devices with AI smarts. The shift to a device that can always listen for a wake word, identify what it's looking at and manage its battery with AI is more progress than the move from 4 to 8-megapixel cameras. But the visibility of change, the technical nature of it and the relatively gradual rollout can catch us off guard. When we refer to the Industrial Revolution we often forget it covers a period of decades, triggered by specific inventions. Those who lived through it didn't immediately identify it as a historical turning point as we now do.

Waves of Innovation

Depending on your point of view, technologies have either connected and informed the world, creating unprecedented wealth and opportunities atop their platforms, or have wreaked havoc on retail, journalism and media. Although the daily deluge of bad news can often make it easy to forget, the world is unequivocally getting better - despite the remaining inequalities, child mortality and the number of people living in poverty is at its lowest level ever, while life expectancy is higher than ever. (Hans Rosling's book *Factfulness* provides a very helpful framework for assessing the true state of the modern world.)

Since the 1700s, there have already been several technology-led waves of change. Each of the last few centuries has been marked by standout technological advances that have dramatically changed how we live. Though marked by regional inequalities and disparities, the world is demonstrably a better place than at any time in our history. Each advance was more technically challenging than its predecessor, but despite that, the pace of innovation is accelerating as shown in the following table recapping past revolutions:

Late 18th -19th	Steam Power, Canals, Textile Automation
Mid 19th	Railroads, Telegraph, Agriculture
Late 19th- Early 20th	Electricity, IC Engine, Aviation, Mass Production, Automobiles
Mid 20th:	Pharmaceuticals, TV, Computers, Space Exploration
Late 20th – Early 21st	Internet, Genetics, Robotics, AI

My intention is not to exhaustively go through every technology wave that's ever occurred, but to provide some context - it's worth reflecting briefly on the massive progress that has brought us to this point. The path governing the adoption of innovation never runs smoothly - it is inextricably linked with deviations, natural events and even luck. During the last 300 years or so since the first industrial revolution there were any number of wars, epidemics and economic events at the macro level, that influenced but never stopped the great waves of innovation. Similarly, I believe that the growth of AI will continue in the coming decades despite any temporary setbacks.

Technologies tend to follow a pattern and we'll talk about that more in just a minute, but the exact route and duration from invention to dispersion to economic impact is hard to predict. The creations of the last couple of centuries have delivered a spectacular change in the quality of life of most people on Earth. As measured by real GDP per capita, average Americans are about eight times better off than their ancestors of just 100 years ago[6].

Figure 2: We now expect free, instant access to any information

In the next wave of innovation, we will see that technology is permeating more and more parts of our lives. More devices come with sensors, connections and screens. We take for granted the fraction of a second Google takes to return results. It even shows us what fraction of a second it took on the results screen, but we ignore it in our haste to click on the desired link. If you actually think about what's happening when we enter a search query, it's amazing that it can happen so fast. Yet, we are utterly unforgiving of delays. Amidst the

---

[6] http://www.libertylawsite.org/2018/06/04/the-great-waves-of-industrial-innovation/

emphasis on speed, it's all too easy to forget what's actually happening and not question the cost of convenience - what will this wave of innovation sweep away?

Back to the Future

"The only constant is change"

Heraclitus

History tells us that all large innovations—whether cars, carriages, canals or cables—have involved great uncertainty. Innovation invites speculation. But our individual ability to influence its direction is interesting. The only certainty is that these technologies will continue to develop - how we choose to use them, and when, is the only open question. The automation genie cannot be put back in the bottle but some of its course can still be controlled and regulated. Just because things have been a certain way for 100 years doesn't mean they should stay that way; nor does the possibility of a new approach mean it's necessarily the correct and immediate way forward. There probably needs to be a balance between the opposite views of "always been this way" vs techno-utopianism.

In 2018, Google CEO Sundar Pichai compared AI to electricity in terms of the importance of its invention and the scale of its impact. That's quite a big claim, but it's also instructive as electricity wasn't an overnight success. It struggled initially to displace the dominant industrial power source, steam. Changes to manufacturing took time. Factories needed to be redesigned to gain maximum benefit from the new technologies. Simply slotting electric motors in to replace steam engines was selling the new technology short. Electric motors could be smaller than steam engines and still be efficient, meaning they could be located differently than their predecessors - steam-powered factories had to be arranged on the logic of the driveshaft. Electricity meant you could organise factories on the logic of a production line. Factory owners hesitated, for understandable reasons.

Likewise, when computers were first introduced, the benefits of insertion into existing processes was limited. By 2000 - about 50 years after the first computer program - productivity was picking up a bit. Two economists, Erik Brynjolfsson and Lorin Hitt, published research[7] showing that many companies had invested in computers for little or no reward while others had reaped big benefits. What explained the difference was whether the companies had been willing to reorganise to take advantage of what computers had to offer. I fully envisage a repeat of this phenomenon as companies struggle to grasp the changes required to truly integrate AI into their operations.

The Pattern

The public perception of, and rate of adoption of, new technologies is well studied. There are 3 curves I find useful to explain how we perceive new technologies as they mature, how they are adopted and how we transition from one set of technologies to the next. We'll look at them in isolation first and then how they can be overlaid to form a more complete view.

- The Hype Cycle
- The Adoption Curve
- S-curves

Together these help frame the debate for the following chapters and are useful tools for a better understanding of technology and our attitudes towards it.

The Hype Cycle

The stages of reaction that an emerging technology goes through are so well known that they have been encapsulated into a simple line chart. Yet media coverage routinely ignores this and reliably moves through the stages when reporting as if they were a surprise, proclaiming the peaks and troughs in sensationalist hyperbole instead of an expected progression.

The following illustration shows the latest annual Gartner Hype Cycle chart (as at August 2018), showing a range of technologies and how

---

[7] http://ebusiness.mit.edu/erik/Beyond%20Computation%20-%20JEP.pdf

they are currently perceived. Some pundits believe that for some AI, we are nearing the infamous "Peak of Inflated Expectations" (see below), and a long let-down is ahead before the technology eventually meets our expectations which, you'll note, don't reach the lofty heights of the peak phase.

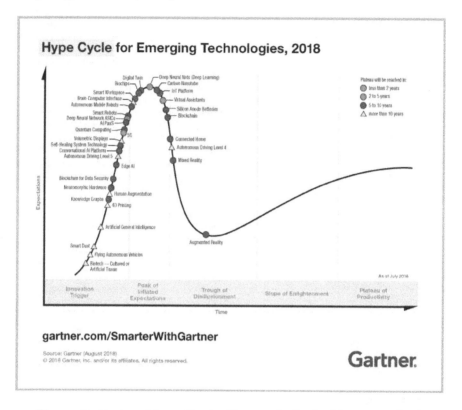

Figure 3: Gartner Hype Cycle (See website for hi-res version)

As each new technology emerges, its proponents and those looking for a story will generally over-exaggerate its potential, leading to an entirely predictable resetting of expectations and then a gradual acknowledgement of its true impact, devoid of the hype and shiny newness factors. Finally, a technology reaches a "normal" state where we no longer perceive it to be anything special.

The Adoption Curve

If the Gartner curve deals with the perception of technologies from a primarily business perspective, the stages of adoption, but from a more consumer segmentation point of view, can also be succinctly summarised in a chart:

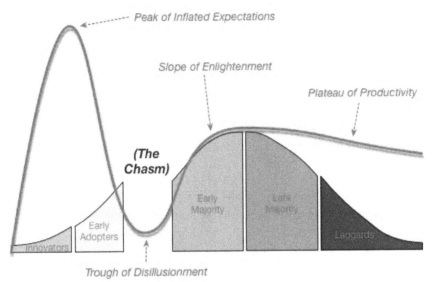

Figure 4: The Adoption Curve

Starting out on the left, only a very small segment of tech-aware people even knows about the emerging technology, before a group of early adopters start to experiment with it. There then follows a gap before the technology matures sufficiently to be of interest and use to the early majority. After they've popularised it and socialised it, demonstrating its benefits, the next cohort gradually adopt it before finally it reaches the laggards - the people with the least interest and means to adopt new technology.

Crucial to these charts is the scale or the speed at which products move along. However, in business and government spheres the second chart (the adoption curve) may no longer apply - the scale at which technology is being deployed and the impact it can have on a population from a central decision may render this chart obsolete as something like AI gets deployed on such a large scale as to immediately influence the entire population. While there are certainly technology, infrastructure, political and social challenges to face, the sheer weight of investment in the AI space is overwhelming. Many of the brightest minds in academia and industry, backed by almost unlimited quantities of capital, are pushing AI technologies forward with great haste, but against a still uncertain timetable. Governments have gotten involved, with China signalling its intent to be a global AI superpower.

As Evans[8] comments, *"there is a point in the cycle of all technologies where pointing out where it will inevitably lead is a route to certain ridicule. For close to a decade, suggesting that essentially everyone on earth would have a mobile was lunacy. Now, with 5 billion phones, it's boring and obvious. Plotting out what effects fully autonomous cars would have, one should assume they'll change things as much as *cars* changed things. The really big innovations don't get x% of y, they change what y is. You couldn't (wouldn't/shouldn't) model cars from horses, jets from liners, PCs from typewriters, mobiles from landlines, rideshare from cabs or AV from cars."*

It is also worth pointing out that these topics do not operate in isolation and the parallel development of many other technologies will also shape our future landscape - for example, many commentators believe that 3D printing may see the term "factory" redefined and lead to mass layoffs in manufacturing. There are also many more anticipated developments in communications, materials sciences and energy production, not to mention healthcare and even forms of transport other than autonomous vehicles, up to and including the mythical flying car (which has recently started to seem less mythical with demonstrations from companies such as Kitty Hawk, Lilium[9] and Uber,[10] among others).

---

[8] https://twitter.com/BenedictEvans/status/771115479393906688
[9] https://lilium.com/
[10] https://www.uber.com/info/elevate/

The Adoption Duration

The length of time a technology or product takes to cross the chasm and reach the late majority varies, but as you can see from the graph below, the number of years elapsing between the introduction of a technology and it reaching a substantial percentage of the population is decreasing rapidly.

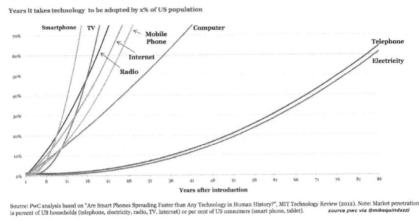

Figure 5: Years to widespread adoption

For example, the telephone took 76 years to reach half of the homes in the US; smartphones less than 10. Of course, some items are obviously slower - an upgrade to an expensive household purchase rather than an individual purchase or - in the case of social networks - a free product that can be adopted anywhere anytime on virtually any device (computer, phone, tablet, etc) at no cost. That's not to take away from the speed of their rise, just to put some context on it that it's hard to compare across products and services and ones limited by physical factors such as size and distribution.

You can build your own graph at the Our World in Data web site[11] if you'd like to compare particular technologies and see how quickly they were adopted.

---

[11]   https://ourworldindata.org/grapher/technology-adoption-by-households-in-the-united-states

The S-Curve

The final curve I want to introduce here is the S-Curve. The purpose of this curve is to illustrate how the pace of change for a particular technology varies during its lifespan. In some cases, it is - as we mentioned about the visibly slowing pace of megapixel upgrades in phone cameras for example. Yet this slow-down is to be expected based on the S-Curve model. This approach helps explain the transition between waves of technologies - how we move from one era to the next. It also clarifies how the pace of an individual technology changes during its lifetime.

As explained by Ben Evans[12]:
While the excitement around a new technology can reach fever pitch, a technology often produces its best results just when it's ready to be replaced - it's the best it's ever been, but it's also the best it could ever be. There's no room for more optimisation - the technology has run its course and it's time for something new, and any further attempts at optimisation produce something that doesn't make much sense.

The development of technologies tends to follow an S-Curve: they improve slowly, then quickly, and then slowly again. And at that last stage, they're really, really good. Everything has been optimised and worked out and understood, and they're fast, cheap and reliable. That's also often the point that a new architecture comes to replace them. You can see this very clearly today in devices such as Apple's new MacBook or Windows 'Ultrabooks' - they've taken Intel's x86 and the mouse and window-based GUI model as far as they can go, and reached the point that everything possible has been optimised.

---

[12] http://ben-evans.com/benedictevans/2016/4/20/the-best-is-the-last

The 'S' Curve model explains how innovations start slow, accelerate, then hit a ceiling requiring companies to jump to a new technology

THE 'S' CURVE

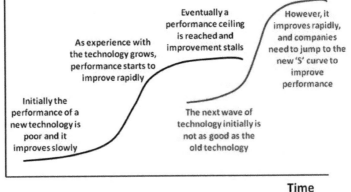

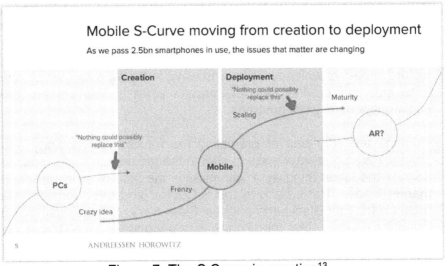

Figure 6: The S Curve in theory

Figure 7: The S Curve in practice[13]

[13] https://twitter.com/BenedictEvans/status/904204619798085638?s=09

The Invisible Revolution

"The next big innovation will happen at the intersection of AI, Software and Hardware"

Rick Osterloh, SVP Google Hardware

As mentioned earlier, one of the key attributes of the current wave of innovations in technology is the lack of visibility of many of the changes. The shiny smartphones that have become so pervasive, have clearly hit a hardware development plateau compared to the obvious rapid annual advances of years gone by. But the focus now has shifted to imbuing them with AI smarts as their physical form reaches the top of the S-curve while their capabilities continue to expand. After decades of wondering how and when AI might arrive, it seems it'll simply be appearing straight into our hands, without many people even realising. This lack of visibility will make it difficult for many people to form an opinion and preference about the future.

As many of the most powerful changes are harder to see, it's more difficult to understand for those outside the technology sector. It's a tough balance, understanding enough tech to make a decision without getting sucked in too deep, into the kinds of platform wars (e.g. iOS vs Android or Windows vs Mac) that distract from the big picture impact of whichever platform wins. In the long run, which one wins may not be the key relevance - what is relevant are the consequences of what emerges.

Humans are very bad at predicting the future of technology and changes are not always easy to spot in the moment. It's very easy to dismiss the latest thing as a "gimmick" in the face of an established market leader. Think back to the S-Curves and then consider the recent history for Blackberry phones. Blackberry unit sales carried on rising for 4 years after the iPhone was announced in 2007 but the arrival of the Apple device was the beginning of the end for Blackberry handsets in the mass market four years later[14].

---

[14] https://twitter.com/BenedictEvans/status/886092937213296642?s=09

Blackberry unit shipments (m)

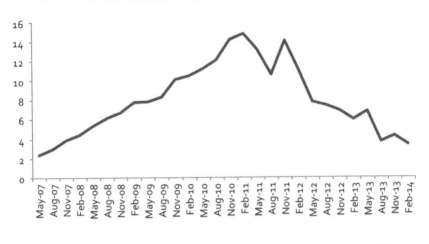

Figure 8: Blackberry sales grew for 4 years after the June 2007 launch of the iPhone

Everything can feel fine for long after the strategic problem arrives - long enough to think the people worrying about it are proved wrong. Yes, there's a healthy cynicism required but there's also a danger of denial, a desire to believe that everything is ok - and an ability to cherry pick data and interpretations to fit the easier belief. I strongly believe that those not taking an interest in AI are like the phone makers who rubbished Apple's entry into the market.

As useful as the curves and charts are, the study of emerging technologies and their adoption often tends to overlook one important point - the reasons for the successful, widespread adoption of some, and the failure of others. As technology moves into new realms, thanks to AI that we'll see in the next chapters, it's worth keeping in mind if these visual frameworks will continue to apply. I suspect that the fact that much AI is invisible to end users will make tracking its progress on these graphs quite challenging.

Our Relationship with Technology

"We used to talk about being 'computer literate', and that meant knowing how to use a mouse or save a file. Today editing video on your pocket computer is banal, but maybe that 'computer literacy' now also means knowing how Facebook makes money, or what machine learning is. That is, maybe tech has become big enough that 'knowing how it works' means not just using the product but knowing where it comes from and how it was created"

Ben Evans[15]

For generations, the decision to adopt a piece of technology has gone no deeper than believing that it will carry out its intended automated function, be it to wash clothes or dispense cash. But as you'll see, we're now contemplating machines that can talk back to us, can listen to us and can take on tasks on our behalf or even defeat us at games. In the brave new world, our technology will have a name and it will know our name. In a twist of irony, the more technologically-savvy may be the least likely to adopt these technologies, more aware and afraid of their invasiveness and believing they command too high a privacy price for the convenience benefits.

Fear of technology is not new - there have, of course, always been people talking about both the salvational qualities and the doom side of technologies. I believe that our relationship with technology is now at an inflection point. The easy changes are made; the hard ones are next - harder to see, harder to understand, harder to control. Technology is going to encroach into areas previously unassailable. And we may not like it. Tech is often accused of living in a bubble - but it is going to break out of its bubble in the coming years to the point where its influence is unavoidable and its impacts on society both good and bad will be of epochal importance. Invisible, passive use of technology is only just beginning and it's not just our relationship with the technology, it's our relationship with the future.

---

[15] https://twitter.com/BenedictEvans/status/986158936578441216?s=09

Cui Bono

As you read the descriptions of new technologies in this book and elsewhere, I strongly recommend you stop to consider the agenda of those involved. It's frequently hard to find the truth between the rose-tinted, self-serving hyperbole of the purveyors of technology, and the negative narratives supported by entrenched interests and media companies themselves threatened by the online giants.

We need to be sceptical of the utopian promises of techno-supporters with their seemingly endless pursuit of speed, based on the buzzwords of the day - disruption, AI, Big Data. No wonder hard-pressed executives struggle to take it seriously and filter the real challenges from the marketing promises attached to each new or resurrected technology idea. But that's not to say there's no truth in the vision on offer. When seismic change does happen, it can take a few years to become clear. The blackberry/iPhone graph above shows the danger of assuming everything is ok, based on indicators. Things change quickly, but as for the frog in boiling water, just not instantly. There's a term in economics called "Intertemporal choice" which describes how an individual's current decisions affect what options become available in the future. With AI, we need to be aware of the future implications of the choices we make today, and of the choices we don't make too.

Chapter 3: The Need for Speed

"A basic function of the great acceleration is that is makes life speedier, and the demands on our time more intense. This panders to some of our most basic biological cravings, but it a way that is more usually invigoration than ruinous. What we need is not to slow things down, but to develop the right strategies to cope."

John Robert McNeill, The Great Acceleration

The speed the earth rotates at changes by tiny amounts - just 2.3 milliseconds every hundred years or so. But while our planet keeps a pretty consistent speed, those of us on it are living life faster than ever, with no sign of slowing down. The assertion that things are speeding up will sound right to some, but to others, they will perhaps require to be convinced. From speed dating to microwave cooking to same day delivery to binge watching, speed is an unavoidable theme of modern life. As we demand instant gratification in more facets of life, technology is both enabling and fuelling this phenomenon.

Inevitably, this acceleration will lead to a point where we start to lose control of technology and we are fast approaching that tipping point in our relationship with it. After decades of fairly obvious/linear developments, we've reached a point that challenges us as much as it supports or enhances us. After decades of anthropomorphic science fiction, our real life automated and automating companions are entering a new paradigm, replete with senses and autonomy - something they've lacked to date. Technology is moving rapidly into new realms: new and threatening realms.

Time Matters

"Until we can manage time, we can manage nothing else"

Peter Drucker

There are lots of things where speed is crucial; the Golden Hour after an accident or the thousandth of a second that decides a race. Even when we can't see or perceive it, the extremes of time matter - a super slo-mo or time-lapse video can change our perspective and let us see things we don't see in real time. For consumers, many of today's gadgets are all about speed and saving time - decades after washing machines, we have robotic vacuums and lawn mowers to save even more time from household chores. For business too, it's about speed and time - businesses that can't respond quickly to consumers desire for speedy, high quality, affordable personal service will fail.

As life gets faster, we change as people - we are harder workers, shorter sleepers, and faster thinkers. We expect the world to offer us what we want, when we want it. Time is our most scarce resource, that is never recyclable but eminently waste-able. Our time is a zero-sum game that spent on Netflix can't be re-spent with kids or on newspapers. Even our movies are faster than before - the average length of a shot has declined from around 10 seconds in the 1930s and 1940s to less than 4 seconds now[16].

Fast and New isn't always better

"It is a mistake to think that moving fast is the same as actually going somewhere."

Steve Goodier

But before we dive into more talk of speed, a word of caution. Speed isn't always without its cost. Attempts to multi-task usually end in sub-optimal performance of each task. In many fields, there is a law of diminishing returns, where faster performance can compromise the

---

[16] James E Cutting - 2011 iPerception

output - for example the news cycle has gone from professional writers and video crews working to edition deadlines to live video from amateur camera phones, compromising the accuracy but giving us a sense of urgency and involvement - instantaneity is the name of the game, even if the end product is of inferior quality.

The current obsession with newness makes little sense in the bigger picture. If you're interested in a topic, the best article or book you could read was very unlikely to have been published in the last 48 hours. Yet our connected lifestyle treats anything that isn't new as if it were instantly obsolete and demotes it in our timelines. We promote the novel in lieu of the worthwhile and fail to reward creators for investing in things of lasting value. While new articles may offer a fresh perspective, or relate to a genuinely new insight, our obsession with chronologically arranged feeds forgets that in many fields 'best' and 'newest' rarely overlap. Ironically, many of the core concepts of the technologies we'll discuss in the next chapter are over 50 years old in origin.

Exponential vs Linear

Any attempt to assess the progress of technology and to quantify its impact requires a discussion of exponential development which explains how developments are cumulative and accelerative. Renowned futurist author Ray Kurzweil writes:[17]

An analysis of the history of technology shows that technological change is exponential, contrary to the common-sense "intuitive linear" view. But because we're doubling the rate of progress every decade, we'll see a century of progress—at today's rate—in only 25 calendar years. When people think of a future period, they intuitively assume that the current rate of progress will continue for future periods. However, careful consideration of the pace of technology shows that the rate of progress is not constant, but it is human nature to adapt to the changing pace, so the intuitive view is that the pace will continue at the current rate. Even for those of us who have been around long enough to experience how the pace increases over time, our unexamined intuition nonetheless provides the impression that

---

[17] http://www.kurzweilai.net/the-law-of-accelerating-returns

progress changes at the rate that we have experienced recently. But the future will be far more surprising than most observers realize: few have truly internalized the implications of the fact that the rate of change itself is accelerating.

For example, when the Internet went from 20,000 to 80,000 nodes over a two-year period during the 1980s, this progress remained hidden from the general public. A decade later, when it went from 20 million to 80 million nodes in the same amount of time, the impact was rather conspicuous. As exponential technological growth continues to accelerate into the first half of the twenty-first century, it will appear to explode into infinity, at least from the limited and linear perspective of contemporary humans. The progress will ultimately become so fast that it will rupture our ability to follow it.

The exponential trend that has gained the greatest public recognition has become known as "Moore's Law." Gordon Moore, one of the inventors of integrated circuits, and then Chairman of Intel, noted in the mid-1970s that we could squeeze twice as many transistors on an integrated circuit every 24 months. There are more than enough new computing technologies now being researched, including three-dimensional silicon chips, optical computing, crystalline computing, DNA computing, and quantum computing, to keep the law of accelerating returns as applied to computation going for a long time.

The Victorian Internet

"Time itself is telegraphed out of existence"

Tom Standage

In The Victorian Internet, Tom Standage explains the impact of the development of the telegraph. During Queen Victoria's reign, a new communications technology was developed that allowed people to communicate almost instantly across great distances. A worldwide communications network whose cables spanned continents and oceans, it revolutionised business practice, gave rise to new forms of crime and inundated its users with a deluge of information. The time it took a messenger covering a distance on horseback hadn't changed for thousands of years. Pre-telegraph, news travelled no faster than the ships that carried it, but suddenly information could travel from London to Bombay in 4 minutes.

The benefits of the network were relentlessly hyped by its advocates and dismissed by the sceptics. Governments and regulators tried and failed to control the new medium. Today the internet is often described as an information superhighway; its nineteenth century precursor was dubbed the highway of thought.

Chronocentrism

The hype, scepticism and bewilderment associated with the Internet - concerns about new forms of crime, adjustments in social norms, and redefinition of business practices - mirror precisely the hopes, fears and misunderstandings inspired by the telegraph. Such reactions are amplified by what might be termed chronocentricity - the egotism that one's own generation is poised on the very cusp of history. But I think it's well justified in the case of AI.

Today's Speed

A lot has changed in the last 35 years or so since I got my first home computer, the venerable Commodore 64. Though I spent many hours playing the game International Soccer, it scarcely bares comparison with today's FIFA 2017 which can at times be hard to tell apart from live television - see Figures 9 and 10. Figure 11 shows how computing power has enabled the rendering of computer game character Lara Croft to evolve over the years from jagged edges and straight lines to subtle shades, curves and even individual hair strands.

Figure 9: Graphics Quality - International Soccer 1983

Figure 10: FIFA 2017

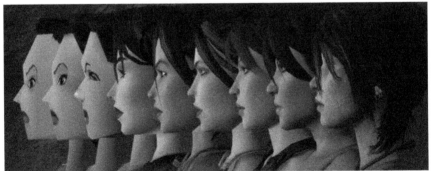

Figure 11: Graphics Quality - Tomb Raider, 1996 to 2014

When I co-founded my first company in 2000, we paid to have a dedicated "high speed" leased line installed into our city centre offices to provide a 64kb link to the Internet. The installation of such a high-tech wonder to a business premises required the 4-lane road outside to be dug up, causing traffic chaos for several days (sorry about that!). Today, a 64kb link would be so slow that it would cause people to assume that the Internet was broken. It wouldn't be enough capacity to show a video the size of a postage stamp, let alone 4K UHD on Netflix. My home broadband connection now runs around 170Mb - a speed increase of over 3,000 times. The chart below shows relative speeds delivered over the technologies used over the last couple of decades.

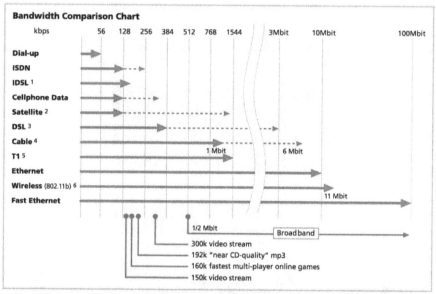

Figure 12: Fixed Line Connectivity Speed Improvements

Today's computers offer not only significantly enhanced graphics capabilities over what we had a few years ago, but they have also become very personal devices that we use to communicate, organise, shop, listen and watch. Looking at the chart below, the amount of activity that takes place wouldn't be possible without super-fast computing and connectivity. We'll take a look in the next few sections at the speedy infrastructure enabling this - and the challenges it faces to keep up.

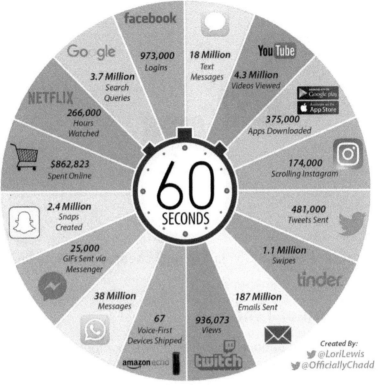

Figure 13: 60 Internet Seconds in 2018

Technology tends to get faster, cheaper and smaller as it matures, not to mention better - not always noticeable on a day to day basis, but very obvious when you take a 10 or 20-year view. Let's take a quick look at some of the changes the last 20 years or so have brought, to give context to how we approach the future. It's worth asking yourself if you noticed these changes as they happened and how much more dramatic the developments are if you take a 5 or 10-year perspective.

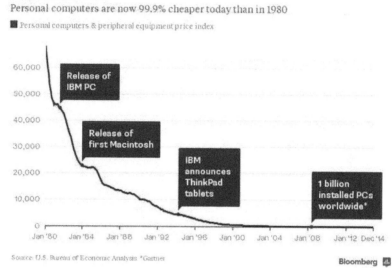

The Price of PCs

Personal computers are now 99.9% cheaper today than in 1980

■ Personal computers & peripheral equipment price index

Source: U.S. Bureau of Economic Analysis *Gartner

Bloomberg

Figure 14: Personal Computing gets cheaper over time (in US$)

A Question of Time

"Technology has been a rapid heartbeat, compressing housework, travel, entertainment, squeezing more and more into the allotted span"

Theodore Zeldin, 1994

Not all time is equal, at least in terms of our perception - our experience of time changes with our moods, with our age, with our level of busyness, with the complexity of our culture. We perceive time differently depending on where we are - research at Google found that 75% of users felt a site was fast when they were at home, but this dropped to 52% when they were out and about even when using the same connection.

Houston airport had a speed issue when passengers were complaining about the wait time for baggage. When planes landed near the terminal it took just one minute for passengers to get to the carousel, so they ended up waiting an average of seven minutes for their bags. The airport "solved" the issue by making the passengers walk further, which saw complaints drop.

As M.I.T. operations researcher Richard Larson says, "Often the psychology of queuing is more important than the statistics of the wait itself". Occupied time (walking to baggage claim) feels shorter than unoccupied time (standing at the carousel). This is also why one finds mirrors next to elevators. The idea was born during the post-World War II boom, when the spread of high-rises led to complaints about elevator delays. The rationale behind the mirrors was similar to the one used at the Houston airport: give people something to occupy their time, and the wait will feel shorter. With the mirrors, people could check their hair or slyly ogle other passengers.

Our expectations further affect how we feel about lines. All else being equal, people who wait less than they anticipated leave happier than those who wait longer than expected. This is why Disney, the universally acknowledged master of applied queuing psychology, overestimates wait times for rides, so that its guests — never customers, always guests — are pleasantly surprised when they ascend Space Mountain ahead of schedule. Professors Carmon and Kahneman have also found that we are more concerned with how long a line is than how fast it's moving. Given a choice between a slow-moving short line and a fast-moving long one, we will often opt for the former, even if the waits are identical. (This is why Disney hides the lengths of its lines by wrapping them around buildings and using serpentine queues.)

Technology Time

"The gods confound the man who first found out how to distinguish hours! Confound him too who in the place set up a sundial to cut and hack my days so wretchedly into small portions".

Plautus

Our view of time is different than that of computers. They operate in a world of Milliseconds (thousandths of a second) or even Nanoseconds (billionths of a second). Consider GPS signals between satellites and receivers on the ground. Those are radio signals that move at the speed of light, which means they travel about one foot every nanosecond. So, if the clocks in GPS satellites and your GPS receiver drift just one millionth of a second - a thousand nanoseconds - out of sync with each other, the system will not pinpoint your location more precisely than within about two-fifths of a mile. If the synchronisation drifts off by one thousandth of a second, the system couldn't tell you for sure what city you're in[18].

Computing operates on a time scale that's hard for humans to fathom. The smallest action in a computer chip - a "cycle" takes just 0.3 nanoseconds. If instead it took 1 second, that would mean that the 40 milliseconds it takes a signal to travel from New York to San Francisco would take 4 years on the same scale.

The Flash Boys

"The construction crews were as bewildered as anyone. The line didn't connect anyone. Its sole purpose, as far as they could see, was to be as straight as possible, even if that meant they had to rocksaw through a mountain rather than take an obvious route around it."

Michael Lewis, Flash Boys

One of my favourite stories about speed, technology and its impact is the 2010 story told in Michael Lewis' book, The Flash Boys. Lewis tells the tale of the creation of a high-speed data connection between the New York and Chicago stock exchanges, created in secrecy, at a cost of about $300 million dollars. The result? A reduction in the time it took for a signal to travel of 3 milliseconds. Yep, just three one-thousandths of a second. By taking a straighter route through mountains and obstacles rather than taking the path of least resistance such as along an existing rail or canal, the Spread cable offered a journey time of 13.3ms.

---

[18]   https://www.smh.com.au/technology/with-earth-spinning-more-slowly-time-isnt-flying-as-fast-as-before-20130925-2udsk.html

These split seconds saved in the transmission of information, an industry expert calculated, were worth an astonishing £12 billion a year to those who knew how to exploit them. The new superfast cable would be used by around 200 trading companies, and its owners were asking each potential client to pay more than £8 million for the privilege - the extremely lucrative world of 'high-frequency trading' (HFT).

However, as you can see from the table below, just two years later there was a conventional (microwave) link between Chicago and New Jersey, which follows an even straighter route than the Spread Networks' 827-mile cable (as microwaves always follow a direct path, whereas cables, by their very nature, must, at least occasionally, detour around physical barriers). The new route also takes advantage of the faster speed of signal travel that is possible through air (compared to signal travel speed through glass fibres, which slow light down). With these two advantages, this new link shaved 4.5 milliseconds off the Spread Networks speed—thus rendering it obsolete.

Express Lanes

New York and Chicago, America's two great trading centers, are 720 miles apart as the photon flies — about 3.9 milliseconds at the speed of light. But variations in transmission technology or how long the route is can make millions of dollars' worth of difference to high-frequency traders. — *Katie M. Palmer*

DETROIT
CHICAGO
CLEVELAND
NEW YORK
0   50 MILES
PITTSBURGH   PHILADELPHIA

ORIGINAL CABLE

Technology
Buried fiber-optic cable

Completion
Mid-1980s

Path length
~ 1,000 miles

Round-trip time for data

14.5
milliseconds and up

Approach
Multiple routes followed the easiest rights-of-way—along rail lines. But that means time-sucking jogs and detours.

SPREAD NETWORKS

Technology
Buried fiber-optic cable

Completion
August 2010

Path length
825 miles

Round-trip time for data

13.1
milliseconds

Approach
Spread bought its own rights-of-way, avoiding a Philadelphia-ward dip in favor of a shorter path northwest through central Pennsylvania.

MCKAY BROTHERS

Technology
Microwave beams through air

Completion
July 4, 2012

Path length
744 miles

Round-trip time for data

9
milliseconds

Approach
Microwaves generally move faster than photons in optical fiber, and McKay's network uses just 20 towers on a nearly perfect great circle.

TRADEWORX

Technology
Microwave beams through air

Completion
Winter 2012

Path length
~ 731 miles

Round-trip time for data

8.5
milliseconds (est.)

Approach
Tradeworx is highly secretive, but the company is open about the price of a subscription: $250,000 a year.

Figure 15: Data Connections between Chicago and New York[19]

The importance of speed (or in tech talk, the reduction of latency) is not just for high speed traders. For companies using Amazon's Cloud services, physical proximity to the data centre storing and processing your services is crucial. For example, Amazon now offer a region

---

[19] http://www.zerohedge.com/news/chicago-new-york-and-back-85-milliseconds

called europe-north1 (in Finland), offering their AWS compute, storage, big data, and networking services. Users in the Nordics can reduce latency by up to 65%, those in Eastern Europe by up to 88% compared to hosting them in the previously closest region.

The 2013 Project Express transatlantic cable cut the round-trip time for data between New York and London from 64.8 milliseconds to 59.6 milliseconds[20]. And to give you an example of the quantities of data that can be transmitted, not just the speed, there's a cable that Microsoft and Facebook laid covering the 6,600 kilometres between the US and Spain. It can transmit data at a speed of up to 160 terabits per second. For reference, that's about 20,000 hours' worth of Netflix HD video.

Chips

Unlike the mechanical innovation of past revolutions, the heart of today's fastest technology has no moving parts. Most of the tech of the electronic age is barely visible - either so small we can't see it or even imagine it (there are 4.3 billion transistors packed into the Apple A11 chip that's less than a square centimetre at 87.66 mm^2 shown here in an iPhone) or invisible to us - cloud based or simply radio waves we can't see.

---

[20]   https://www.bloomberg.com/news/articles/2012-03-29/stock-trading-is-about-to-get-5-dot-2-milliseconds-faster

Figure 16: An Apple A11 CPU in situ in an iPhone

The CPUs that have powered our computers for decades have progressed incredibly, in line with Moore's Law. A 1993 Intel Pentium CPU had 3.3 million transistors compared to the staggering 4.3 billion of the 2017 iPhone X CPU shown above. Moore's Law has been the go-to example of increasing technological speed for commentators for decades. While the doubling of transistors every 18 months doesn't sound particularly meaningful in isolation, the increasing performance coupled with decreasing size and cost is massively important in the modern world.

Custom Chips

After decades of emphasis on CPUs (particularly Intel X86 for PCs), there's been increasing interest in Graphics Processing Units (GPUs) and custom chips. CPUs are excellent at a variety of tasks and therefore ideal as general-purpose brains for general purpose computing. Ever faster CPUs have enabled our PCs to run more demanding applications faster but even they have struggled with some of the computationally intensive tasks we've thrown at them such as graphics rendering. But a CPU's versatility is not as important in some use cases as pure speed. Some of the applications we'll see in the next few chapters place such strain on computing resources that they wouldn't yet be practical if all we had were CPUs. And after decades of CPU dominance for Intel in PCs and ARM in phones, other types of chips are coming to the forefront. AI is bringing new players into the chip world. Names you'd recognise from the software world are jumping into the expensive and challenging world of designing and manufacturing dedicated chips in the quest for more speed. Before we look at more types of chips, let's briefly look at how speeds are measured for chips.

FLOPS

Floating point operations per second (FLOPS) is one popular measure of computer performance - how many mathematical operations per second can be performed. To put it in more meaningful terms, here's the performance growth over the last 10 years in gigaflops (gflops = 1 billion flops).

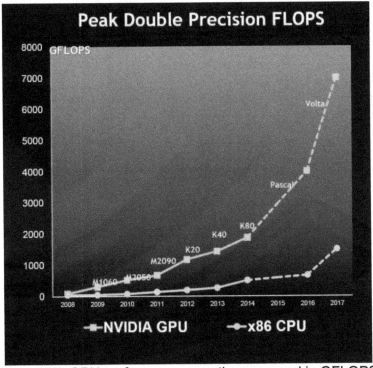

Figure 17: GPU performance growth, measured in GFLOPS

GPU

Once the staple of PC games, GPUs have risen to prominence recently outside of games due to their high performance running calculations for cryptocurrencies and AI. Thanks to their highly parallel structure they are more efficient than general-purpose CPUs for algorithms where the processing of large blocks of data is done in parallel. In research done by Indigo, it was found that while training deep learning neural networks, GPUs can be 250 times faster than CPUs. That's a difference between one day of training and almost 8 months and 10 days of training for the kinds of algorithms we'll talk about in the next chapter.

Figure 18: An NVidia GPU fits in a standard desktop PC and contains 12 billion transistors

FPGA

A Field Programmable Gate Array (FPGA) is a type of chip that can be reprogrammed for different tasks. This is different from CPUs that belong to a class of microprocessors called Application Specific Integrated Circuits (ASICs) and are designed to do only one thing which can't be changed once the circuit is designed. In 2017, Microsoft[21] used thousands of these chips at once to translate all of English language Wikipedia into Spanish—3 billion words across five million articles—in less than a tenth of a second.

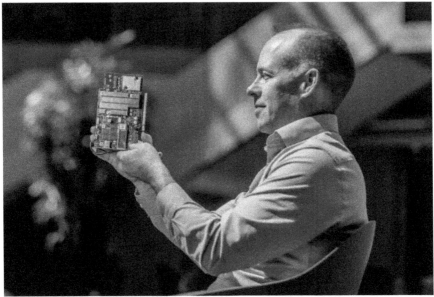

Figure 19: A Microsoft executive holding an FPGA board

---

[21]https://www.microsoft.com/en-us/research/blog/microsoft-unveils-project-brainwave/

TPU

While FPGA's offer flexibility by being programmable, Google decided to seek ultimate AI speed by designing a single-purpose chip that could handle AI-specific tasks (training and inference - more on these later) at a lower cost than GPU/CPUs, with higher performance, while consuming less power. The Tensor Processing Unit (TPU), is designed to do one thing extremely well: multiply tensors (integer matrices) in parallel that are used to represent the (deep) neural networks used in Machine Learning for AI.

In operation, running Google Photos, an individual TPU can process over 100 million photos a day delivering 180 teraflops of computing performance. When combined into a pod of 64 TPUs, Google can offer 11.5 petaflops of performance. This level of performance offers practical benefits when working with complex models: for well-known AI datasets (ResNet-50 and Transformer), training times drop from the better part of a day to under 30 minutes on a full TPU pod[22]. Google Cloud customer eBay saw one of their ML tasks, that took more than 40 days to run on in-house systems, completed in just four days on a fraction of a TPU Pod, a 10X reduction in training time.

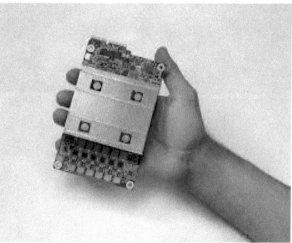

Figure 20: A Google TPU

[22]

https://supercomputersfordl2017.github.io/Presentations/ImageNetNewMNIST.pdf

Figure 21: A Google Edge TPU

Google also credits the TPU with making the provision of voice search to their massive Android user base viable - without the TPU, the computational expense of its deep learning models would have been tremendous, Google said. "If we considered a scenario where people use Google voice search for just three minutes a day and we ran deep neural nets for our speech recognition system on the processing units we were using, we would have had to double the number of Google data centers!" wrote Google hardware engineer Norm Jouppi. Google has also announced smaller TPUs for use in mobile scenarios and embedded devices[23]. If you'd like to learn more about how TPUs work, check out the Google Cloud blog[24].

---

[23] https://aiyprojects.withgoogle.com/edge-tpu/
[24] https://cloud.google.com/blog/products/ai-machine-learning/what-makes-tpus-fine-tuned-for-deep-learning

Supercomputers

In 1997, the first supercomputer to break the teraflop barrier achieved 1.3 teraflops. It cost $46 million dollars, took up 1,600 square feet of space[25], and was made up of 104 "cabinets". Just 10 years later in 2007, the Sony PS3 offered 1.8 teraflops and could sit under your TV in a game console for $400.

If you crave even more performance, super computers now offer petaflop performance - 1,000 times faster than the teraflops that were just a few years ago supercomputers. At the time of writing in mid-2018, the world's fastest (publicly known) supercomputer is called "Summit". Designed by IBM for the Department of energy and installed at Oak Ridge National Lab in Tennessee where it takes up an area about the same as two tennis courts, it is comprised of 9,000 CPUs and 27,000 GPUs. At a cost of about a quarter of a billion dollars, it's outside the price range of most organizations but as we know, the cost of such power will fall rapidly. The inclusion of GPUs shows that it was designed for artificial intelligence operations, and can use machine learning and deep learning to power research into health, physics and climate modelling, among other domains.

Figure 22: The Summit Supercomputer

---

[25] https://en.wikipedia.org/wiki/ASCI_Red#cite_note-MIT-3

It can process an incomprehensible 200,000,000,000,000,000,000 (200 quadrillion) calculations per second or 200 petaflops. "If every person on Earth completed one calculation per second, it would take the entire world population 305 days to do what Summit can do in 1 second," according to its owners[26]. For perspective, in one hour, Summit can solve a problem that it would take a powerful desktop computer 30 years to crack.

Quantum Computing

While the evolution of chips over the past 50 years has continued to deliver exponential advances in performance, there is work going on to create the next generation of computing, known as Quantum computing. The topic is worthy of its own book, so I'll just highlight it here as something to keep a watch on. It is likely to become a reality in the coming years and something that will once again offer a step-change in what computers can achieve. As we've already seen, 'classic computers' have been improving at an astonishing rate for the last half-century. Every two years we have been able to roughly double the number of transistors that we can fit onto a microchip. Transistors are the fundamental building blocks of computing, the switches that control the flow of electrical input, that allow for the binary on/off, zero/one system that is the basis of classic computers.

Unlike classic computers, in which information is represented in 0's and 1's, quantum computers rely on particles called quantum bits, or qubits. These can hold a value of 0 or 1 or both values at the same time — a superposition denoted as "0+1." They solve problems by laying out all of the possibilities simultaneously and measuring the results. It's equivalent to opening a combination lock by trying every possible number and sequence simultaneously. Although there's still a long way to go from the laboratories to practical applications, some simulations[27] suggest that quantum computing could be 100 million times faster than classic computers in some calculations. All the big tech players are investing in quantum computing research - in March 2018, Google unveiled its Bristlecone[28] proof of concept quantum

---

[26] https://www.ornl.gov/news/ornl-launches-summit-supercomputer

[27] https://ai.googleblog.com/2015/12/when-can-quantum-annealing-win.html

[28] https://ai.googleblog.com/2018/03/a-preview-of-bristlecone-googles-new.html

device. In Google's own words, it is cautiously optimistic that it can be the basis for a demonstration of quantum supremacy - where a quantum device can dramatically outperform today's best conventional supercomputer on some computational tasks.

Figure 23: A Google Bristlecone Quantum chip

Storage

Alongside processors, another key component of computing is data storage. The ability to cheaply store large quantities of data is almost as important an innovation as the ability to process it. If we weren't able to save and retrieve information, all of the data generated by sensors wouldn't be available to our ultra-fast processors. Thankfully, storage capacity has increased exponentially in recent years.

In 1956, an IBM Model 350 4Mb hard disk unit was over 5 feet tall and 5 feet wide and was transported on a forklift.

Figure 24: 4Mb in 1956

Figure 25: 1.44Mb in 1987 on a Floppy Disk and (top) a Micro SD
which can hold 512Gb in 2018

Floppy disks from the 1990s could store 1.44Mb of data. At the time
of their launch, their small size of 3.5" relative to the preceding
generation of 5.25" made them a marvel of miniaturisation. However,
today's preferred portable storage medium, micro SD cards, measure
about 0.6" and yet can store 512GB of data. That's over 365,000
times the capacity of a floppy disk.

Web Speed

While the computing power underlying our modern experiences is growing, it's worth focusing for a few minutes on the experiences modern consumers crave and the emphasis on speed of experience.

Although most of us aren't directly involved in high speed trading, our daily interactions with technology increasingly display a dependence on speed similar to those traders we discussed earlier fighting over milliseconds. Although many people have only had mainstream access to the Internet for a little over 20 years, we've become hugely demanding of it and dependent on it. So, while the core networking technologies underpinning the Internet have remained largely the same since their inception (for example, TCP/IP, DNS and HTTP), the quest for speed that underpins so much of Internet tech in recent years has seen the emergence of new techniques such as compression, CDN, AMP, preloading and caching all vying with the inherent opposite pull of ever-richer content.

As early as the 1990s, as people were just starting to gain access to the world wide web, research was already showing that web users had a short attention span. Almost 70 percent of respondents in a survey[29] reported that it "took too long to download web pages," making lack of speed the most widely-cited problem for 'net surfers. Back then, it was more a connection issue, as we didn't have high speed broadband networks. Now, it's most likely a page optimisation issue as the user interface struggles to render, or the page is actually made up from multiple different servers, with unseen calls being made to frantically piece together a dynamic page to please both the user who requested it and the advertisers paying good money for the user's attention.

New research shows that 90 percent of visitors will leave a site if they have to wait more than ten seconds for it to load. According to content delivery network service provider CDNlion[30], optimum speed is no more than four seconds, though some studies suggest two seconds is closer to visitor expectations today. As amazing as it sounds, a

---

[29] http://www.peer1.com/knowledgebase/how-slow-website-impacts-your-visitors-and-sales

[30] http://cdnlion.com/what-is-cdn-how-does-cdn-work/

couple of seconds can make the difference in keeping visitors on your website or driving traffic away at an alarming rate.

Consumers have little patience with slow web sites or apps. One example Google gives is that of Walmart, where in the fall 2014, visitors to Walmart's mobile site faced a 7.2 seconds load time. After 12 months of work to optimise performance, Walmart reduced that to 2.9 seconds. In the end, for every second of improvement, Walmart.com experienced up to a 2% conversion rate increase. In a Google analysis[31] of 10,000+ mobile web domains, it found the average load time for mobile sites is 19 seconds over 3G connections. The study found that 53% of mobile site visits are abandoned if pages take longer than 3 seconds to load. In Google's Site Performance for Webmasters video, it states that *"2 seconds is the threshold for e-commerce website acceptability. At Google, we aim for under a half second."*[32] A lack of speed officially counts against you for your ranking on Google Search[33], the lifeblood of many online businesses. Sites that are slow to load are ranked lower than others, even if their content is deemed relevant to the search.

Tricks of the Trade

As developers strive to deliver rich content but avoid slow page load times, or require large app downloads, a number of initiatives has emerged in recent years to further reduce wait times for users. One such high profile effort to improve the speed of mobile pages is Accelerated Mobile Pages, (AMP)[34] created by Google as an open source technology. Google reports that AMP pages served in Google Search typically load in less than one second and use 10 times less data than the equivalent non-AMP pages

For experiences richer than typical web pages, developers can also opt for Progressive Web Apps[35], (PWA). Progressive web apps are

---

[31] https://www.doubleclickbygoogle.com/articles/mobile-speed-matters/

[32] https://www.youtube.com/watch?v=OpMfx_Zie2g

[33]https://webmasters.googleblog.com/2018/01/using-page-speed-in-mobile-search.html?m=1

[34] https://www.ampproject.org/

[35] https://developers.google.com/web/progressive-web-apps/

regular web pages or websites, but can appear to the user like native mobile applications. This means that users can get a good user experience without having to download and install a high-performance app. While web experiences are typically slower than a well-written native app, PWAs employ technologies from native apps such as icons on the home screen and notifications to provide fast experiences. UK retailer Debenhams[36] doubled the speed of their mobile web experience with a PWA.

Connectivity

While the processing speed of our devices has increased, the feed of information to them is also vital in determining our user experience, and connection technology has struggled to keep pace with our insatiable demand for ever richer web content. A web page of 20 years ago was perhaps just a few kilobytes, with some text and maybe some images. Now, web pages are averaging 3Mb[37], featuring multiple high-resolution images, often dynamically personalised for us. The graph below shows the growing size of pages, projected to exceed 4Mb in 2019. And that's before we talk about Video content - a 480p resolution video takes about 2MB per minute but when streaming, consistency is vital and it's recommended to have at least 2-3 megabits per second (Mbps).

---

[36]https://www.mobilemarketer.com/news/debenhams-doubles-speed-of-mobile-site-with-progressive-web-app/509870/

[37] https://speedcurve.com/blog/web-performance-page-bloat/

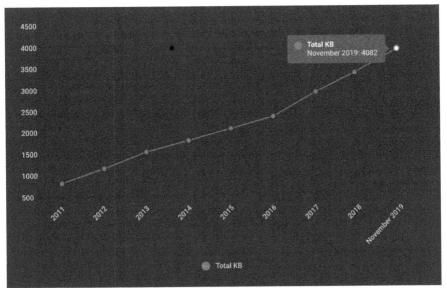

Figure 26: Average web page size, in KB

My first "high-speed" mobile phone in 2002 could theoretically manage 64kps but it certainly couldn't sustain it. But it didn't have a colour screen, nor a screen capable of video, so it didn't really matter. But that's only 16 years ago. As each generation of mobile technology has been developed, the emphasis has been on speed - just as with the evolution of Wi-Fi. This chart shows successive generations of Wi-Fi growing from 54 Mbps to speeds approaching 1 Gbps.

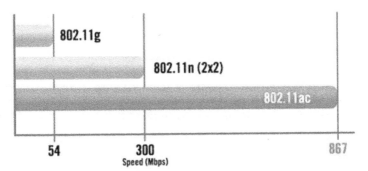
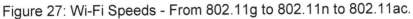

Figure 27: Wi-Fi Speeds - From 802.11g to 802.11n to 802.11ac.

Mobile handset manufacturers and Mobile Carriers now talk about theoretical speeds competing with fixed fibre broadband - in 2017, UK mobile network EE demonstrated a 360 Mbps download on their live network using a standard 4G handset[38].

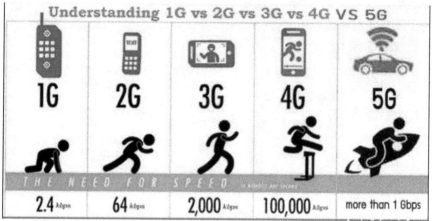

Figure 28: Accelerating Cellular Connectivity Speeds

Putting the Speed to Good Use

"Anticipate Needs. Being quick is knowing what your customer wants before they want it."

Google[39]

On a practical level, what does the increase in computing performance mean? How we harness the computational speed, the data we have available to feed it via fast connectivity, and the costs involved combine to drive progress in ways greater than the sum of the parts - the combinatorial effect. One example from the medical world is the decrease over time of the cost to sequence a genome. Just 18 years ago (as I got my first touch-screen mobile phone), it cost $100m dollars to sequence a genome. Now that cost is below

---

[38] http://newsroom.ee.co.uk/ee-launches-next-phase-of-4g-for-the-worlds-fastest-smartphones/

[39] https://www.thinkwithgoogle.com/marketing-resources/experience-design/speed-is-key-optimize-your-mobile-experience/

$1,000[40] and you can see below the dramatic reduction in the cost over time.

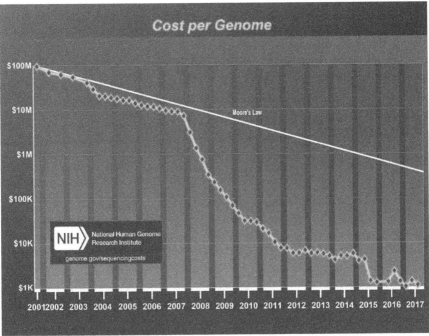

Figure 29: Genome Sequencing Costs over time

As we'll see in the next chapter, the increase in the speed of computing power has been a major driver in the progression of AI, and thus the associated areas of computer vision and natural language processing. But before we dive into that, let's look at a few other examples and implications of speed.

---

[40] Wetterstrand KA. DNA Sequencing Costs: Data from the NHGRI Genome Sequencing Program (GSP) Available at: www.genome.gov/sequencingcostsdata. Accessed July 30th 2018.

Speeding Up

As Google became the dominant search engine, one of the things people loved most about it was the speed at which it delivered its usually pretty accurate and useful results. Displayed proudly at the top of each query was the time taken to trawl the mammoth amount of data available and give you a list of what you were probably looking for:

About 329,000,000 results (1.07 seconds)

Figure 30: Google Search Results Speed is shown on all searches

But perhaps unnoticed by many, in 2010, Google significantly enhanced its service with an update known as Google Instant[41]. This was where it changed to predict the most likely completion and streams results in real-time for those predictions—yielding a smarter and faster search. Google claimed it could save the average searcher two to five seconds per search. Now the same predictive approach is coming to everything from simple text responses to full-blown email completion, now in Gmail, all thanks to AI.

Many of the tools that have become popular over the last decade are largely speed driven - the move to asynchronous communication in some cases (text ahead of voice) and to synchronous in others (chat ahead of email) have sought to increase the pace and number of our conversations.

Speedy Pizza

While there has been much emphasis on improving web site performance (which is frequently very necessary), some companies that are embracing the trend for speed have been looking beyond page load speeds and optimisations for even more innovative ways to make their business faster. As Amazon patented the concept of 1-Click purchasing, some people wondered what was faster than 1 click? Zero click! In April 2016, Domino's Pizza launched a new app

---

[41] https://googleblog.blogspot.ie/2010/09/search-now-faster-than-speed-of-type.html

that removed all the clicks from the order process. Simply open the app to start a 10 second countdown - if you don't cancel the timer, when it hits zero, it will place your standard order.

Dominos are an interesting mini-case study in how speed has changed consumer expectations and how they've responded. Modern customers are impatient, expecting brands to intuitively know what they need, when they need it, and deliver it without delay. The early Dominos website ordering experience was cumbersome. It often took more than 25 steps to order a pizza. Dominos introduced customer profiles for regular customers, which allowed auto-filling much of the information previously entered by customers bringing the number of steps down to five. Fast forward to today and Dominos receives 60% of orders online and 70% of those from mobile. Dominos has continued to experiment with new, faster ways to order Pizza, with voice-ordering and even emoji ordering. We'll see in Chapter 5 how voice interfaces are offering even faster ways to order.

On Demand Delegation

In many cases, our impatience with web-based solutions has led us to embrace a plethora of apps, each dedicated to a single function of convenience. If you want a product or service in the fastest possible time, you can be sure there's a smartphone app devoted to meeting your whims with little more than the touch of a finger on an icon. With rapid connectivity and (often) flexible workers from the gig economy to flex with demand, you can now delegate virtually any chore in most cities.

Humans have long had a desire for immediacy - the famous Marshmallow Test[42] showed only ⅓ of people deferred long enough to receive the second marshmallow. We have a chemical reaction to speed - with pleasurable endorphins/dopamine. Our neurological need for new experiences explains our lack of patience with loading screens and preference for faster services. Whether you need a lift, a personal shopper, a doctor, a dog walker, people to do your laundry, clean your house or carry out home repairs, you can summon these services the moment you need them. Gone are the

---

[42] http://psycnet.apa.org/record/1971-02138-001

days of booking services weeks in advance. While flower delivery and valet parking aren't new, the on-demand economy is reimagining them by making these services more convenient, more affordable and available with a few taps.

When we do free up our time, what we choose to do with it is crucial, and this will be even more of an issue as we delegate tasks to technology. Steven Pinker, in his book Enlightenment Now, points out how *time spent doing laundry fell from 11.5 hours a week in 1920 to an hour and a half in 2014. This might sound trivial in the grand scheme of progress. But the rise of the washing machine has improved quality of life by freeing up time for people—mostly women—to enjoy other pursuits. That time represents nearly half a day every week that could be used for everything from binge-watching Ozark or reading a book to starting a new business.* What will the equivalent time saving be and what will we do with the new time?

Pre-empting (is) the Future

There has been a shift away from products and services delivering convenience in isolation, and towards all-encompassing platforms geared to ensure everything is not just available, but ready – before, or just as, a need arises.

Telefonica Blog[43]

Telefonica has identified a series of emerging behaviours and grouped them under the banner of 'nowism' – acting on needs only as they arise (which, over time, come with using on demand services habitually), valuing time more than ever before and spending on services that can help save or protect it. So-called 'choice paralysis', from trawling and comparing endless options for everything one might need or want, has increased a desire for abdicating these time-consuming processes to someone or something else. In turn, with a desire to spend their time on things that are meaningful or enjoyable, rather than on searching, planning, and grappling with abundance,

---

[43] http://en.blogthinkbig.com/2016/03/21/3-themes-to-watch-in-2016-about-product-innovation/

people will continue to seek out products and services that promise effortless decision making, immediate fulfilment, and improved relevance.

In the always-connected digital era with unlimited choice, price transparency, time poverty, channel blur and frenetic multitasking, we can't or won't wait for anything anymore. Instant gratification is the name of the game. There is only so far you can go with speeding things up before there's no more scope to remove steps from the user interaction. The next logical advance is to remove all steps from the interaction by pre-empting the user, or at least offering solutions to the user rather than asking for inputs.

This will come in one of two ways - predictions based on your past behaviour or responses to your signalled intentions.

So that could be a prediction that you might order a pizza because it's Saturday night, you're home, there's nothing in your calendar or correspondence suggesting any plan to go out, no indications that you've already eaten and a prior history of ordering pizzas on Saturday night. Or you could simply signal your desire to eat, a time, how hungry you are, any exclusions and a system could auction that intent to a variety of suppliers who would bid for your order - the opposite to how you currently search their offerings on a web site. Instead you'd post your desire to eat and they would respond with offers - this concept is explored in detail in the 2012 Book, The Intention Economy[44] but seems likely to be widely enabled by AI.

Move Fast and Break Things

"There is more to life than simply increasing its speed."

Mahatma Gandhi

Faster and better are often used interchangeably but that is clearly not always the case. The famous early motto of Facebook to "Move Fast and Break Things" is perhaps indicative of the mentality

---

[44]https://www.amazon.com/Intention-Economy-When-Customers-Charge/dp/1422158527

prevalent in much of the technology industry, especially start-ups, prioritising speed over quality; done is better than perfect. How sustainable is this mentality? You could argue it's imperative to get momentum, and then you can mature into something more stable, but all the time wary of the next fast mover who may steal the momentum from you.

It is also a useful way of looking at the difference between technology optimists and those in the real world. While Silicon Valley wants to move as fast as possible regardless of collateral damage, there are a lot of situations where more caution is required and the consequences of innovation heeded. The potential for misuse or harm must also be considered. *"If you're not embarrassed by your first version, you waited too long to ship it"* said Reid Hoffman, co-founder of LinkedIn - that maybe ok in a social app, but not in a medical one.

In The Everything Store[45], the author tells how Amazon implemented a 4 hour "click to ship" metric for online shopping at a time when the industry typically operated at 12 hours. Very soon, users came to expect such fast service and suddenly perceived anything less as "slow", despite having been satisfied with the previous levels of service. The goalposts moved and businesses that didn't or couldn't respond were "Amazoned". As perhaps the best example of these trends, we'll see multiple instances of Amazon's aggressive innovation in later chapters.

The insatiable tech view of the world leaves very little time for business to evaluate, deploy and benefit from advances before they must be looking to the next shift:

As soon as you really understand something in tech it's probably time to stop paying attention to it - it's no longer part of the future. So tech is a continuing process - what should I start forgetting about, and what do I need to start trying to understand next?

Ben Evans[46]

---

[45]https://www.amazon.com/Everything-Store-Jeff-Bezos-Amazon-ebook/dp/B00BWQW73E

[46] https://twitter.com/BenedictEvans/status/904782356178911232

Unpopular Speed

"I recognise that, in the Valley, people are obsessed with the pace of technological change. It's tough to get that part right... We rush sometimes, and can misfire for an average person. As humans, I don't know whether we want change that fast – I don't think we do."

Sundar Pichai, CEO, Google[47]

Not everyone is happy about speed. As you go about increasing speed by removing steps in a process, that tends to also have the effect in many cases of removing intermediaries or value adds. This collapsing of the value chain in many industries is causing resistance and resentment from incumbents disintermediated by technology and a more direct service provider-to-consumer relationship based on speed. Many countries have seen protests against services like Uber which offers a streamlined experience compared to traditional providers.

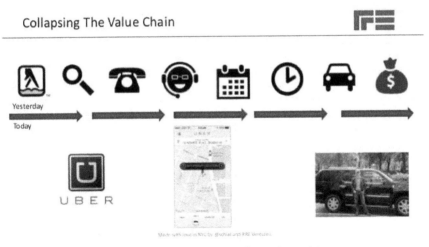

Figure 31: Uber speeds up a decades-old process

---

[47] https://www.theguardian.com/technology/2017/oct/07/google-boss-sundar-pichai-tax-gender-equality-data-protection-jemima-kiss

Going Online

One phrase that illustrates our changing relationship with technology is 'going online'. In the 1990s, going online was a conscious and not always easy or satisfying experience. It was a specific, temporary state, separate from daily life. It took time, dedicated computer hardware, your phone line, patience and offered quite little reward in return. You had to buy a modem, connect your phone line to your computer and navigate what were quite hard to use interfaces. Although services like AOL and MSN made things easier, cafes and homes didn't have Wi-Fi, phones didn't connect to the internet and there was no internet of things. In short, connectivity was slow, rare and expensive.

Just two decades later, in the developed world, you don't really go online anymore. It's simply there, almost omnipresent, waiting for you to want something. Your devices assume connectivity, as does your office, car, home, and public space. Many airlines offer Wi-Fi at 30,000 ft. The term misleads us by suggesting that opting out remains an option. Already there's been concern by the move to a cashless society in China that foreigners can't transact and in Sweden that older people uncomfortable with new technologies are being pushed out.

In 1999, Stewart Brand published his pace layers in The Clock of the Long Now, highlighting the different paces that elements of our society move at, and the need for each to provide balance. I would add technology as an influence skewering through virtually all layers with differing impacts.

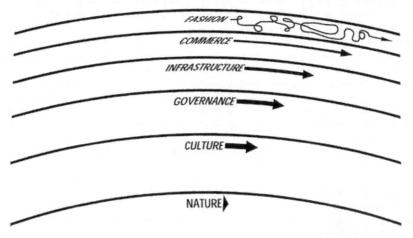

Figure 32: "Pace Layers" - Fast Layers innovate, while slow layers stabilise[48]

It's worth keeping in mind these competing forces as we move on to explore the technologies now emerging to boost the next wave of innovation and add fuel to the race for speed. We'll look at commerce in detail in Chapter 7 and come back to talk about some of the non-technical issues in Chapter 9, but for now, let's dive into the power behind the New Acceleration - the exciting world of Artificial Intelligence.

---

[48] https://twitter.com/stewartbrand

Chapter 4: Unpacking Artificial Intelligence

"Success in creating AI could be the biggest event in the history of our civilisation. [It will be] either the best, or the worst thing, ever to happen to humanity. We do not yet know which."

Professor Stephen Hawking[49]

"There are perhaps 700 people in the world who can contribute to the leading edge of AI research, perhaps 70,000 who can understand their work and participate actively in commercializing it and 7 billion people who will be impacted by it."

Ian Hogarth[50]

> **Note**: This chapter is not a highly technical introduction to AI technologies - it introduces some high-level concepts and terminology (you'll learn a lot of new acronyms!) but aims only to give a broad understanding of some of the technologies to enable a better understanding of the kinds of possibilities that now exist, particular those we'll explore in Chapters 5 & 6. My aim here is to give you enough information to critically assess the commentary on AI you'll see in the media, and to inspire you to give careful consideration to the merits and challenges of AI. For readers who wish to dive deeper into the technicalities, I've included a list of recommended reading, videos and courses in Appendix 1. And for those who want to try it themselves, I've also included details of some great resources you can download for free to try AI hands-on.

Narrowing the Debate

AI is simultaneously one of the hottest, least understood and most contentious areas of technology. Depending on which narrative you believe, it will be the end of humanity, the greatest human invention ever or amount to nothing. There is a near endless torrent of stories

---

[49] http://www.cityam.com/251814/major-new-ai-research-centre-opening-uk
[50] https://www.ianhogarth.com/blog/2018/6/13/ai-nationalism

in the media as well as a rush to include AI in every technology company's pitch. Given the proclivity of technology advocates to proclaim every new invention as the next big thing, it's understandable that many have grown weary of predictions of impending revolution.

In order to assist in understanding AI, I think it's important to clarify some of the terminology and cut through the marketing hyperbole. First things first. Forget everything you've seen in the movies about AI. For some people, "artificial intelligence" immediately conjures a vision of the creation of a sentient, self-aware, conscious machine intelligence that can emulate or exceed human cognitive ability. However, I can't find a single credible expert who believes we are near creating what's known as Artificial General Intelligence (AGI) which is as broadly flexible as that of humans. That's not to say we'll never get there, but there is no known path to it at present.

But we are most definitely already able to create Artificial *Narrow* Intelligence (ANI) - systems that are able to display human-like skills at very specific tasks. As you'll see, ANI is mastering an increasing number of these narrow domains - and that can be scary enough on its own, without spending (wasting) any time thinking about AGI just yet. Narrow AI can be exceptionally useful - it's hard to imagine anyone thinking that ANI that can diagnose disease more effectively than humans is not important.

While demonstrations of AI prowess in specific domains such as the victory of Deep Mind over a leading Go[51] player or IBM's Debating computer[52] are impressive, each system is capable only in its own narrow tasks and useless at any other activity. Tasks for AI systems are often framed in narrow contexts for the sake of making progress on a specific problem or application. While machines may exhibit stellar performance on a certain task, performance may degrade dramatically if the task is modified even slightly. So, for now at least, we should consider AI as best suited to solving specific problems rather than possessing any form of general reasoning abilities or sentience.

---

[51] https://deepmind.com/blog/alphagos-next-move/
[52] https://www.ibm.com/blogs/research/2018/06/ai-debate/

In 2016, the Obama Whitehouse published a report[53] urging both public and private sectors to take heed of AI:

"After years of steady but slow progress on making computers "smarter" at everyday tasks, a series of breakthroughs in the research community and industry have recently spurred momentum and investment in the development of this field.

Today's AI is confined to narrow, specific tasks (emphasis mine), and isn't anything like the general, adaptable intelligence that humans exhibit. Despite this, AI's influence on the world is growing. The rate of progress we have seen will have broad implications for fields ranging from healthcare to image- and voice-recognition. Like any transformative technology, however, artificial intelligence carries some risk and presents complex policy challenges along several dimensions, from jobs and the economy to safety and regulatory questions.

There are tremendous opportunities and an array of considerations across the Federal Government in privacy, security, regulation, law, and research and development to be taken into account when effectively integrating this technology into both government and private-sector activities."

Origins: What's in a Name?

New words will make their way into common parlance, even if people aren't totally sure of what they mean....Much like "the cloud" and "big data" before it, the term "artificial intelligence" has been hijacked by funding-hungry start-ups, marketers and advertising copywriters. Much of what people are suddenly calling "artificial intelligence" is really just data analytics—in other words, fairly standard statistics.

Artificial Intelligence isn't a simple term in itself. Marvin Minsky, a pioneer in artificial intelligence, often described AI as a "suitcase term." It's a concept that seems fairly clear but is in fact actually complex and packed – like a suitcase – with lots of other ideas,

---

[53] https://obamawhitehouse.archives.gov/blog/2016/05/03/preparing-future-artificial-intelligence

concepts, processes, subtleties, distinctions, sub-disciplines and problems. Bear with me while we unpack some of the components of Minsky's suitcase in this chapter.

Underpinning much of the impending change discussed in this book is a family of technologies frequently referred to collectively as Artificial Intelligence. An imprecise term for a number of advanced techniques, it's a broad discipline with the goal of creating intelligent machines - usually referring to the concept of a computer performing tasks with near-human or even superhuman abilities. Simply put, AI is a branch of computer science in which computers are cajoled into doing things that normally require human intelligence. This includes areas such as learning, reasoning, problem-solving, understanding language and perceiving a situation or environment. AI represents the next era of computing, after the tabulating era (very early computers) and the programmable systems era (where computers are programmed line by line to complete a specific task).

If you get too much into the detail of how AI works, it quickly gets very complicated. As one writer[54] cautions those covering AI, *"keep in mind: AI is a big field, and very diverse in terms of topics and methods used. The main AI conferences (such as IJCAI, AAAI, ICML and NIPS) have thousands of attendees, and most of them only understand a small part of what goes on in the conference"*.

Despite the hype, AI isn't a new idea. First coined as a term by researchers at Dartmouth in 1955, artificial intelligence was also posited by Alan Turing in 1950, but without the now familiar moniker and his concept of the imitation game. Researchers at the time recognised that the computers at their disposal were far from able to realise their ambitions and for much of the next 50 years, this held true. But as we have seen in chapter 3, the exponential growth of computer power, and the development of new types of chips mean we now have unprecedented computing power at our disposal, with more to come.

Over the decades, interest in the ambition of creating AI waxed and waned, and researchers followed many potential paths. The tasks that experts expected to conquer quickly frequently escaped them,

---

[54] http://togelius.blogspot.ie/2017/07/some-advice-for-journalists-writing.html

leading to the concept of 'AI Winters', where interest in the field ebbed away and to assertions like *Moravec's Paradox* - the discovery by researchers in artificial intelligence and robotics that, contrary to traditional assumptions, high-level reasoning requires relatively little computation, but low-level sensorimotor skills (such as movement) require enormous computational resources.

An Ordinary Phenomenon

AI is also something of a moving target - as Author Pamela McCorduck explains: *"It's part of the history of the field of artificial intelligence that every time somebody figured out how to make a computer do something—play good checkers, solve simple but relatively informal problems—there was chorus of critics to say, 'that's not thinking'.*[55]" AI researcher Rodney Brooks sums it up: *"Every time we figure out a piece of it, it stops being magical; we say, 'Oh, that's just a computation"*.

As we progress through the stages of development of new technology, what users once considered as intelligent and noteworthy, tends to become ordinary over time, usually quite quickly. For example, improving Search so that it was accurate and fast could be regarded as highly intelligent at the time but now it's the minimum we expect. As we move through technical advances in AI, the bar becomes ever higher. We now expect intelligence to transform our lives in a more drastic way than ever before.

The AI Hype

"It's hard to overstate how big of an impact AI is going to have on society over the next 20 years."

Amazon CEO Jeff Bezos

---

[55] https://en.wikipedia.org/wiki/AI_effect#cite_note-1

There's no shortage of commentary on AI but in an attempt to quantify it, I've found the AI Index from Stanford provides some useful metrics. AI Index is an open, not-for-profit project to track activity and progress in AI. It aims to facilitate an informed conversation about AI that is grounded in data rather than opinion. You can find its annual report online: AI Index 2017 Report.[56] Figures 33 and 34 are examples of the information available in the report.

The Volume of Activity metrics capture the "how much" aspects of the field, like attendance at AI conferences and VC investments into start-ups developing AI systems. The Technical Performance metrics capture the "how good" aspects; for example, how well computers can understand images.

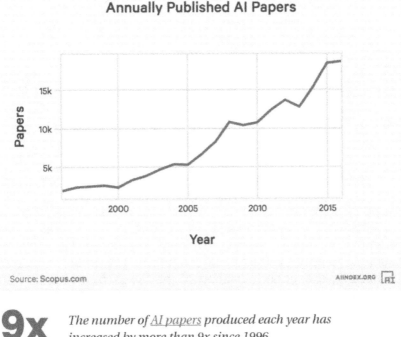

Annually Published AI Papers

Source: Scopus.com   AIINDEX.ORG

9x *The number of AI papers produced each year has increased by more than 9x since 1996.*

Figure 33: Publication of AI Papers

---

[56] https://ai100.stanford.edu/

The amount of annual funding by VC's into US AI startups across all funding stages.

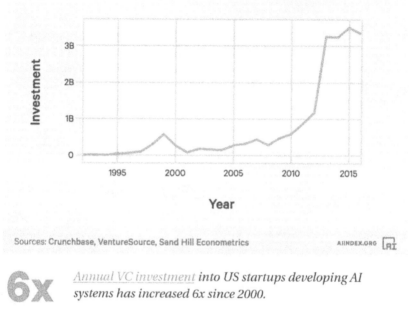

Annual VC Investment in AI Startups

Sources: Crunchbase, VentureSource, Sand Hill Econometrics   AIINDEX.ORG

6x  *Annual VC investment into US startups developing AI systems has increased 6x since 2000.*

Figure 34: Venture Capital Investment in AI Start-ups

The report also notes increases in conference attendances, AI course enrolments in top universities and job listings seeking AI skills, as well as dramatic increases in the developer interest in ML tools like Tensorflow. Activity by itself is, of course, no guarantee of progress but it does give a good indication of the levels of investment and therefore the levels of expectation.

Machine Learning (ML)

Perhaps the best place to start in discussing the current state of AI is with a set of techniques known as machine learning. Artificial intelligence has become a focal point for the global tech community largely thanks to the recent renaissance in machine learning. The vast majority of articles and advances I've seen in recent years that purport to be "AI", are more accurately examples of machine learning. As illustrated below, AI dates back to 1955, while ML came to the fore in the 1990s, with progress to Deep Learning (DL), that we'll discuss later in this chapter, emerging in the last decade.

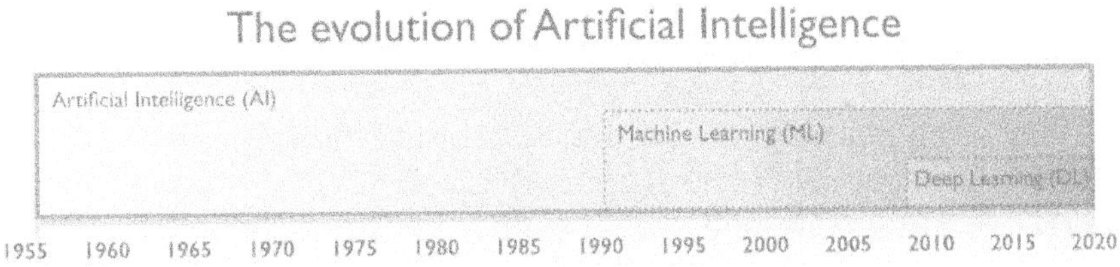

The evolution of Artificial Intelligence

Figure 35: The emergence of AI, ML and DL[57]

Machine Learning is a subset of AI that uses statistical techniques to give machines the ability to "learn" from data without being explicitly given the instructions for how to do so. Machine learning was defined by Arthur Samuel in 1959 as the science of getting computers to learn and act without being explicitly programmed. It can be traced back to statistical pattern recognition, and is integral to popular online services you use already, such as searches, spam filters and recommendation engines. It came into its own as a discipline in the 1990s as availability of datasets and computational power increased.

The key concept of ML is **training** a model using a learning algorithm that progressively improves model performance on a specific task by analysing large quantities of data. Once the training is complete, the model can be applied to new datasets to arrive at outcomes, a process known as **inference**.

Machine Learning itself is a broad term, with many sub divisions making up the field. Within the divisions of types of learning, there are further distinctions into types of networks. Don't worry if you don't understand these - unless you're planning to become a ML practitioner, awareness that there are different approaches suiting different tasks should be more than enough.

---

[57] https://medium.com/mmc-writes/the-fourth-industrial-revolution-a-primer-on-artificial-intelligence-ai-ff5e7fffcae1

Three of the most widely adopted machine learning methods are **supervised learning** which trains algorithms based on example input and output data that is labelled by humans, **unsupervised learning** which provides the algorithm with no labelled data in order to allow it to find structure within its input data and **reinforcement learning** where training is based on rewarding successful outcomes.

Supervised Learning

In supervised learning, the computer is provided with example inputs that are labelled with their desired outputs. The purpose of this method is for the algorithm to be able to "learn" by comparing its actual output with the "taught" outputs to find errors, and modify the model accordingly. Supervised learning therefore uses patterns to predict label values on additional unlabelled data.

For example, with supervised learning, an algorithm may be fed data with images of sharks labelled as fish and images of oceans labelled as water. By being trained on this data, the supervised learning algorithm should be able to later identify unlabelled shark images as fish and unlabelled ocean images as water.

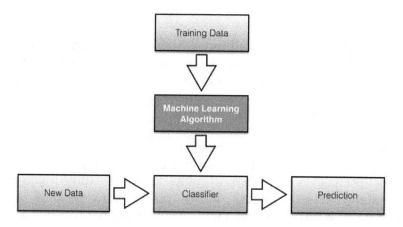

Figure 36: Machine Learning

A common use case of supervised learning is to use historical data to predict statistically likely future events. It may use historical stock market information to anticipate upcoming fluctuations, or be employed to filter out spam emails. In supervised learning, tagged photos of dogs can be used as input data to classify untagged photos of dogs.

Unsupervised Learning

In unsupervised learning, data is unlabelled, so the learning algorithm is left to find commonalities among its input data. As unlabelled data are more abundant than labelled data, machine learning methods that facilitate unsupervised learning are particularly valuable. The goal of unsupervised learning may be as straightforward as discovering hidden patterns within a dataset. Unsupervised learning is commonly used for transactional data. You may have a large dataset of customers and their purchases, but as a human you will likely not be able to make sense of what similar attributes can be drawn from customer profiles and their types of purchases.

Without being told a "correct" answer, unsupervised learning methods can look at complex data that is more expansive and seemingly unrelated in order to organize it in potentially meaningful ways. Unsupervised learning is often used for anomaly detection including for fraudulent credit card purchases, and recommender systems that recommend what products to buy next. In unsupervised learning, untagged photos of dogs can be used as input data for the algorithm to find likenesses and classify dog photos together, without actually knowing it's a dog.

Reinforcement Learning

Reinforcement Learning is an area of ML that has received particular attention over the past decade. It is concerned with software agents that learn goal-oriented behaviour by trial and error in an environment that provides rewards or penalties in response to the agent's actions towards achieving the goal.

In reinforcement learning, the computer program will interact with a dynamic environment in which it must perform a particular goal (such as playing a game with an opponent or driving a car). The program is provided with feedback in terms of rewards and punishments as it navigates its problem space. Using this algorithm, the machine is trained to make specific decisions.

The Power of ML

The fundamental concept behind machine learning is letting the computer program learn from examples. For example, with supervised learning you can train the computer to recognise a cat in an image by feeding it huge quantities of images labelled as cats. Eventually, it will learn to identify a cat in an image it hasn't seen before - and will offer a confidence score as to how certain it is that the new image is a cat.

In humans, the label "cat" gets connected to every cat we see, such that certain neural pathways are weighted and others aren't. For "cat" to fire in our brains, what we perceive has to be close enough to our previous cat encounters. Although humans probably don't need to see millions of cats of every different breed from every conceivable angle to infer what a cat looks like in general, how machine learning works isn't dissimilar to how we teach infants concepts - we show them labelled images and point and say "cat" until they get familiar enough to identify cats. We tend to forget the years we spend learning and labelling the world, and we make a lot of mistakes along the way - we've all seen kids point at a cat and say dog as they learn.

The power of machine learning is that it's a way of using massive amounts of data to have machines operate more like humans do without giving them explicit instructions. Instead of describing "cat-ness" to a computer, instead just plug it into the Internet and feed it millions of pictures of cats. It can then have a general idea of "cat-ness." Next test it with even more images. Where it's wrong, humans can correct it, which further improves its "cat-ness" detection. Repetition of this process results in a computer that knows what a cat is when it sees it, for the most part as well as we can. The important difference, though, is that unlike us, it can then sort through millions of images within a matter of seconds.

This shift from pre-programmed tasks to learned knowledge entirely changes what computers can do. Previously, if we couldn't explicitly codify it, we couldn't get a computer to automate it. Yet much of human knowledge is tacit, meaning that we can't easily explain it. Try writing down instructions that would enable another person to learn how to ride a bike or to recognize a dog. This is referred to as *Polanyi's Paradox*[58]. This not only limits what knowledge we can transfer in written form to another person but has historically placed a fundamental restriction on our ability to automate. ML will end much of the paradox as computers learn rather than relying on being told, but ironically, as we'll see in chapter 9, there's a new paradox, as computers can't always tell us how they've reached a decision.

Deep Learning

Deep Learning is a type of ML that is particularly popular in recent years. Based around the concept of layers in a neural network, it attempts to mimic the activity in layers of neurons in the human brain so as to recognise complex patterns in data. It has been very effective as recent computing advances facilitate much deeper and more complex layers than were previously possible. Deep learning has seen significant advances in applications such as:

- Language Translation
- Image recognition
- Speech Recognition
- Medical Imaging Analysis
- Textual Analysis (e.g. for sentiment)

The 'deep' in deep learning refers to the large number of layers of neurons in the artificial neural networks. The 'input layer' receives information the network will process—for example, a set of pictures. The 'output layer' provides the results. Between the input and output layers are 'hidden layers' where most activity occurs. Typically, the outputs of each neuron on one level of the neural network serve as one of the inputs for each of the neurons in the next layer.

---

[58] http://philosophicaldisquisitions.blogspot.com/2015/10/polanyis-paradox-will-humans-maintain.html

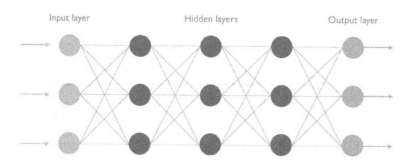

Figure 37: Layers in a (simplified) Neural Network[59]

To put it another way, the "intelligence" in a Deep Neural Network, its reasoning, is built upon the behaviour of thousands of simulated neurons, arranged into dozens or even hundreds of intricately interconnected layers. The neurons in the first layer each receive an input, like the brightness of a pixel in a photo, and then perform a calculation before outputting the value to the next layer, and so on, until the combination of processing through the layers leads to a conclusion. DNN also uses a process called back-propagation that refines the calculations of individual layers so that the network can "learn".

Ready for some more acronyms? There are lots of kinds of neural network, but four broad kinds of Neural Networks are popular at the moment:

1. **Multi-Layer Perceptrons** (MLP): MLPs are suitable for classification prediction problems where inputs are assigned a class or label.

2. **Convolutional Neural Networks** (CNN): are especially effective for any type of prediction problem involving image data as an input. A CNN has several layers through which data is filtered into categories. These are primarily used in image recognition and text language processing. If you've got a billion hours of video to sift through, you could build a CNN that tries to examine each frame and determine what's going on. One might train a CNN by feeding it

---

[59] https://medium.com/mmc-writes/the-fourth-industrial-revolution-a-primer-on-artificial-intelligence-ai-ff5e7fffcae1

complex images that have been tagged by humans. AI learns to recognise things like stop signs, cars, trees, and butterflies by looking at pictures that humans have labelled, comparing the pixels in the image to the labels it understands, and then organizing everything it sees into the categories it's been trained on.

3. **Recurrent Neural Networks** (RNN): were designed to work with sequence prediction problems. While RNNs were traditionally difficult to train, a type of RNN called **Long Short-Term Memory**, or LSTM, is perhaps the most successful RNN because it reduces the problems of training a recurrent network and in turn has been used on a wide range of applications including:

- Text data
- Speech data
- Classification prediction problems
- Regression prediction problems

4. **Generative Adversarial Networks** (GAN): neural networks comprised of two arguing sides — a generator and an adversary — that 'fight' among themselves until the generator wins. If you wanted to create an AI that imitates an art style, like Monet's for example, you could feed a GAN a bunch of his paintings. One side of the network would try to create new images that fooled the other side into thinking they were painted by Monet. Basically, the AI would learn everything it could about Monet's work by examining the individual pixels of each image.

A CNN or RNN model is rarely used alone. These types of networks are used as layers in a broader model that also has one or more MLP layers. Perhaps the most interesting work comes from the mixing of the different types of networks together into hybrid models. For example, consider a model that uses a stack of layers with a CNN on the input, LSTM in the middle, and MLP at the output. A model like this can read a sequence of image inputs, such as a video, and generate a prediction.

Despite the success of ML/DL in some areas, as a technique it is not suitable for all challenges. It typically requires large data sets for training; it takes extensive processing power to train a neural network.

And as we'll discuss in Chapter 9, it has an 'explainability' problem — it can be difficult to know how a neural network developed its predictions.

Training vs Inference

A key concept in ML is understanding training vs inference. The two phases of Neural Networks are called training (or learning) and inference (or prediction), and they refer to development of a model versus its ultimate use in solving a problem. Once you train a model it can then work away processing new data. But you need to train different models for different things - these are narrowly optimised; think of them like athletes that are great at one discipline but not necessarily very good at another.

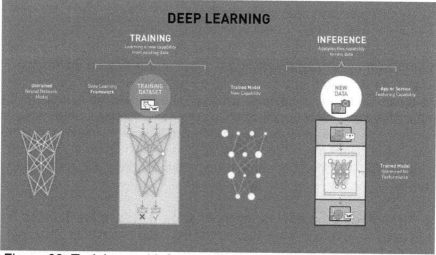

Figure 38: Training and Inference in Deep Learning – (see web site for hi-res version)

While training requires a lot of computing power, like the GPU/TPUs we discussed in the previous chapter, once trained, they can be run on less demanding hardware, and it some cases can be "pushed to the edge", which is tech-speak for small 'computers' such as Phones or IoT devices that are not dependent on connectivity for all functions. So, for example, while a model to identify plant types might be trained on a powerful system in a datacentre, the model might be run on a smartphone without a data connection and still allow for plant identification in the field.

Speeding Up AI

It is virtually impossible to measure the performance of AI in a meaningful comparative way, as the applications are so diverse, the problems it seeks to solve so disparate and the approaches so varied. But there is little doubt that the results, even if only in laboratory style applications, are accelerating. We saw in Chapter 3 how computer chip designs are being optimized specifically for the field of ML, both to improve training and inference performance. Let's take a look at what GPUs and TPUs have actually delivered, now that we know more about deep learning.

In March of 2016, the AlphaGo system developed by the Google DeepMind team beat Lee Sedol, one of the world's greatest Go players, 4-1. In October 2017 a Nature paper[60] detailed a new version, AlphaGo Zero, which beat the original AlphaGo system 100-0. That's a lot of progress for 18 months.

Apple unveiled an ML training acceleration tool called Create ML at their 2018 developer conference which boasts an improvement in the speed of training for one of their customers from 24 hours to 48 minutes on a laptop and just 18 minutes on a high-end workstation.

---

[60] https://www.nature.com/articles/nature24270

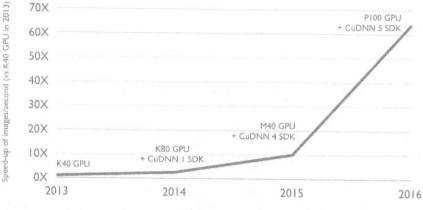

Source: NVIDIA

Figure 39: GPUs driving improvements in Training Speeds

New GPU supercomputers eclipse older chips

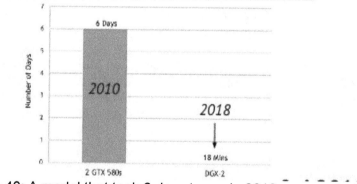

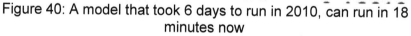

Figure 40: A model that took 6 days to run in 2010, can run in 18 minutes now

Data - Feeding the Monster

The neural networks used for deep learning typically require large data sets for training—from a few thousand examples to many millions. Fortunately, along with processing power, data creation and availability have grown exponentially. Today humanity produces 2.2 exabytes (2,300 million gigabytes) of data every day; 90% of all the world's data has been created in the last 24 months. While as a species we transferred 100GB of data per day in 1992, by 2020 we will be transferring 61,000GB per second.

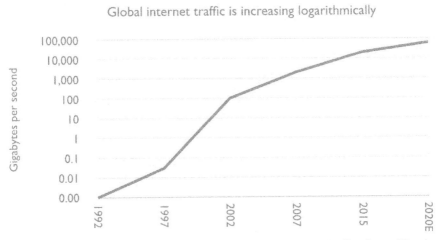

Global internet traffic is increasing logarithmically

Figure 41: Global Internet Data Traffic below—note the logarithmic scale

This chart shows the rapidly rising growth in data created, with an increasing % of it being in structured/tagged format which is easier for machines to process and/or learn from.

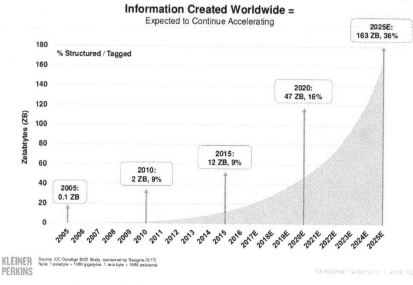

Figure 42: Data Creation Rate in Zettabytes

AI for Everyone

"Deep learning is going to be in every industry, in every business and non-profit, a tool in everyone's hands"

Francois Chollet, AI Author

Despite the technological complexity of ML, several popular frameworks are readily available which abstract much of the mathematical detail - if you know how to use them, and you have data to train them, they are tools to achieve a lot. The most popular tool at present is called TensorFlow and it's available for free download. This chart shows the key tools as rated on popular developer site GitHub (more stars equals more popular among developers)

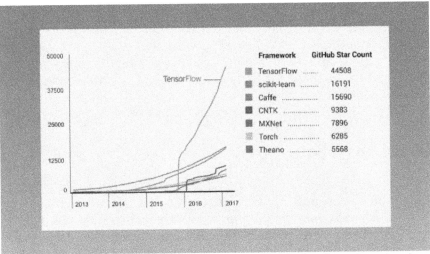

Figure 43: Popular AI Frameworks available for free download

As Francois Chollet, the creator[61] of Keras the popular ML framework for working with TensorFlow, explains:

"One thing that's really fascinating about our field is the sheer diversity of problems that you can solve with our techniques and our tools. I've seen Keras being used for so many problems I didn't even know existed. Like optimizing the operation of a salmon farm. Allocating micro-loans in developing countries. Building automated checkout systems for brick-and-mortar stores. In general, there seems to be a gap between the set of problems that people here in Silicon Valley are aware of, and all the problems that people are facing out there and that could be solved with these technologies. Making frameworks like Keras and TensorFlow free to use and as accessible as possible is a way to initiate a kind of large-scale distributed wave of problem-solving: it's the people who understand the target domains that are going to be building the solutions, on their own, using our tools, having 100x the impact that we alone could have".

But Chollet also sounds a note of caution that we'll pick up on again in chapter 9:

---

[61] https://www.pyimagesearch.com/2018/07/02/an-interview-with-francois-chollet/

"Applying machine learning inappropriately can potentially lead to simplistic, inaccurate, unaccountable, un-auditable decision systems getting deployed in serious situations and negatively affecting people's lives. And if you look at some of the ways companies and governments are using machine learning today, it's not a hypothetical risk, it's a pressing concern".

ML/DL in Action

In chapters 5 and 6, we'll delve into detail about advances in Computer Vision and Speech Recognition, but for now, these two graphs illustrate very clearly the impact Deep Learning has had on these two fields - we'll focus later on what these improvements mean in practice. In Figure 44 below you can see how computer image recognition performance has improved rapidly to now match human performance, while Figure 45 shows similar rapid improvements in Speech Recognition.

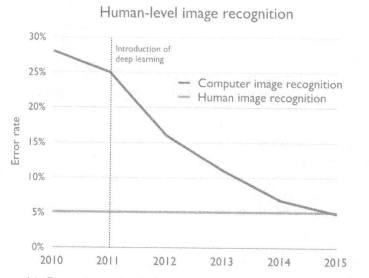

Figure 44: Deep Learning's Impact on Image Recognition Tests

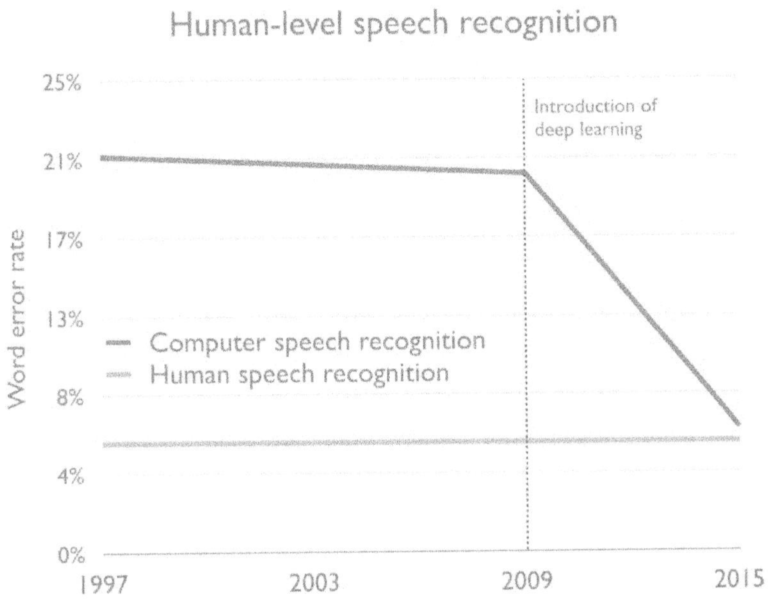

Figure 45: Deep Learning's Impact on Speech Recognition Tests

Examples - AI in Action

Whether you realise it or not, it's likely you already have multiple examples of advanced AI in operation around you. Later, in chapters 7 and 8, we'll see how many businesses and even whole industries will take on AI in the coming years, but let's begin with what several of the tech giants have already put at our fingertips.

Amazon

Throughout this book, I draw frequently on examples from Amazon's use of AI and other technology to speed up their business. And having grown from nothing to a company worth around $1 trillion dollars, making its founder Jeff Bezos the richest man in the world along the way, there is clearly much to be learned from Amazon's approach.

AI has long been at the core of Amazon's business. *"A lot of the value we're getting from machine learning is actually happening beneath the surface,"* Bezos said at the Internet Association's annual gala in May 2018. It is things such as improved search results, improved product recommendations, improved forecasting for inventory management and hundreds of other things. AI also powers Amazon's recommendation engine, which generates about 35% of the company's sales. By using data from individual customer preferences and purchases, browsing history and items that are related and regularly bought together, Amazon can use ML to create a personalized list of products that will likely appeal to the individual. And as we'll see in later examples, AI is key to Alexa, Amazon's voice-powered virtual assistant, as well as the growth of the market-leading Amazon Web Services (AWS) division and other initiatives like Amazon Go, the checkout-less store.

Google

"The last 10 years have been about building a world that is mobile-first...in the next 10 years, we will shift to a world that is AI-first"

Sundar Pichai, CEO, Google

Just as we'll draw on multiple examples from Amazon in later chapters, we'll frequently look at examples from Google and its parent company, Alphabet, as we examine the impact of technology and our changing relationship with it. Google has stated its intent to become an AI-led company and it is involved in many of the most prominent projects. Google's ubiquity means that any technologies it deploys can reach vast numbers of users. It already uses AI across commonly used products like Search, Translate, Gmail (to suggest automatic replies) and Photos (to make photos searchable). The latest version of Android (Android 9, 'Pie') uses AI to identify music, improve your battery life and take better photos. The Google Flights service predicts delays even before the airlines![62] The following graph from Google shows the growing influence of ML model use in the company.

---

[62] https://techcrunch.com/2018/01/31/google-flights-will-now-predict-airline-delays-before-the-airlines-do/

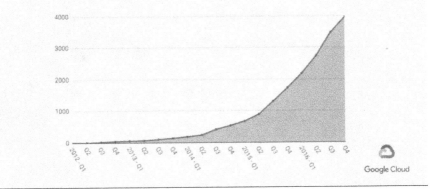

There are over 4000 TensorFlow machine learning models in production at Google, and it has transformed our company

Figure 46: ML use in Google

DeepMind

In 2014, Google bought a UK-based AI company called DeepMind for over $500m. Since then, it has gained significant publicity for its AI called AlphaGo that conquered the World Champion Go player in March 2016 in a match that was watched by over 200 million people worldwide. More recently, DeepMind has unveiled an updated version called AlphaGo Zero that used only Reinforcement Learning. Despite using less hardware, the new version beat its predecessor AlphaGo by 100 games to none, and is entirely self-taught. What is more, it achieved this performance after just 72 hours of practice.

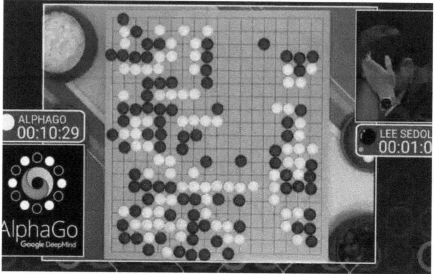
Figure 47: AlphaGo in action

While DeepMind is involved in lots of theoretical research as well as supporting AI efforts across Google, it is also partnering with leading medical institutions, as we'll discuss in chapter 8.

Facebook

Many of the experiences and interactions people have on Facebook today are made possible by AI. Given the unprecedented scale at which Facebook operates, with some 2 billion users, it is among the biggest users of AI to deal with the incredible volume of data and the need to personalize every feed. Its internal AI tool, FBLearner Flow, is used by more than 25 percent of Facebook's engineering team. Since its inception, more than a million models have been trained, and Facebook's prediction service has grown to make more than 6 million predictions per second[63]. Facebook's machine learning systems handle more than 200 trillion predictions and five billion translations per day. Its algorithms also automatically remove millions of fake accounts every day.

---

[63] https://code.facebook.com/posts/1072626246134461/introducing-fblearner-flow-facebook-s-ai-backbone/

Facebook uses both "traditional, old-school machine learning" and deep learning Multi-Layer Perceptrons (MLP), Convolutional Neural Networks (CNN), and Recurrent Neural Networks (RNN/LSTM)[64]

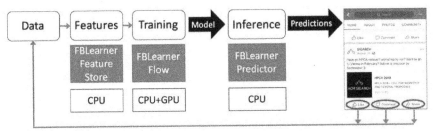

Figure 48: Example of Facebook's Machine Learning Flow for its FBLearner product into a FB Feed.

Facebook uses these tools to identify people in photos and to guess what articles you are most likely to read, as well as to translate languages. It also powers the services offered to advertisers - Facebook can comb through its entire user base of over 2 billion individuals and produce lists of millions of users who are "at risk" (based on the AI's prediction) of jumping ship from one brand to a competitor. These individuals could then be targeted aggressively with advertising that could pre-empt and change their decision.

Instagram

Having grown rapidly since its acquisition by Facebook, Instagram now boasts over a billion users. However, its reverse chronological feed was resulting in users missing 70% of all posts and 50% of their friends' posts. Instagram now users a ML algorithm based on each user's behaviour to create a unique personalised feed for everyone. Even if you follow the exact same accounts as someone else, you'll get a personalized feed based on how you interact with those accounts. Instagram also uses ML to combat bullying and delete offensive comments.

---

[64] https://www.zdnet.com/article/how-facebook-scales-ai/

Netflix

"We don't have one product but over a 100 million different products with one for each of our members with personalized recommendations and personalized visuals"

Netflix Blog[65]

Netflix also makes extensive use of AI to profile users and to personalise the tiles displayed on their home screens. And I don't just mean the titles they show; the image used for the movie or show is personalised in an effort to make it more individually appealing than the generic promo image. So, if you've a tendency to watch comedies, you'll be shown a still image featuring Robin Williams for Good Will Hunting, but if Netflix's AI thinks you're more of a romance viewer, it'll show you artwork containing Matt Damon and Minnie Driver. This level of personalised selection for each asset means handling a peak of over 20 million requests per second. The specific machine learning framework used by Netflix is "contextual bandits" - a type of simplified reinforcement learning and an intriguingly named one!

Figure 49: Three prior movie choices influence the personalised tile displayed for Good Will Hunting

---

[65] https://medium.com/netflix-techblog/artwork-personalization-c589f074ad76

The Business of AI

So, if that's a quick look at how 5 of the most technically advanced firms in the world use AI in their daily business, what does AI mean for the rest of us? How do regular businesses even know where to start? We'll look further at the business impact of AI in chapters 7 and 8 once we've explored two of the key areas of progress powered by AI.

Understanding what's possible, understanding how that maps to specific business needs, and being aware of the challenges inherent in AI are crucial. Make no mistake, this represents massive organisational challenge which is cross functional, not just an 'IT problem'.

For most people outside the technology word, the field is still largely shrouded in uncertainty at best and scepticism at worst. For those who see an opportunity and recognise an imperative to embrace AI for competitive advantage, the gap between ambition and execution is large at most companies. AI is not a magic solution to business challenges and no doubt, even among those who master the terminology, many will be disappointed at the effort involved in acquiring data, training algorithms, ensuring quality and the probabilistic rather than definitive outputs.

Leading Stanford researcher Andrew Ng created a useful table[66] summarising some generic ML applications in which some input data (A) is used to quickly generate some simple response (B).

---

[66] https://hbr.org/2016/11/what-artificial-intelligence-can-and-cant-do-right-now

What Machine Learning Can Do

A simple way to think about supervised learning.

INPUT A	RESPONSE B	APPLICATION
Picture	Are there human faces? (0 or 1)	Photo tagging
Loan application	Will they repay the loan? (0 or 1)	Loan approvals
Ad plus user information	Will user click on ad? (0 or 1)	Targeted online ads
Audio clip	Transcript of audio clip	Speech recognition
English sentence	French sentence	Language translation
Sensors from hard disk, plane engine, etc.	Is it about to fail?	Preventive maintenance
Car camera and other sensors	Position of other cars	Self-driving cars

Figure 50: Machine Learning Applications

Being able to input A and output B will transform many industries. Today's supervised learning software has an Achilles' heel: it requires a huge amount of data. You need to show the system lots of examples of both A and B. For instance, building a photo tagger requires anywhere from tens to hundreds of thousands of pictures (A) as well as labels or tags specifying if there are people in them (B). So what can A→B do? Here's one rule of thumb that speaks to AI's disruptiveness: If a typical person can do a mental task with less than one second of thought, we can probably automate it using AI either now or in the near future.

A lot of valuable work currently done by humans — examining security video to detect suspicious behaviours, a driver deciding if a car is about to hit a pedestrian, a moderator finding and eliminating abusive online posts — can be done in less than one second. These tasks are ripe for automation. However, they often fit into a larger context or business process; figuring out these linkages to the rest of your business is also important. Understanding what AI can do and how it fits into your strategy is the beginning, not the end, of that process.

Fear Factor

"While it is hard to calculate the cascade upon cascade of new developments and their positive effects, we already know the dire consequences and frightening scenarios that threaten to engulf us. A great transformation of human society is under way, greater than Gutenberg's revolution – greater I would submit than the Industrial Revolution (though clearly dependent on it) – the greatest change to our ways of living since we moved from hunting and gathering to settling down in farms, villages and seaports and started to trade and form civilisations."

Stephen Fry[67]

Much discussion of AI tends to involve fears about whether our continued pursuit of greater computational powers will lead to the demise of humans as AI gains sentience and disposes of us. While it is obviously worth proceeding carefully, at present there does not seem to be a significant risk of such a development. Currently, there is no known path from even the current best narrow A.I. tools (such as DeepMind's AlphaGo Zero) to "general" A.I. — self-aware computer programs that have mastered general common-sense reasoning, knowledge acquisition across multiple domains, emotions and other such human characteristics.

But the lack of imminent general AI and the so-called Singularity[68] doesn't mean AI poses no risk. As we'll see in later chapters, there are very real concerns about the threat AI poses to jobs, to justice and to the global balance of power. The real fear should relate to our ability to harness the positives of AI whilst mitigating these risks.

Making Senses - The Capabilities built on ML

Although we've touched on some examples of the potential of ML, I want to look in much more detail in the next chapters at two areas - the advances that are giving computers not intelligence but "senses" - capabilities that allow them to move into whole new areas and

---

[67] http://www.stephenfry.com/2017/05/the-way-ahead/

[68] https://en.wikipedia.org/wiki/Technological_singularity

capabilities that will forever change our relationship with technology.

Although the recent advances in creating Artificial Narrow Intelligence have impacted myriad areas, the advances in the areas of image and voice are particularly striking, as they veer towards the creation of anthropomorphic computers. Machine learning is enabling computers to have senses, which is more important than the physical anthropomorphism of humanoid robots we were expecting - it gives computers the ability to interact with us on our own familiar terms. As we shall see in the next two chapters, the radical advance of computer vision and natural language processing, two of AI's most important and useful functions, are directly related to the creation of deep learning artificial neural networks.

Chapter 5: See++

"We're going from computers with cameras, that take photos, to computers with eyes, that can see"

Ben Evans[69]

For the first half-century of computing, computers were blind. For input, they relied on a steady stream of data, from punch cards or keyboards, largely in the basic form of letters and numbers (as opposed to images, sound or video). And they got really really good at analysing it and extracting value from it. Feed a computer a list of structured information and it's quite easy to get valuable insights from it; show a computer a photograph that a 3-year-old human could identify as a cat or a dog, and it was flummoxed. But not anymore. This new capability for computers to see has huge implications for society and the economy. If computers can "see", they can do a lot more than they could before, and they can do it much faster than humans.

Learning to See

"The relation between what we see and what we know is never settled..."
John Berger, Ways of Seeing

You may think that the ability for computers to see what's in an image isn't all that useful. After all, humans are very good at recognising and labelling images, so maybe it's not an area we particularly need help with? But speed and scale are the two things to consider. A computer can instantly compare any image it sees with a perfect recall of every previous image it has seen. And it can do it in milliseconds without ever getting tired. And this applies to video as well as photos. A computer can pick out 100 distinct faces in a crowd before a human can spot two. So, for applications from image recognition to self-driving cars to surveillance, computers that can see are a breakthrough - the progression from just taking photos to seeing the world is key: it will unlock numerous areas previously impervious to automation.

---

[69] https://twitter.com/BenedictEvans/status/760174699263385600?s=09

In this section, we'll look first at the proliferation of digital cameras (a vital source of visual data), and then at how the technologies described in the previous chapter enable computers to make sense of all these visual inputs.

Computers being able to see the photos they're taking allows for massive improvements to the end product for us. If computers can learn what makes a photo better through ML training, they can apply that knowledge to the photos we take - already, features such as portrait mode, exposure correction and object removal are all possible thanks to ML. But before we explore this in more detail, it's useful to first understand how digital photography works as the technology underlying this revolution - the digital eyes that are now connected to digital brains that can interpret the images.

Faster Photos

It's not long since the process of taking a photo involved waiting about a week from pressing the shutter button to actually getting to see your photos. Nothing could be done if you'd missed the moment you thought you'd captured. Sharing photos involved holding negatives up to the light to try to discern which one you wanted reprints of, then waiting another week for them to come back. While timelines improved when one-hour photo minilabs became popular during the 1980s, they commanded a significant price premium over waiting a few days for your photos.

Digital photography changed all that - bringing unprecedented speed to the entire process. Now you can preview a digital photograph in real time, print glossy copies of it on a home printer that costs less than $50 and email it to anywhere in the world in an instant. Those that grew up with photo film processing delays and limited shots per roll will find it odd that there's now an app (Gudak Cam) that recreates that 'slow' experience for today's incredulous teens.

In digital photography, when you press the button, the "picture" hits the image sensor chip, which breaks it up into millions of pixels. The sensor measures the colour and brightness of each pixel and stores it as a number. Your digital photograph is effectively an enormously long string of numbers describing the exact details of each pixel it contains. This technology has taken a couple of decades to become ubiquitous but has completely changed the way we take photos.

The Second Coming of the Camera

"It only took 50 milliseconds to capture the image, but it took 23 seconds to record it to the tape. I'd pop the cassette tape out, hand it to my assistant and he put it in our playback unit. About 30 seconds later, up popped the 100 pixels by 100 pixels black and white image."

Steven Sasson, Kodak[70]

The first digital camera (created by Kodak in 1975) wasn't very good. It was large, expensive, had no screen of its own and created terrible images (about one hundredth of one megapixel - by comparison, my phone today creates 23-megapixel images). Things have advanced rapidly since then, and in November 2000, Sharp launched the first phone with a camera in Japan and thus began the modern era of everyone carrying an image sensor in their pocket.

Steven Sasson with the prototype digital camera.

Figure 51: The first digital camera

[70] https://lens.blogs.nytimes.com/2015/08/12/kodaks-first-digital-moment/

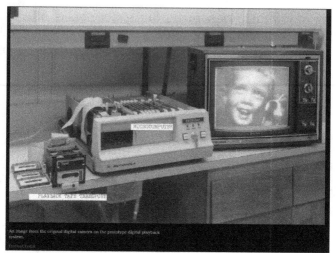

Figure 52: The machine to display the output

Today, there are over 3 billion digital cameras in the world - the vast majority embedded in phones. 98.4% of the consumer 'cameras' sold in 2016 were built into smartphones – only 0.8% were compacts, 0.5% DSLRs, and 0.2% mirrorless."[71] If you look at the graph below, only a tiny sliver represents dedicated camera devices, while the vast grey tower represents cameras in mobile phones. Laptops, tablet devices, and even cars now have multiple cameras.

---

[71] https://petapixel.com/2017/03/03/latest-camera-sales-chart-reveals-death-compact-camera/

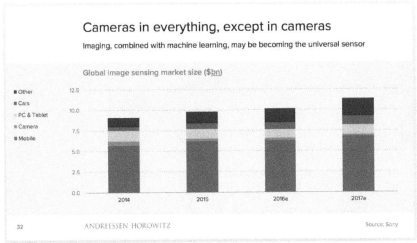

Figure 53: Very few camera sensors end up in "cameras"

Most phones today actually boast two cameras with cameras on both the front and rear of all but the very cheapest devices. Several high-end models now have more - with two or even 3 on the back. Amazon built a phone with 5 cameras on the front! Things might not have turned out this way - for many years, mobile carriers were urging phone makers to remove the front-facing camera to save cost as nobody was using video calling. Then apps happened. Video calling worked, selfies became a thing, and filters like bunny ears swept apps like Snapchat and Snow to hundreds of millions of users. There was also a brief period when you could buy webcams as accessories for computers. Now, it's almost impossible to get a computer without a camera already built in.

Looking at this next graph shows the cost of digital sensors declining rapidly as, first, compact digital cameras and then phones, drove volumes. Now, the cost of a sensor is so low that adding a camera to practically any device is possible - which is why we see cameras in everything from cheap phones to doorbells to vending machines.

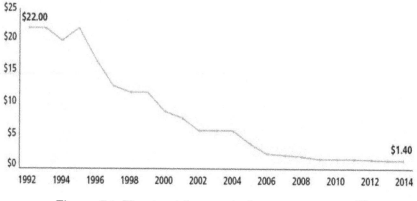
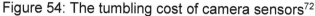

Figure 54: The tumbling cost of camera sensors[72]

The move to digital photography and video capture changed everything. Gone were the restrictions of film, the delays, the physical size of the device required to hold a canister of gelatin and silver halide crystals. Capturing has changed: cameras in our hands, cameras on lampposts & buildings and wearable cameras. Smartphones, Dash Cams, GoPro, Drones. Over 300 hours of video are uploaded to YouTube every minute. The following chart shows the dramatic growth in the capture of photos since the advent of digital photography.

---

[72] http://itac.ca/uploads/events/execforum2010/rob_lineback_10-6-10-2.ppt

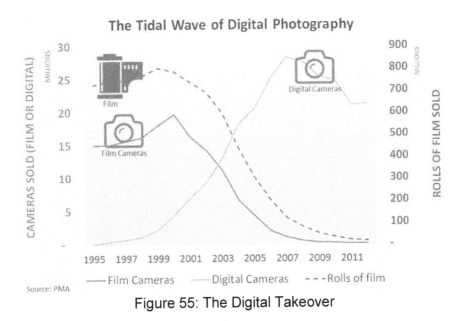

Figure 55: The Digital Takeover

Better Photos

"The result, when applied to Apple scale, has the power to be transformative for modern photography, with millions of amateur shots suddenly professionalized"

John Paczkowski, Managing Editor, Buzzfeed[73]

We've all been disappointed with how a photo we've taken has turned out, and most of us don't have the post-processing skills to fix it. Basic errors in exposure can leave a photo too bright or too dark. Similarly, few who haven't studied photography know how to achieve the nice professional looking blurred effect common on portrait photos (known as bokeh).

But thanks to improved sensors and AI processing, photos can be automatically fixed. "*It's all seamless; the camera just does what it needs to,*" says Apple Exec Phil Schiller. "*The software knows how to take care of it for you. There are no settings.*" An MIT and Google

---

[73] https://www.buzzfeed.com/johnpaczkowski/iphone-portrait-lighting

research paper[74] describes an algorithm that can enhance a photo in real time - even before you press the shutter. Their neural network was trained with more than 5,000 professionally edited photos, which taught it specific editing rules associated with "good" photos.

Despite some concerns about the loss of skills, AI removes technical barriers to good photos for many people: *But isn't something lost when you use software to simplify and automate a process that's historically been artistic? After all, there's something a bit dystopian feeling about pushing a button and essentially flattening the playing field between professionals and amateurs. "This is not about dumbing things down," Apple Human Interface Team member Johnnie Manzari observes, noting that as devices become more professional, they often become more intimidating. "This is about accessibility. It's about helping people take advantage of their own creativity."*[75]

Not Just Photos

"The camera system in the iPhone is becoming the central focus of its technological advancements. And it's not just about pictures anymore. With augmented reality and computer vision emerging as contenders for the next major wave in platform development, the camera system is an input mechanism, a communications system and a statement of intent".

TechCrunch[76]

Today's leading smartphones take better photos than ever - stabilised images, better focus, better exposure, super slow motion, even bokeh effects for professional looking portraits, etc. These features will quickly trickle down from top end models to all but the cheapest phones in just a couple of years. But as mentioned in the quote above, cameras are no longer just about taking photos. They also enable multiple new applications. The old maxim was that a picture's worth a thousand words, but, it's now a lot more - it's deconstructed, it's analysed, it's located, it's timed and dated. It's compared and

---

[74] http://groups.csail.mit.edu/graphics/hdrnet/data/hdrnet.pdf

[75] https://www.buzzfeed.com/johnpaczkowski/iphone-portrait-lighting

[76] https://techcrunch.com/2017/09/19/review-iphone-8/

categorised. And as models trained using ML pour over it, multiple new applications for photos are unleashed. If you have cameras creating high quality digital images everywhere, generating data, what can you now do with it? What can AI do beyond making our photos look better? That's the next revolution in photography - the AI vision revolution.

Two Pizzas on a Stove

"There are fundamental changes that will happen now that computer vision really works, now that computers have opened their eyes."

Jeff Dean, Head of Google AI[77]

This seemingly mundane image of pizza is actually one of the most remarkable I've ever seen. Perhaps not very aesthetically pleasing to human eyes (unless you're hungry), its importance is derived from the caption: it was added automatically by a computer; a computer was able to identify that this is a photo of a pizza and add a caption. What may seem simple to a human is a game changer for the capabilities of computers. They are starting to open their eyes and *see*.

---

[77] http://fortune.com/ai-artificial-intelligence-deep-machine-learning/

Figure 56: Two Pizzas on a Stove

Computer Vision, the branch of computer science devoted to enabling computers to see, is not something people are necessarily conscious of - if you ask most people, they probably think they don't use computer vision, but most of us use it several times a week. Whether in a basic form such as barcodes, or an ANPR camera reading your license plate at a toll booth, computers have already started to watch us in limited ways.

But computer vision is no longer confined to barcodes. Researchers have been working for years to get computers to recognise the contents of images. But until recently, results have been too poor to use in most settings. While performing Optical Character Recognition (OCR) on a pre-defined form has been relatively easy, computers have typically failed more than a quarter of the time to identify even simple images. The recent advances in deep learning described in the previous chapter have had a dramatic impact on image recognition and the ability of computers to correctly identify objects in an image. So, what specifically does machine learning bring to the field of computer vision?

Object Detection & Visual Search

As we saw in the pizza example above, computers are getting significantly better at identifying objects in photos, which means they can also search photos looking for items. As you can see from the graph below, showing AI performance on a standard object detection test, performance has improved dramatically in the years since Deep Learning was applied. Just a few years ago, it would take a month or longer to train an image recognition model on the ImageNet dataset (a standard databank of training images). Today, with more recent processors, Facebook can do the same in under an hour.

The performance of AI systems on the object detection task in the Large Scale Visual Recognition Challenge (LSVRC) Competition.

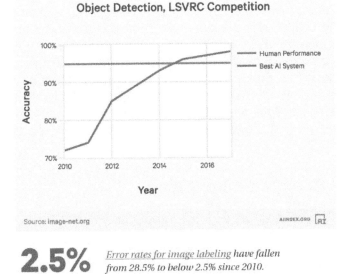

Object Detection, LSVRC Competition

Source: image-net.org

2.5% *Error rates for image labeling have fallen from 28.5% to below 2.5% since 2010.*

Figure 57: ML-derived improvements in Object Detection

Google offers a cloud-based application program interface, which can detect faces, signs, landmarks, objects, and text within a single image.

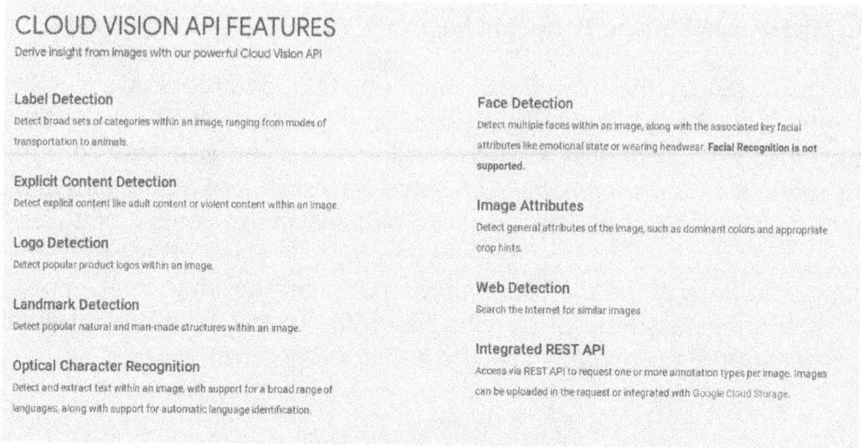

CLOUD VISION API FEATURES
Derive insight from images with our powerful Cloud Vision API

Label Detection
Detect broad sets of categories within an image, ranging from modes of transportation to animals.

Explicit Content Detection
Detect explicit content like adult content or violent content within an image.

Logo Detection
Detect popular product logos within an image.

Landmark Detection
Detect popular natural and man-made structures within an image.

Optical Character Recognition
Detect and extract text within an image, with support for a broad range of languages, along with support for automatic language identification.

Face Detection
Detect multiple faces within an image, along with the associated key facial attributes like emotional state or wearing headwear. Facial Recognition is not supported.

Image Attributes
Detect general attributes of the image, such as dominant colors and appropriate crop hints.

Web Detection
Search the Internet for similar images.

Integrated REST API
Access via REST API to request one or more annotation types per image. Images can be uploaded in the request or integrated with Google Cloud Storage.

Figure 58: Google's Cloud Vision API Features

In case you're thinking that such image recognition requires massive computing power, it is possible to run an image recognition service with near human levels of accuracy on just a mobile phone. Google provides a range of different size models[78] (the larger the model, the better it performs) that are already trained for use in mobile apps. The Convolutional Neural Network (CNN) model can perform chores like object detection, face attribute recognition, fine-grained classification (recognising a dog-breed, for instance) and landmark recognition.

Object Recognition in Video

So far in this section, we've talked about how digital cameras and AI techniques can both enhance photos visually as well as learn what's in a photo. It's extremely important to note at this point that much of what applies to photos also applies to video, although the sheer volume of data in a moving image, as opposed to a still image, requires different techniques.

Google's Video Intelligence[79] service automatically recognises objects in videos and makes videos searchable. As well as object detection, it also allows tagging of scene changes in a video or detecting suspected adult content.

---

[78] https://ai.googleblog.com/2017/06/mobilenets-open-source-models-for.html
[79] https://cloud.google.com/video-intelligence/

Figure 59: Google's Video Intelligence Service recognises a Tiger in a video

Visual Search

"A lot of the future of search is going to be about pictures instead of keywords"

Ben Silbermann, CEO, Pinterest

As computers learn to detect objects in photos and videos, the next obvious question is what can be done with these new capabilities. Some applications are focused on identifying the content - for example Google Lens allows you to point your camera at an object and see what it is, at a sign or menu and have the text translated; or even identify a target item of clothing for purchase. Pinterest uses visual search to identify more pins like one you select - in this case, it's identified more pizzas based on a visual search from the top left example.

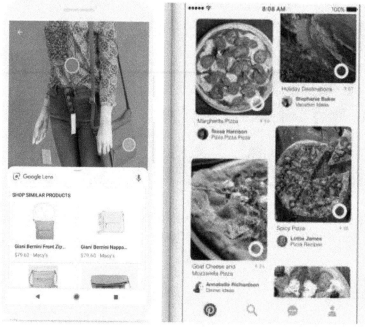

Figure 60: Google Lens Visual Search (L) and Pinterest Visual Search (R)

This simplicity of visual search is a big improvement. It enables people to find information without requiring them to type into a search box. Some things are hard to describe, or you may not know the word for it to be able to type or voice search it.

Face Recognition

As computers begin to be able to reliably identify what's in a photo, they can also now tackle other questions: the next step after being able to determine what is in a photo, is *who* is in an image. Then follow up questions like where was the photo taken, when was the photo taken? What's the emotion associated with the expression of the people in the photo?

Google Photos, with over 1 billion users, is one of Google's most popular products and may be one of the most widespread examples of AI in consumer use today. Over a billion photos per day are uploaded to the service, offering a huge data set to train on. Thanks to ML, uploaded images (including videos) are now searchable - for people, places, things, words. I can pick up my phone, open Google photos and search for the word dog. Every photo I have taken that contains a dog is shown. Similarly, it has grouped photos by faces it sees frequently, allowing me to see all the photos containing any one of my friends. Its accuracy amazed me recently when going through old photos to prepare a montage for a family event: it was able to pick out photos of me that were 40 years old and correctly identify me, based only on the facial recognition machine learning had identified from recent photos of me. Google Photos will also now suggest sharing a photo with any of your contacts it has identified in it.

Likewise, Facebook's Moments app will suggest sharing photos with friends in an image. Facebook has an internal ML-trained system called Lumos that enables image searching by keywords on your Facebook photo albums. Facebook also has an Alternative (Alt) Text Tool[80] that provides descriptions of photos for visually impaired users. People using screen readers will hear a list of items a photo may contain. Previously, people using screen readers would only hear the name of the person who shared the photo, followed by the term "photo" when they came upon an image in the News Feed. Now, they'll get a richer description of what's in a photo thanks to automatic alt text. For instance, someone could now hear, "Image may contain three people, smiling, outdoors."

Face Unlock

Face recognition is not only useful for identifying who is in a photo. Both phones and laptops can now securely unlock simply by looking at them. For years I thought the fastest way to unlock a phone was a fingerprint - now I don't even have to touch a sensor. For example, the iPhone X uses a camera to check over 30,000 points on your face, while Windows Hello unlocks laptops with a near infrared camera to ensure you're not trying to trick it with a photo instead of a real person.

---

[80] https://newsroom.fb.com/news/2016/04/using-artificial-intelligence-to-help-blind-people-see-facebook/

On some laptops, the camera that was put there ostensibly for video calls has been repurposed to carry out instant facial recognition. The Windows Hello face recognition engine[81] consists of four distinct steps that allow Windows to understand who is in front of the sensor:

1. Find the face and discover landmarks - the algorithm detects the user's face in the camera stream and then locates facial landmark points (also known as alignment points), which correspond to eyes, nose, mouth, and so on.

2. Head orientation - to ensure the algorithm has enough of your face in view to make an authentication decision, it ensures the user is facing towards the device +/- 15 degrees.

3. Representation vector - Using the landmark locations as anchor points, the algorithm takes thousands of samples from different areas of the face to build a representation. The representation at its most basic form is a histogram representing the light and dark differences around specifics points. For privacy reasons, no image of the face is ever stored – it is only the representation.

4. Decision engine - Once there is a representation of the user in front of the sensor, it is compared to the enrolled users on the physical device. The representation must cross a machine-learned threshold before the algorithm will accept it as a correct match.

Once computers can detect a face and identify it, the potential for new features doesn't end there. A few years back, I was amazed by the app that can tell my heart rate and breathing rate using just an iPhone camera. But once I understood that it's sensitive enough to detect changes (invisible to our eyes) in face colour due to the blood flow of my heart beat and infer my heart rate from that, it made sense. But it also leads to more questions about what more computers can see when they look at us.

---

[81] https://docs.microsoft.com/en-us/windows-hardware/design/device-experiences/windows-hello-face-authentication

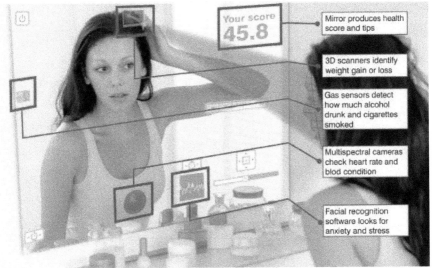

Figure 61: A future bathroom mirror watching us - credit: The Next Web[82]

Sentiment Analysis

The field of Sentiment Analysis via computer vision will be able to assess faces and look for signs of anxiety, stress, happiness and more. Microsoft Azure[83] offers a range of services including the ability to analyse faces to detect a range of feelings and personalise an app's responses. The emotions detected are anger, contempt, disgust, fear, happiness, neutral, sadness, and surprise. These emotions are understood to be cross-culturally and universally communicated with particular facial expressions. As well as in still images, it can recognize emotions in video by extracting frames of a video and then sending those frames to the API.

Similarly, Google offers a service to do sentiment analysis on an uploaded photo shown here:

[82] https://thenextweb.com/insider/2016/05/13/the-internet-of-eyes-and-the-personification-of-everything-around-you
[83] https://azure.microsoft.com/en-us/services/cognitive-services/emotion/

Joy						Very Unlikely
Sorrow						Very Unlikely
Anger						Very Unlikely
Surprise	▪ ▪ ▪ ▪					Likely
Exposed						Very Unlikely
Blurred						Very Unlikely
Headwear						Very Unlikely

Roll: 4°   Tilt: 12°   Pan: -4°

Confidence   99%

Figure 62: Google's Sentiment Analysis API

Much of this technology is somewhat reminiscent of scenes from the then-futuristic Terminator movies but it is already in widespread use, frequently without much public awareness. Retailers in particular are using sentiment analysis to track customer mood, and we'll talk more about this in chapter 7. In China, for example, fried chicken franchise KFC recently unveiled its first "smart restaurant" that uses facial recognition to predict what meal customers are likely to want, based on their age, gender, mood and the time of day.

Figure 63: The Terminator Visual Scanning and Object Recognition
- © 1991 Carolco Pictures

Applied Computer Vision

As computers start to see, we'll notice them infiltrating numerous walks of life - both an increase in the number of physical cameras watching us in more and more places, and an increase in what they are looking for as ML continues to improve their capabilities. Importantly, these developments will also mean things we never thought of as computer vision issues will have technology applied to them.

Cameras in the Home

You might have noticed in the graph earlier that cameras in non-camera devices are a growing category, and that includes the emergence of image sensors in places you wouldn't have previously expected them. Central to home security and smart homes, the idea of private security cameras is relatively recent. But even more recent is the addition of "smart" technology that goes beyond simple motion detection - some devices can identify a person as opposed to an animal, and in the case of a known person ringing your smart doorbell, your phone can even announce the name of the person at the door. I expect market leaders Nest, Amazon/Ring and Netatmo to continue to add smarts to their cameras. Meantime, Amazon has also announced a smart camera for your home that can take your photo and use machine learning to analyse your outfit to give you daily fashion advice (Echo Look). Perhaps even more unexpectedly, the camera in my fridge lets me check if there is anything missing, while I'm in the supermarket. Hold on a minute, there's a camera for my fridge?? Some of these use cases may seem like distinctly first world problems!

Cameras in the High Street

For all the commentary and concern about online privacy, web site cookies and worries that online shopping sites are tracking you, when you walk into most retail premises on the high street, a sensor is used to count you. For years, stores have used this basic footfall measure to keep track of how many people come into their locations. It helps planning for staffing levels, working out sales conversion levels and other retailer KPIs. But as the sophistication of the technology available increases, these devices are being replaced with cameras that can do far more than simply count something as vague as "people". One London company[84] offers a system using foot-level cameras to anonymously examine retail footfall (literally) by assessing footwear and using ML to figure out if they are male or female. By placing cameras at ground level throughout the store, you can anonymously track a person's journey through the store. We'll talk more about related advances in retailing again in chapter 7.

Assistive Technologies

Encouragingly, there are already several examples of AI capabilities being used to help people with disabilities or challenges in daily life.

For the vision-impaired

An extremely promising area for computer vision and its new ML-learned skills is the emergence of apps to assist those (numbering over 250 million people worldwide[85]) with visual impairments. This is an area where technological advances can make meaningful improvements to individuals' lives. Microsoft offers an experimental app called Seeing AI[86] that uses computer vision to describe the world for the visually impaired. It offers a number of modes to help identify people (and their emotions), products, documents, images and currency.

---

[84] https://www.hoxtonanalytics.com/

[85] http://www.who.int/news-room/fact-sheets/detail/blindness-and-visual-impairment

[86] https://www.microsoft.com/en-us/seeing-ai

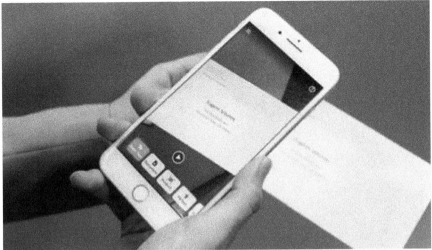

Figure 64: Microsoft's Seeing AI App

Some of the features are available via ML models on the phone itself (known as "at the edge" in technology terms - where the AI runs on the device rather than requiring a connection back to a data centre). However, some of Seeing AI's more experimental features — like describing an entire scene or recognizing handwriting — require an internet connection.

Similarly, the Google Lookout app[87] helps people who are blind or visually impaired by giving auditory cues as they encounter objects, text and people around them.

---

[87] https://www.blog.google/outreach-initiatives/accessibility/lookout-app-help-blind-and-visually-impaired-people-learn-about-their-surroundings/

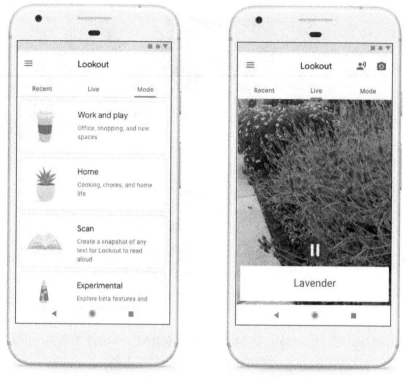

Figure 65: Google's Lookout App

It is designed to be used installed on your phone worn in a lanyard around your neck, or in your shirt pocket, with the camera visible and pointing away from your body. Depending on the mode Lookout processes items of importance in your environment and speaks information it believes to be relevant—text from a recipe book, or the location of a bathroom, an exit sign, a chair or a person nearby.

For example, in Home mode, you'll hear notifications that tell you where the couch, table or dishwasher is. It gives you an idea of where those objects are in relation to you, for example "couch 3 o'clock" means the couch is on your right. The core experience is processed on the device, which means the app can be used without an internet connection.

For the hearing impaired

Lip reading apps are likely to become available in the not too distant future. In 2016, Google's Deep Mind and Oxford University published a study[88] describing how they had used TensorFlow to train a convolutional neural network using LSTM on almost 5,000 hours of BBC footage to "lip read" and annotate the video footage with 46.8 percent accuracy. That might not seem too impressive but for comparison, a professional human lip-reader was correct only 26.2 percent of the time. The following sequences of images shows a computer closely watching lips to infer what was spoken.

Figure 66: Lip Reading - The mouth motions for 'afternoon' from two different speakers

What Else?

Two other hugely hyped areas of technology, Self-Driving Cars (SDC) and Augmented Reality (AR) rely heavily on cameras and computer vision. SDC combine images from cameras with other types of inputs, such as LIDAR, in a process known as sensor fusion. Together, these inputs can give SDC superhuman sight, which is then processed by a variety of algorithms to determine how to proceed safely. Tesla's driver assistance system, Autopilot, uses 8 cameras (and radar) to provide enhanced cruise control that, while not fully autonomous, can for example enable the car to park itself in a garage. Augmented Reality, whether in phones (for example, Apple's ARKit and Google's ARCore) or glasses (for example Magic Leap), depends heavily on computer vision advances. While augmented reality is a powerful and

---

[88] https://arxiv.org/pdf/1611.05358v1.pdf

promising technology that can overlay digital images or interfaces onto a real-world view, the ease with which we can now change what we see gives pause for thought.

The Camera Never Lies

There are plenty of times when you'd like to be able to fix a photo - not to manipulate in a deceptive way but to, for example, remove visual obstructions. AI-powered systems are becoming increasingly proficient at such activities. Consider the example Google showed at their IO developer conference in 2017:

Figure 67: Google's Object Removal Technology (Unreleased)

This kind of capability raises questions about authenticity. Although clearly a better picture, it's also somewhat inaccurate in that it's not actually what the taker saw - it may well represent what they wanted, and it may also be a true reflection of what would have been possible from a slightly better location and doesn't have a malicious intent, but it certainly doesn't fit with the maxim that the camera never lies.

Or this example[89] which can remove the distortion of raindrops on lens using a generative adversarial network:

Figure 68: ML removes raindrops from image (see website for hi-res version to appreciate the detail)

As an important reminder of the power of algorithms when combined, looping back to the earlier section on object detection, the paper also shows how the removal of raindrops improves the recognition by 10%:

[89] https://arxiv.org/pdf/1711.10098.pdf

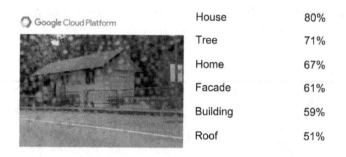

House	80%	
Tree	71%	
Home	67%	
Facade	61%	
Building	59%	
Roof	51%	

(a) Recognizing result of original image

Property	89%	
House	87%	
Real Estate	70%	
Road	64%	
Home	63%	
Facade	62%	

(b) Recognizing result of our removal result

Figure 69: Raindrops removal improves Object Detection scores

Just Add Beauty

Popular apps, Snap and Instagram, include extensive camera-based features to change how their users look. Apps like Snow and B612 have 100's of millions of users even though the sole purpose of the app is to produce photos with funny or cute effects. These use ML to analyse the camera feed and add digital embellishments for sharing on social sites. They have sliders to control how much to "beautify" your photo, with face slimming and skin smoothing algorithms working in real time. This may seem harmless but has led to concerns about the impact of these images on people's body image, especially among teenagers.

Figure 70: Snow AR App Beauty Effects

Such manipulations are largely intended for humorous effect or social sharing, but of course the ability to alter a photo opens a pandora's box of opportunities to make changes far more nefarious than removing obstructions. Computers that can see and understand photos and videos will quickly be able to manipulate them too, without our direct supervision. For decades, we'd been able to rely on authenticity of photos, and then came Photoshop. But that required a relatively skilled person and some time to "touch up" photographs. But we're now entering an era when materially altering photos can be instant, indiscernible and also applies to video - where AR will change what we see, and tools such as Deepfakes[90] can be used to "put words into people's mouths" - which represents the next generation of fake news. We are perhaps used to scouring an image for some incongruous shadow or unlikely juxtaposition that alerts our mind to the likelihood of tampering but we are not trained to question video in the same way. "Read My Lips" will take on a whole new meaning!

---

[90] https://en.wikipedia.org/wiki/Deepfake

Fake News

In an age of Photoshop, filters and social media, many of us are used to seeing manipulated pictures – subjects become slimmer and smoother or, in the case of Snapchat, transformed into puppies. Photoshop has conditioned us to question images, but it's a post-processing tool that requires quite a lot of skill and time to use; it's not a real-time change that requires no user skill.

However, there's a new breed of video and audio manipulation tools, made possible by the advances in artificial intelligence discussed in the previous chapter, that will allow for the creation of realistic looking footage of public figures appearing to say, well, anything. For example, software developed at Stanford University is able to manipulate video footage of public figures to allow someone to put words in their mouth – in real time. Face2Face[91] captures the second person's facial expressions as they talk into a webcam and then morphs those movements directly onto the face of the person in the original video. Although user intentions may be well-meaning, voice-morphing technology could be combined with face-morphing technology to create convincing fake statements by public figures. Some academics have already developed ML solutions to detect fakes[92].

At a time of increasing volumes of accusations of fake news and the use of social networks to instantly and widely disseminate materials of questionable provenance, these technologies present a very real risk of adding fuel to the fire. While forgeries involving high profile speakers are likely to be scrutinised and discredited at some point, there exists the likelihood that some people will take these videos at face value and not be aware of any subsequent clarifications or retractions.

---

[91] https://web.stanford.edu/~zollhoef/papers/CVPR2016_Face2Face/page.html
[92] https://arxiv.org/abs/1806.02877

Nobody Behind the Camera

Given the advances enabled by deep learning to now recognise many of the elements of a good photograph: people, smiles, pets, sunsets, famous landmarks and more, one logical extension would be to consider if a computer could decide when to take a photo, based on these components thus raising the question - can the camera become the photographer?

Photography has always required a photographer. For nearly 200 years, there's been someone in charge of the shutter button. In 1900, the Kodak Brownie popularised amateur photography, while a century later, the rise of the smartphone has seen photo taking soar to 1.2 trillion every year. But we're just at the start of a new revolution in photography - where we're no longer the ones even taking the photos. With all the recent talk about robots and AI replacing humans, who would have thought that photographers would be among the activities in the firing line so soon? Yet, there are already multiple indications that point to an impending sudden change where we're no longer the ones composing the best images.

In December 2017, the Research at Google team quietly released the innocuous looking free Selfissimo app[93]. With barely any interface at all, this app snaps Selfies of you when it detects a change in your pose. It's a camera app with no shutter button - it decides when to take the photos. In early 2018, heavily funded start-up Skydio[94] unveiled their first product - an autonomous drone that can follow a person (even when they run) while dodging any obstacles in its way. Travelling at up to 25 miles per hour, it can track a person and record them in high quality video, with a smooth aerial perspective once the preserve of Hollywood movies. Although rather pricey at $2,500, I would expect such functionality to become more affordable very rapidly.

In early 2018, the Google Hardware team launched the Clips "camera". It decides when to take the photos, its purpose to recognise and unobtrusively capture moments that you wouldn't otherwise. Moments where you are in the photo rather than taking the photo.

---

[93] https://ai.googleblog.com/2017/12/introducing-appsperiments-exploring.html
[94] https://www.skydio.com/

Moments that your phone would ruin. It is intended to identify and record "interesting" moments as short videos. It's self-contained (i.e. no Internet connection required), with an internal processor to assess what it sees and save what it deems to be important. Its focus is on capturing candid moments of people and pets, rather than the more abstract and subjective problem of capturing artistic images. It's surprisingly small in real life, which may prompt a reaction of "it's creepy". At $250, it's not especially cheap, but may appeal to parents or pet lovers seeking images a little different from the bland predictability that populates Facebook and Instagram feeds.

Figure 71: Google Clips Smart Camera powered by AI

The Clips is an experiment and a showcase. Although it features a shutter button to reassure hesitant folk for whom a camera device without a button is a step too far; it's not intended to be used but more a vestigial sop to a bygone era. Clips is not a mass market device that will appeal to everyone but it's a signal of what's to come - intelligent devices that are watching us. In this instance at least, they are benevolent devices seeking to capture precious moments for us that we might otherwise miss.

A detailed blog post from Google[95] explained the training process behind the Clips: *the engineers assembled a dataset of videos and then employed expert photographers and video editors to select the best short video segments. These early curations provided "good" examples for algorithms to emulate. However, in order to create a smooth gradient of labels from "perfect" to "terrible" the team also*

---

[95] https://ai.googleblog.com/2018/05/automatic-photography-with-google-clips.html

rated pairs of clips - this pairwise comparison approach, instead of having raters score videos directly, because it is much easier to choose the better of a pair than it is to specify a number. Given this quality score training data, our next step was to train a neural network model to estimate the quality of any photograph captured by the device. We started with the basic assumption that knowing what's in the photograph (e.g., people, dogs, trees, etc.) will help determine "interestingness". To identify content labels in our training data, we leveraged the same Google machine learning technology that powers Google image search and Google Photos, a subset of the over 27,000 different labels describing objects, concepts, and actions that were most relevant to predicting the "interestingness" of a photograph. We then trained a MobileNet Image Content Model (ICM) to recognizing the most interesting elements of photographs, while ignoring non-relevant content.

First Make Photos Pretty, next....Surveillance?

For anyone who has seen the Tom Hanks & Emma Watson movie, The Circle, the notion of an artificially intelligent miniature camera will arouse immediate suspicion. Already fairly common in surveillance and security, the "leisure" applications of computers that can see are starting to emerge. The Clips is essentially constantly thinking: Is that person important? Do they look happy? Will this make a good photo? If it thinks so, it'll store the photo for you. It's intended for capturing parties not criminals but the underlying technology is flexible.

There are already plenty of home security cameras that can detect faces, or tell animals from humans so as not to set off an alarm. While premium devices such as the Nest camera retail at $299, Wyze, created by former Amazon employees, offers a HD camera with motion detection for just $20. Although these cameras are designed to be active primarily when you're out of the house, applying AI to devices capable of watching us, not just intruders, may be a tough sell to many people. Do you want an invisible, candid camera in your own home? Is it creepy or useful?

This is the beginning of a new era. We're moving from enhanced photography to enhanced photographers, and even automated photographers. We are in the early days of computers that can make qualitative judgements on the photographic merits of what they are observing. With Clips, the AI happens right on the device and your photos aren't shared unless you choose to upload them. That should reassure most people, but as with voice assistants like Alexa and the Google Assistant which we'll discuss in the next chapter, many people are sceptical about putting listening devices in their homes - and now we're talking about watching devices too. Are we rushing into a world of the Panopticon[96]?

Supercharged Surveillance

"$10 cameras everywhere that can do perfect face recognition pose a much more realistic and proximate threat of dystopia than 'general AI'"

Ben Evans[97]

Somewhat ironically, 'In camera' when used as a legal term, means in private. Yet outside legal circles, cameras are all about capturing images. George Orwell's seminal book 1984 was published in 1949. In it, Orwell presaged "telescreens" everywhere that watched citizens' every movement.

We've had surveillance for years now - CCTV is common place but it's a hard technology to scale. It's expensive to have staffed control rooms, and very inefficient to have police forces scouring large quantities of CCTV footage after a crime. So what's changed? Thanks to AI, we can now pretty much automate surveillance. The work of a control room, if now done by a single computer, gives CCTV networks the scale to become significantly more effective - and that's where concerns about just how effective probably need to be addressed. We'll come back to a more detailed discussion of ethics and AI in Chapter 9, but for now let's look at some of the developments.

---

[96] https://en.wikipedia.org/wiki/Panopticon
[97] https://twitter.com/BenedictEvans/status/859414903689314305?s=09

There are certain security-conscious areas where we perhaps expect facial recognition to be active - it's common place in airports for example. Most of us are also used to seeing CCTV in public places and in shops for the purposes of crime reduction. Less obviously, in many jurisdictions, police cars are increasing fitted with cameras for ANPR purposes. These can check for tax and insurance compliance, as well as identification of cars of interest to inquiries.

The market for CCTV is growing rapidly worldwide as AI makes cameras far more practical than they have even been.

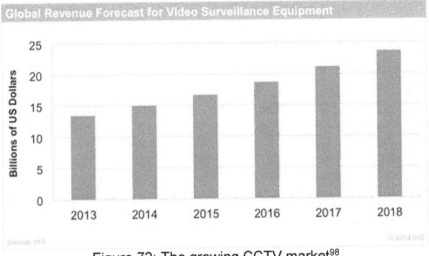

Figure 72: The growing CCTV market[98]

Most large cities have already eagerly embraced CCTV and many are accelerating its deployment as AI multiplies its effectiveness without increasing staff costs. In Moscow, there are over 160,000 cameras in the city's CCTV network, and five full days of video retained at all times, which can be searched by police for wanted faces. New York City today has roughly 20,000 officially run cameras in Manhattan alone, while Chicago has over 32,000 CCTV devices in its inner city. Camera-equipped drones are being used by over 350

98

https://archive.eetasia.com/www.eetasia.com/ART_8800694603_499489_NT_fade 546c.HTM

US agencies[99] - with some early efforts to create an algorithm to spot antisocial/violent behaviour in a crowd from a drone[100], alongside their use in search and rescue. Body cameras have grown beyond police use to include hospital staff and teachers. Tony Porter, the UK Home Office Surveillance Camera Commissioner said in an interview[101] *"the question I'd put forward is: What kind of society do we want to live in? Is it acceptable for all of us to go around legitimately filming each other, just in case somebody commits a wrong against us?"*

China in particular has used its growing AI skills to widely deploy facial recognition systems. Chinese face recognition start-up Megvii, is valued at over $2bn. A recent New York Times article[102] detailed how, in some cities, cameras scan train stations for China's most wanted. *Billboard-sized displays show the faces of jaywalkers and list the names of people who can't pay their debts. Facial recognition scanners guard the entrances to housing complexes. Already, China has an estimated 200 million surveillance cameras—four times as many as the United States. "This is potentially a totally new way for the government to manage the economy and society,"* said Martin Chorzempa, *a fellow at the Peterson Institute for International Economics. "The goal is algorithmic governance,"* he added. A Citizen Score concept due to be rolled out in 2020, called the Social Credit System, will use Facial Recognition as a key technology pillar[103].

---

[99] http://www.thedrive.com/aerial/15092/drones-in-law-enforcement-how-where-and-when-theyre-used

[100] https://www.theverge.com/2018/6/6/17433482/ai-automated-surveillance-drones-spot-violent-behavior-crowds

[101] https://www.nationalgeographic.com/magazine/2018/02/surveillance-watching-you/

[102] https://medium.com/the-new-york-times/inside-chinas-dystopian-dreams-ai-shame-and-lots-of-cameras-ff18d45bfc13

[103] https://www.wired.co.uk/article/chinese-government-social-credit-score-privacy-invasion

Figure 73: Police officer in China wearing A.I.-powered smart glasses.
Photo: -/AFP/Getty Images

The world over, much new technology receives significant funding from not only the Government sector, but specifically the military and law enforcement. GPS and the Internet itself owe their origins to the US Military. Google courted much controversy in early 2018 around its involvement in Project Maven - a Pentagon project to use AI to assess drone images. Similarly, law enforcement is interested in the benefits of emerging technologies and Microsoft and Amazon among others are reconsidering their positions on Governmental uses of AI.

Surveillance and Law Enforcement

"As a country, we have not yet come to grips with, if you're in public and your face is visible, what is appropriate for the government to do with it."

Dr. Chris Boehnen, IARPA[104]

---

[104] https://www.iarpa.gov/

Law enforcement suppliers are jumping on the AI bandwagon. Axon, the leading maker of body cameras for law enforcement in the USA, is adding artificial intelligence to its arsenal proclaiming that *"Investments in artificial intelligence will have a transformative impact on Axon products by making workflows smarter including deep data analysis on the more than 5.2 petabytes of customer data hosted across the Axon Network"*.[105]

The FBI Next Generation Identification[106] (NGI) system boasts a facial recognition search that enables authorized law enforcement to submit a probe photo for a search against over 30 million criminal mugshot photos and receive a list of ranked candidates as potential investigative leads. Amazon specifically promotes use of its ML-based facial recognition service (Rekognition) to law enforcement[107] and boasts of its ability to offer real-time face recognition across tens of millions of faces, and detection of up to 100 faces in challenging crowded photos[108].

Amazon Rekognition Example: Finding Missing Persons using Social Media Video

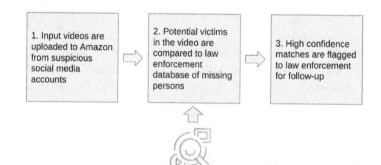

Figure 74: Amazon's Rekognition Video product use case

---

[105] http://investor.axon.com/news-releases/news-release-details/taser-makes-two-acquisitions-create-axon-ai

[106] https://www.fbi.gov/services/cjis/fingerprints-and-other-biometrics/ngi

[107] https://aws.amazon.com/rekognition/?nc2=h_a1

[108] https://aws.amazon.com/blogs/machine-learning/amazon-rekognition-announces-real-time-face-recognition-support-for-recognition-of-text-in-image-and-improved-face-detection/

The Washington County Sheriff's Office has been using Amazon Rekognition over the past year to reduce the identification time of reported suspects from 2-3 days down to minutes while an Orlando proof-of-concept uses the Amazon technology to search for "people of interest" through city cameras, prompting the ACLU[109] and a coalition of other groups to write to Amazon demanding they cease provision of service to law enforcement.

Figure 75: Amazon's Rekognition picks out multiple faces (see website for colour version)

Citizen Surveillance

The affordability of cameras has also driven a new trend - surveillance by non-State actors. Domestic installations of CCTV cameras are at an all-time high and this is a priority area for Google (Nest) and Amazon. While the emergence of a new category of small personal cameras such as GoPro is led mainly by hobbyists, another category is that of dashcams. With dash cams starting at less than $20, the market is growing rapidly.

---

[109] https://www.aclunc.org/docs/20180522_AR_Coalition_Letter.pdf

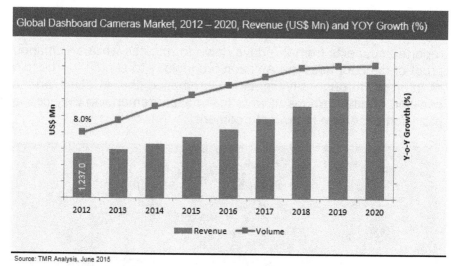

Source: TMR Analysis, June 2015

Figure 76: Growth in Dashcam market

Ostensibly a means of capturing a record of events in the case of a disputed collision or insurance claim, they can, of course, also be used to capture alleged transgressions by other drivers. Police appeals for witnesses now routinely mention "people who were in the area who may have dashcam footage". Road users in the UK are now able to submit footage of alleged dangerous driving to police forces in England and Wales, using a service created by a dashcam manufacturer[110]. The website allows visitors to upload videos before sending footage to the right police force or redirects visitors to those forces operating their own submission websites. Privacy groups have cautioned that, while safe roads and good driving are desirable, a culture of citizen surveillance may emerge.

Seeing in the dark

"Only in the darkness can you see the stars"

Martin Luther King

---

[110] https://www.nextbase.co.uk/national-dash-cam-safety-portal/

Human eyes aren't great at seeing in the dark. Although our pupils can dilate to let more light in, as light levels fall, the monochromatic rods in our eyes take over from the more colour sensitive cones. But electronic cameras have an advantage in that they can see far beyond the human visible spectrum. So, when we talk about cameras and their ability to feed data to ML algorithms, we should remember that they can "see" far more than we can. They can rely on infrared light to not only see but also to measure - using a technique called time of flight, calculating how long it takes an infrared beam sent from an emitter to bounce off an object and back to a camera next to the emitter. It's essentially radar with light.

These images[111] shows how a new IR sensor from Panasonic can see through a container with Soy sauce to make the labels on the bottles in the sauce legible while totally impervious to human eyes.

Tank containing soy sauce

Figure 77: An IR sensor can see through Soy sauce

The images show what a human will see vs what a Sony camera can see by the light of two candles. You can see the video of it online[112].

Figure 78: A digital camera's view (L) vs ambient light (R)

[111] https://www.businesswire.com/news/home/20170209005586/en/Panasonic-Worlds-First*1-Organic-CMOS-Image-Sensor/
[112] https://www.youtube.com/watch?v=0lx3o9VWqX8

Alongside the development of the AI that lets computers see, advances will continue in the sensors that feed them, the optics that supply the light and even in areas such as lensless flat cameras[113] that will lead to dramatically smaller cameras than we have today. Combined, these technologies will give computers super-human vision.

Seeing (is) the future

Computers were blind for the first few decades of their existence. Now, they are starting to see. And we may never see the world the same way again. As computers learn to see, we're facing profound changes; not being able to believe what we see - even in video; relying on computers to see what we can't; being watched not by a mindless CCTV camera but a sophisticated algorithm that can infer our actions and intent. AI is watching....is it also listening?

---

[113] http://www.caltech.edu/news/ultra-thin-camera-creates-images-without-lenses-78731

Chapter 6: Talking (to) Machines

Interacting with computers has for decades required learning of their language and using precise written communication (code) rather than speaking to them in a human language. Languages computers are good at: C++, Assembler, Java, Python. Languages computers are bad at: all human languages. For those who can't code, interacting with computers has required mastery of a keyboard to type oblique commands or more recently, a mouse to navigate around icons.

Simply talking to computers has been an ambition for decades and a staple of all science fiction imagined futures. The "Turing Test[114]", so long seen as the holy grail for artificial intelligence, is based on an interaction with a computer being so natural as to be indistinguishable from a human conversant. And just as the technologies outlined in Chapter 4 are helping computers to see, so too advances in Machine Learning are bringing us closer to computers that can listen and talk. Although technically daunting, enabling the ability to communicate naturally with computers will be a game-changer.

Fast Talk

Typing isn't a very efficient means of communication - most people talk faster than they can type. On average, we can speak at a rate of about 150 words per minute, compared with the standard of 40 words per minute required to be considered a competent though not outstanding typist. People also frequently can't spell very well (as my editor will attest). Different languages require different keyboards, while we all use the same basic physiology to speak. Anthropologically, the spoken word predates even the earliest forms of writing by thousands of years.

---

[114] https://en.wikipedia.org/wiki/Turing_test

So, although much harder for computers than other methods, those looking for better human computer interfaces (HCI) persevered with speech due to its importance to humans. This has been an area of study in computer science for decades, but recent advances in machine learning have made dramatic improvements such that natural human-computer interaction is now practical in certain domains. This represents a turning point in how and where we interact with computers. Although their core capabilities are unaffected by the interface involved, with a speech interface, we humans perceive and treat them differently, and we expand the range of people who can interact with them. Though some people are working on direct brain interfaces, for now, voice is the easiest means of communication for humans, more natural and faster than typing. If we can make computing power accessible to virtually everyone, without requiring them to learn SQL to query data, or even learn a simple GUI, we can change the definition of what it means to be computer literate.

There are many limitations of speech as a means of communicating with computers - it's not always a convenient input mechanism; speaking to your phone in the middle of a meeting is not popular. And speech also faces the uphill battle of changing societal norms. Regardless of these frictions, speech is much faster and far more accurate irrespective of language. This speed advantage will ultimately render speech to be the primary form of input to computers, initially with mobile phones, but then with laptops.

Verbal Communication is not Easy

Although humans generally learn to begin to talk after a couple of years, it takes many more before they master it. It may take more than a decade before humans have mastered grammar, vocabulary and intonation. For computers, learning vocabulary and grammatical rules is the relatively easy part as these are easily codified into computer-friendly data. But computers have struggled with anything more advanced than that. Early attempts at voice-driven computing were frustratingly inaccurate.

Verbal communication is made up of several distinct sub-features, each of which needs to be solved before we can have "natural" conversations with a computer. The computer needs to recognise the words it's heard, then understand the meaning and then it must be able to formulate a relevant response and finally annunciate it. And to add to the challenge, all this has to happen very quickly if it is to be useful.

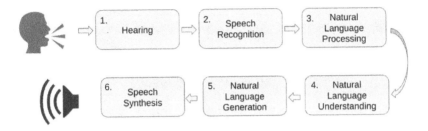

Figure 79: The 6 stages of Voice

Step 1 Hearing

The actual hearing is the easiest part. Microphones have existed for over 100 years, employing different methods to convert the air pressure variations of a sound wave to an electrical signal Along with recent advances in quality and miniaturisation, the introduction of techniques such as far field technology can assist in collecting the spoken inputs to give the next stages the best chance of success, even in challenging noisy environments. With each generation of the iPhone, there has been an increase in the number of microphones, from one in the first iPhone to four in the iPhone 5 and 6S. In devices like Amazon Echo that may be across the room from the person speaking, algorithms for far-field processing help to suppress certain surrounding noises in the environment, and focus on the dominant voice signal in the room, ensuring that the speech recognition rates are very high. The Echo uses an array of 7 mics; the delay between each microphone receiving the signal enables the device to identify the source of the voice and cancel out noise coming from other directions. This is known as beamforming.

Once the "clean" audio signal is ready to be processed and we can say that the computer has heard the input, the hard work starts - the computer must now make sense of what it's heard.

Step 2 Automatic Speech Recognition (ASR)

Speech recognition is a crucial step in voice-driven computers. The challenge is in correctly identifying the words that the human has spoken, despite the potential for confusion of similar sounding words or the challenge of accents. There are over 200,000 words in English, and that's before you count technical things like chemical names or words that can be both a noun and a verb with very different meanings. While everyday conversation only utilises a few thousand words, we still need our computer listeners to have an extensive vocabulary.

Serious efforts to develop ASR gained momentum in the 1980s with techniques such as Hidden Markov Models (HMMs) and Gaussian Mixture Models (GMM). In 1990, a software program for personal computers called Dragon Dictate launched for an eye-watering $9,000, touting a dictionary of 80,000 words. It required each user to train it, and to talk in a stilted manner at about 30 words a minute - about a quarter of a natural talking pace. It worked well enough to gain followers in specific domains like healthcare and law but didn't become broadly popular.

Deep Learning to Recognise

As we mentioned briefly in Chapter 4, recent years have seen spectacular progress in Speech Recognition. After decades of slow progress, there have been huge advances both in accuracy and scale of vocabulary. The change from 70% to 90% accuracy changes the user experience from one of total frustration to a nearly usable system.

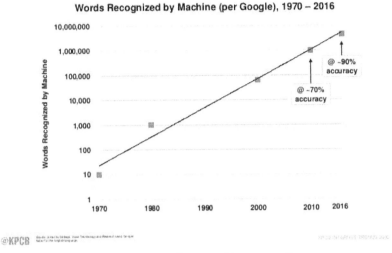

Next Frontier = Recognition in heavy background noise in far-field & across diverse speaker characteristics (accents, pitch...)

Words Recognized by Machine (per Google), 1970 – 2016

Figure 80: Word Recognition over the years

This Google graph in Figure 81 below shows how the word error rate is continuing to decline and is now approaching human accuracy levels. By applying Deep Learning to Speech Recognition in 2012, Google saw a 30 percent reduction in error rate compared against the existing non-AI system. This was the biggest single improvement in speech recognition in 20 years[115].

---

[115] http://www.techworld.com/personal-tech/google-deepmind-what-is-it-how-it-works-should-you-be-scared-3615354/

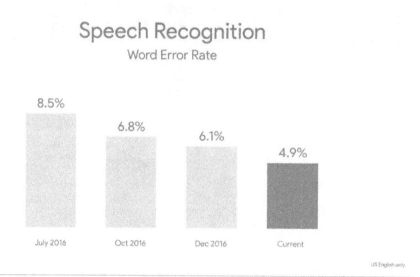

Speech Recognition
Word Error Rate

8.5%

6.8%

6.1%

4.9%

July 2016   Oct 2016   Dec 2016   Current

US English only.

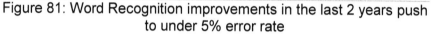

Figure 81: Word Recognition improvements in the last 2 years push to under 5% error rate

These improvements have been made possible by deep learning and in particular RNNs using Long short-term memory (LSTM). In practical terms, this makes a big difference for using speech input - in a Stanford study on Deep Speech 2[116], a neural network based speech recognition system was three times faster than typing, and the error rate was 20.4 percent lower, making voice input highly preferable.

Steps 3, 4 and 5 Natural Language Processing (NLP)

Assuming the words have been heard and correctly identified, the next stage is to then understand what those words mean in that particular ordered combination. There's plenty of room for mistakes in recognising words. Humans generally do a terrific job of hearing the right variant of similar sounds, based on context and our expectation of what is likely to be said. But we're far from perfect - we

---

[116] https://arxiv.org/abs/1512.02595

even have a word, mondegreen, to describe those times we mishear song lyrics.

Picking out similar sounding words is a big challenge - the phonemes that make up 'euthanasia' sound the same as 'youth in Asia'. Or if you say 'I saw a new display', it could be understood in some contexts as 'I saw a nudist play'. Picking out a command from a fairly limited range of possibilities is relatively easy but understanding a sentence, particularly without a context is exponentially harder. Given that 15% of all Google searches have never been asked before, despite there being 1.2 trillion searches a year, it's clear you couldn't predict what a search query might be. Computers don't have human experience comprehension advantages and will inevitably make some errors. But we shouldn't be too hard on them - though we tend to expect perfection, even we mishear on occasion.

Although often grouped under the heading of NLP, this stage of the process contains 3 siblings:

- Natural Language Processing (NLP) - computers reading language
- Natural Language Understanding (NLU) - computers understanding language
- Natural Language Generation (NLG) - computers writing language

NLP is what happens when computers turn the words they've heard into structured data. After converting speech into text, NLU software comes into the picture to decipher its meaning. It is quite possible that the same text has various meanings, or different words have the same meaning, or that the meaning changes with the context. Knowing the rules and structure of the language, understanding the text without ambiguity, are some of the challenges faced by NLU systems.

NLU can be used for things like:

- Simple profanity filters (e.g. does this forum post contain any profanity?)
- Sentiment detection (e.g. is this a positive or negative review?)
- Topic classification (e.g. what is this tweet or email about?)
- Entity detection (e.g. what locations are referenced in this text message?)

If you're collecting acronyms as you go through this book, a popular technique in this space is Topic Modelling and Latent Dirichlet Allocation (LDA). Topic modelling is a type of statistical modelling for discovering the abstract "topics" that occur in a body of text. Latent Dirichlet Allocation is an example of topic model and is used to classify text in a document to a particular topic.

But even the words are heard clearly and correctly identified, there are still semantic challenges. One example proposed as a test of machine intelligence is a Winograd Schema Challenge[117] which requires the resolution of what's known in linguistics as anaphora - the use of an expression whose interpretation depends upon another expression in context. In this example, the test is to identify the antecedent of an ambiguous pronoun in a statement: "The city councilmen refused the demonstrators a permit because they feared violence." What does the word "they" refer to here — the councilmen or the demonstrators?

---

[117] https://en.wikipedia.org/wiki/Winograd_Schema_Challenge

For developers who want to analyse text, there are services available to save them becoming experts in NLP. For example, Google's service[118] offers several methods for performing analysis and annotation on a snippet of text including:

- Sentiment analysis - identifies the prevailing emotional opinion within the text, especially to determine a writer's attitude as positive, negative, or neutral.
- Entity analysis inspects the given text for known entities (Proper nouns such as public figures, landmarks and so on. Common nouns such as restaurant, stadium, etc.)

The next step we're likely to see in NLP is emotion analysis - should a voice assistant respond differently if it detects a particular emotion in our request? Combined with sentiment analysis, this could influence how to shape a response. This sort of technology is already in use in some call centres to identify irate customers who need priority assistance, but will soon be part of the processing that our spoken requests goes through

When NLP and NLU have understood the meaning of what the Microphones and ASR have heard, it's time to respond. That's where NLG comes into play - it is the software process that automatically transforms data into a written narrative. For example, if you've determined that the person speaking requested a weather forecast, you would source weather data and use NLG to turn it into a response.

---

[118] https://cloud.google.com/natural-language/docs/basics

Figure 82: Visual Weather Forecast Data

If the data was visually as shown above, NLG might create a response to be spoken of *"it'll be cloudy until Thursday, with showers the rest of the week. Temperatures range from the high 40s to the mid-60s."*

NLG can create huge quantities of text very quickly, and is widely used for tasks such as automated reporting of business intelligence dashboards or stock market reports. Narratives written with NLG are designed to read as though a human wrote each one individually. A financial services firm, for example, can deliver portfolio summaries to thousands of clients with each summary using the customer's unique set of information to speak directly to the individual.

Step 6 Text To Speech (TTS)

So even if the text of a conversational response has been constructed accurately and quickly, there still remains the challenge of delivering it back to the human interlocutor. The NLG text may be grammatically and syntactically perfect but convincing speech synthesis is difficult. The spoken word is full of nuances, inflections and even disfluencies that make it sound natural.

Although the discipline around image recognition we talked about in the previous chapter is quite new, there have been multiple attempts over the years at making computers recognize speech and, more successfully, attempts to make computers talk. Early attempts were very instantly recognisable as computer synthesised voices, devoid of any of the inflections of a human voice. But although they were not very natural-sounding, at least they worked. These early solutions were based on an approach known as concatenative TTS - where a very large database of short speech fragments are recorded from a single speaker and then recombined to form complete utterances. This makes it difficult to modify the voice (for example switching to a different speaker, or altering the emphasis or emotion of their speech) without recording a whole new database

Sounding Human

The latest approach to generating natural-sounding speech is based on neural networks that synthesize more natural-sounding speech. One example is WaveNet[119], a generative model for raw audio created by DeepMind. It's trained with a large volume of speech samples and is able to create audio waveforms from scratch. During training, the network extracts the underlying structure of the speech, for example which tones follow one another and what shape a realistic speech waveform should have. When given text input, the trained WaveNet model generates the corresponding speech waveforms. Using the TPUs we discussed in Chapter 3, the WaveNet model can generate one second of natural-sounding speech in just 50 milliseconds.

For the voice of its Alexa assistant, Amazon offers developers a mark-up language enabling them to add the intonation that makes synthesized speech sound more natural. This allows Alexa to do things like whisper, pause, bleep out expletives, and vary the speed, volume, emphasis, and pitch of its speech. App developers using Alexa can verbally distinguish 2018 from 2,018, or a panda that eats shoots and leaves from one that eats, shoots, and leaves. What these new capabilities don't address, though, is when they should and shouldn't be used - just because Alexa can use colloquialisms doesn't

---

[119] https://deepmind.com/blog/wavenet-generative-model-raw-audio/

mean it should. While it might sound more natural, it begs the question if digital assistants should try to be like us or should simply offer cold efficiency. It stands to reason that an AI more capable of analysing and expressing emotions would also be more capable of manipulating your own.

Ready Made Solutions

As with the computer vision services we looked at earlier, the major platforms offer powerful voice-related services:

Google Cloud Speech-to-Text enables developers to convert audio to text by applying powerful neural network models via an API. The API recognizes 120 languages and variants. You can enable voice command-and-control, transcribe audio from call centres, and more. It can process real-time streaming or pre-recorded audio, using Google's machine learning technology. Cloud Speech-to-Text comes with multiple pre-built speech recognition models so you can optimize for your use case (e.g., voice commands). The pre-built video transcription model is intended for indexing or subtitling video and/or multi-speaker content, and uses machine learning technology that is similar to YouTube captioning. Similarly, AWS provides Amazon Transcribe which can analyse audio files and have the service return a text file of the transcribed speech. Microsoft likewise offers its Azure Speech to Text service via its Cognitive Services APIs.

Bringing Voice to the Mass Market

Besides smartphones, only one other technology in history has been adopted by a ¼ of Americans in just 2 years - AI-powered voice assistants. Their growth has been aided by their low price (less than $50) but also clearly by consumer interest.

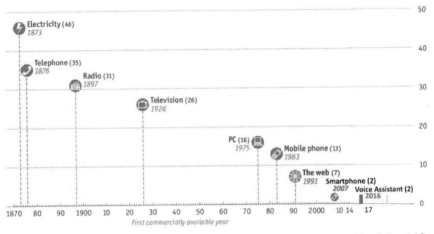

Technology adoption
Years until used by one-quarter of American population

Figure 83: Years before a technology was adopted by ¼ of the US population

The top 3 voice systems in widespread use are Apple's Siri, Amazon's Alexa and Google Assistant. Each is available via phone and home speakers, though the speaker market is led by Amazon with its plethora of shapes and sizes (Dot, Echo, Echo Plus, Spot, Show and Look), and Google who offer 3 sizes (Mini, Home & Max), with Apple selling only the high-end HomePod speaker.

Siri

Siri's launch in 2011 brought voice recognition and intelligent responses to widespread notice on mobiles. Previous attempts on desktops with Dragon Dictate and Windows had limited success as had Microsoft's Pocket PC offerings in the early 2000s. Although it had its limitations and was prone to mishearing, Siri was better than anything that had gone before it and good enough to persuade people that voice interactions on mobile were feasible. Siri now receives over 2bn requests per week and has expanded from the iPhone to the Apple Watch, Apple TV and the HomePod speaker.

Figure 84: L-R: Google Home, Apple HomePod and Amazon Echo
Voice-enabled speakers

Alexa

Although Apple had launched Siri to a mixed response in 2011, Amazon surprised the tech world in 2015 by unveiling a home speaker product, Echo, with a resident assistant called Alexa. Featuring far field technology that assisted in delivering excellent speech recognition, the speaker impressed early adopters with good performance playing music and controlling home automation.

At the start of this chapter, I explained the various steps involved in talking to a computer and having it understand and respond to you. It's worth highlighting once again the speed element of all this. If the milliseconds in the fibre optic story connecting Chicago and New York in Chapter 3 are hard to relate to, here's another story about the origins of Alexa on the Amazon Echo that's a bit easier to grasp in everyday life: Business Insider[120] reported on how Amazon CEO Jeff Bezos challenged the Echo team to surpass the latency goals they had set themselves. With industry best performance about 3 seconds

---

[120] http://uk.businessinsider.com/the-inside-story-of-how-amazon-created-echo-2016-4?r=US&IR=T

to process a spoken request, the Amazon staff had targeted improving that to 2 seconds, but Bezos told the team in a meeting *"Your target for latency is one second."* The team were dismayed at the severity of the challenge, but in fairness to them, the Echo sitting on my desk as I type responds to my requests for songs from Spotify with staggering speed, a testimony both to Amazon and to Spotify engineers.

There are over 5,000 people at Amazon working on Alexa and it shows with weekly updates over the last 3 years. Amazon has expanded the availability of Alexa with its own range of Echo Devices (which now includes two options with screens, as well as one designed for fashion advice and another that can control your TV), adding Alexa to the main Amazon shopping app, and enabling Alexa in numerous third-party speakers. With strong developer support, there are now over 50,000 skills for Alexa - 3rd party integrations and services that offer everything from games to news to smart home control. This is a key example of the importance of other technologies enabling AI - the AI itself would be blunt without the rise of APIs to provide access among systems so that they can act on our behalf. But the rapid rise in popularity has also hit the headlines over privacy concerns and cases where law enforcement has sought transcripts from Amazon[121].

Google

Google's application of DNN techniques in 2012 saw its voice search accuracy improve by over 20%. Replacing older techniques of GMM, RNNs featuring new technology (and more acronyms) such as Connectionist Temporal Classification (CTC) offered improvements in speed and accuracy. Google's voice search (which accounts for 20% of all searches on its Android app) has evolved into Google Assistant, which is now found in Phones, Watches, Android TV and a range of smart speakers. The Google Assistant is a ubiquitous part of the organisation's strategy to bring AI to the largest possible population.

---

[121] https://www.cnet.com/news/amazon-echo-alexa-agrees-to-hand-over-data-in-murder-case/

Embracing Speech

Although it's still relatively early days for this technology, the low price point and good initial experience, enthusiastic adoption of voice speakers means they have already crossed the chasm we spoke about in Chapter 2 between early adopters and the early majority. Research[122] has shown that, so far, people primarily put voice-activated speakers at the centre of their homes where everyone can access them.

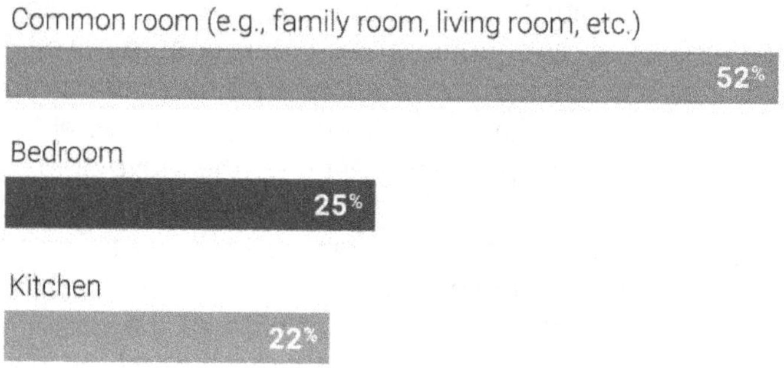

Common room (e.g., family room, living room, etc.)

52%

Bedroom

25%

Kitchen

22%

Figure 85: Location of Smart Speakers in Homes

Another survey[123] shows that people use their smart speakers an average of 3 times per day.

---

[122] https://www.thinkwithgoogle.com/consumer-insights/voice-assistance-consumer-experience/

[123] https://voicebot.ai/2018/04/02/smart-speaker-owners-use-voice-assistants-nearly-3-times-per-day/

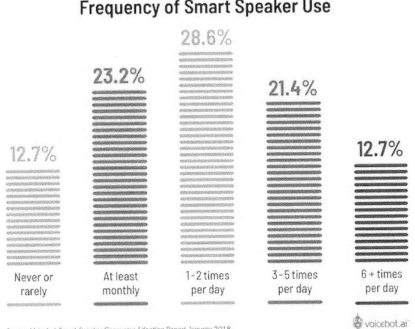

Figure 86: Frequency of use of Smart Speakers

72% of those surveyed said that their devices are used daily; checking commute times and setting reminders for things to buy later are now accomplished by talking to their virtual assistant. In a trend that I'm sure will be studied in great detail, 41% of them said it had changed their relationship with technology, being more akin to talking to another person, and using phrases like "please," "thank you," and even "sorry."

As an example of continuing rapid development from both a technological and sociological point of view, Amazon and Google have announced plans to add politeness features to their platforms that can be configured to insist on politeness towards the ethereal assistants so as to help educate children.

Evolving Speech

With a recognition of how important a new paradigm this is, there is something of an AI arms race far beyond politeness features, to develop the technology powering these voice platforms. The current digital assistants can interpret speech very well compared to the systems of just a couple of years ago, but they are not the conversational interfaces that the technology providers want them to be. Despite their many capabilities with links to up to the minute news, sports and entertainment as well as connections to near endless systems that order products, control hardware in our homes or make video calls, they are currently incapable of responding to us in an empathetic or even apparently engaged manner.

Google added an optional feature called Continued Conversation to their Assistant where it continues to listen after delivering an answer to your first query to see if there is a follow-up. Previously you had to re-awaken it by saying "Hey Google" again, which was very unnatural. The ability to chain commands may be only the removal of one "Hey Google" invocation, but makes the interaction feel a lot more natural.

Was	Now
You: "Hey Google, did the Patriots win today" Assistant: "Yes, the Patriots won 22-10 today" You: "Hey Google, when's their next game" Assistant "Patriots play again on Tuesday"	You: "Hey Google, did the Patriots win today" Assistant: "Yes, the Patriots won 22-10 today" You: "When's their next game" Assistant "Patriots play again on Tuesday"
Hey Google, Turn on the Bedroom Light Hey Google, Turn off the Hall Light	Hey Google, Turn on the bedroom light and turn off the Hall light Or Hey Google, Goodnight (runs a routine you've created that groups multiple actions under a single command

Assistants become AI-ssistants

"Echo has a way of sneaking into your routines. When Alexa reorders popcorn for you, or calls an Uber car for you, when your children start asking Alexa to add Popsicles to the grocery list, you start to want pretty much everything else in life to be Alexa-enabled, too."

New York Times[124]

A major part of the new voice-led paradigm is an Intelligent Agent (also known as Intelligent Assistant). Over time, all of us will have many, perhaps dozens, interacting with each other and acting on our behalf. These Intelligent Agents will be the "ghost in the machine" in voice first devices. They will be dispatched independently of the fundamental software and form a secondary layer that can fluidly connect between a spectrum of services and systems. They'll know the places we go, the people we interact with, our habits, our tastes and preferences, and more. Then they'll use this data to anticipate our needs.

Google Duplex[125]

You have to listen to this to believe it - It's a digital assistant making a call to book a hair appointment, talking to a real person in a salon - I highly recommend you listen to the audio sample[126].

---

[124] https://www.nytimes.com/2016/03/10/technology/the-echo-from-amazon-brims-with-groundbreaking-promise.html?_r=3
[125] More info on Duplex is at - https://ai.googleblog.com/2018/05/duplex-ai-system-for-natural-conversation.html

[126]http://www.gstatic.com/b-g/DMS03IIQXU3TY2FD6DLPLOMBBBJ2CH188143148.mp3

Figure 87: Google Duplex - Ask your assistant to book an appointment and it'll call the salon in the background and update your calendar

Designed to let the user delegate certain mundane tasks to their Assistant, Duplex will allow the Assistant to make phone calls and complete transactions on the user's behalf. Starting with restaurant reservations and scheduling hair salon appointments, just provide the date and time, and your Assistant will handle the arrangement. If a business uses an online booking service, the Assistant will book through that. Otherwise, the Assistant will call the business on your behalf. Yep, with a good old phone call. Once your reservation or appointment is booked, the Assistant will then add a calendar reminder for your appointment and allow you to cancel if needed, again with just a request from you.

Google believes this technology will be helpful to the many small businesses that rely on phone calls to accept appointments today—they argue that their research shows that 60 percent of small businesses don't have an online booking system. Yet many people simply don't reserve with businesses that don't take online bookings. This may therefore be an important interim technology. There has already been a somewhat divided response to this—some wowed by the technical ability, others worried about it being deceitful and portending an explosion of sophisticated nuisance robocalls. The next demo Google gave included a change where the AI clearly identified itself at the opening of the call.

As long as it stays limited to domains such as booking appointments, Duplex is surely little different than an executive having their PA make a reservation on their behalf. Perhaps for businesses who do not want to accept such reservations, there will be a mechanism to opt out of receiving these calls, much as they can prevent Google from indexing their website today. For many commentators, the visibility of it being an AI entity conducting the call seems crucial. Is it fair that a business may not know it's a computer making a reservation? Should the Assistant identify itself explicitly as an AI? The logical conclusion, though, is that more reservations will likely be completed without any human interaction—until everyone has an AI that makes and takes bookings without voice calls.

According to Google, *Duplex technology is built to sound natural, to make the conversation experience comfortable. It's important to us that users and businesses have a good experience with this service, and transparency is a key part of that. We want to be clear about the intent of the call so businesses understand the context. We'll be experimenting with the right approach over the coming months. One of the key research insights was to constrain Duplex to closed domains, which are narrow enough to explore extensively. Duplex can only carry out natural conversations after being deeply trained in such domains. It cannot (yet) carry out general conversations.*[127]

Duplex raises some important questions about how we want to use technology, and will inevitably expose differing levels of acceptance. Given how many of these scenarios lie ahead, it's important to tackle these concerns now. The ultimate aim for voice solutions is known as *ethopoeia* - the rhetorical ability to capture the ideas, words, and style of delivery suited to the person for whom an address is written - the ultimate in personalisation. It also involves adapting a speech to the exact conditions under which it is to be spoken. While not anthropomorphism, it brings computers and our relationship with them to a whole new level, and suggests they will soon develop an ability to not only orchestrate our lives, but perhaps even to manipulate them.

---

[127] https://ai.googleblog.com/2018/05/duplex-ai-system-for-natural-conversation.html

Advanced AI-ssistants

So far, most AI-ssistants can complete discrete commands, or even a sequence of commands. However, none has yet stitched together the abilities to complete complex commands that a human assistant would be easily able to achieve.

AIssistants are only partially about voice - they are also about awareness: our habits, our preferences, our location, our services; we connect them to our lives with APIs and our contacts. They are way deeper than the simple voice interface. Impressive as they are, what we have today are very much 1st generation products. They respond well to simple commands (and now even chained commands) and save time with routines (multiple actions triggered by a single command). But proactive, they are not. If you tell Alexa every day to do the same thing, she doesn't twig that it might be worth automating. Nor does she understand what room you're in and what can be inferred from that, if anything. But these features will come soon, perhaps even by the time you read this.

What will life be like if everyone can have a personal assistant totally attuned to their needs and focused only on predicting and satisfying their every whim? Over time, all of us will have many, perhaps dozens, interacting with each other and acting on our behalf. They will automatically deliver you the information you need to know, just as you need to know it. Rather than relying on a single input screen, or even a series of screens, we'll instead interact with computers with less friction. In our modern age of information, the average adult makes more than 20,000 decisions a day—some big, like whether or not to invest in the stock market, and some small, like whether to glance at your mobile phone when you see the screen light up. New AIssistants promise to prioritize those decisions, delegate them on our behalf, and even to autonomously answer for us, depending on the circumstance. Much of this invisible decision-making will happen without our direct supervision or input. What makes ambient design so tantalizing is that it should require us to make fewer and fewer decisions in the near-future. Think of it as a sort of autocomplete for intention. We will interact both actively and passively with our AIssistants, found in our wearables, thermostats, cars and pockets. They will listen and observe in the background, sometimes asking questions—other times offering up text, audio or haptic notifications as needed, and those will all be decided by 'intelligent' algorithms in the pursuit of speed.

Away from factories and offices, one of the most interesting questions of the AI acceleration will be the automation of life. Not only of physical tasks like household chores, but of our needs and wants. We've already talked about automated ordering but only in the context of replenishment. Soon there will be no more 'Life Admin' - not spend time paying bills, making mundane decisions. The next step will be for your AIssistant to tackle the things you don't even realise are "friction" - usually get a taxi when you get off the train? Your Assistant will have it waiting for you in a perfectly choreographed routine. Instead of landing at an airport and firing up the Uber app to book a ride to a hotel where you wait to check in, future systems will work together to ensure that happens seamlessly, stepping straight into a waiting car and then going straight to the room that's expecting you, exactly as might happen for a person with a dedicated concierge or entourage of assistants.

Imagine a scenario of a leak in your home - your smart home will detect it and ask Alexa to call a plumber. Alexa will give the plumber your zip code, and agree a suitable time and a price. Your AI may share some details about your setup to help the plumber know what parts to bring. You may or may not be home when the plumber calls - but that's ok as your AI will open the door, guide them to the problem, all the while watching them via CCTV. Your AI will also likely authorise payment for them as they leave, and recoup any money from your insurance or warranty provider if relevant.

The New User Experience - No UI

"Our goal in Speech Technology Research is to make speaking to devices--those around you, those that you wear, and those that you carry with you--ubiquitous and seamless."

Google[128]

---

[128] https://ai.google/research/pubs?area=SpeechProcessing

As we get better at each step along the way to creating computers that can hear, listen, construct a meaningful reply and deliver that reply in an agreeable tone, we are fundamentally changing how we interact with computers for the first time in decades. So how significant is this?

Steve Jobs was reported to have said that "great technology should be invisible", Although he was heavily involved in the interaction revolutions of popularising the GUI and then the touchscreen (he described our fingers as the ultimate pointing device), he purchased the start-up behind Siri to spearhead Apple's move into voice recognition.

We've seen successive big changes in how we interact with technology since the original punch cards, progressed to keyboards, then graphical user interface (GUI) and then touchscreens. But each required a proximate interaction with a device on your desk, lap or in your hand. It also created a barrier for those not familiar with the interface. But voice is a dramatic difference - my mother uses a computer only since she can talk to it.

Peak Screen

The touchscreen revolution has brought computing to more people than ever. But today's interfaces also tend to be solo affairs. Although they facilitate and promote communications, they can also severely inhibit personal interactions. The near-addiction people have for the phone in their hand has raised many questions about whether we are using our phones too much and whether this form of interaction with technology is becoming detrimental.

At Google's and Apple's 2018 summer developer conferences, executives took the stage to show how their latest software was brining important features but then both companies unveiled something else: software to help you use your phone a lot less. So, two tech giants are building the beginning of something new: a less insistently visual tech world, a digital landscape that relies on voice assistants to take some pressure off our eyes and our fingers. It is perhaps serendipitous timing that, as we reach addictive levels of device usage, the companies now have the beginnings of technology to abstract the technology - letting us delegate to an invisible agent we can speak to, who works on our behalf and remains just a word away.

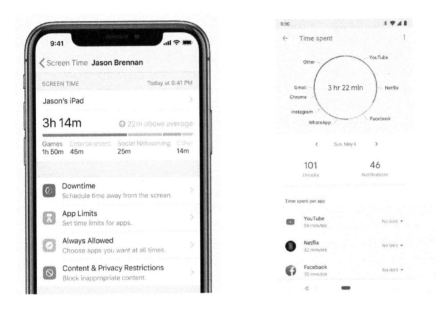

Figure 88: iOS (L) and Android (R) features to reduce usage

"2018 marks the beginning of the end of traditional smartphones. During the next decade, we will start to transition to the next era of computing and connected devices, which we will wear and will command using our voices, gesture and touch. The transition from smartphones to smart wearables and invisible interfaces—earbuds that have biometric sensors and speakers; rings and bracelets that sense motion; smart glasses that record and display information— will forever change how we experience the physical world. This doesn't necessarily signal a post-screen existence. We anticipate foldable and scrollable screens for portable, longer-form reading and writing."

Future Today Institute Report[129]

---

[129] https://futuretodayinstitute.com/2018-tech-trends-annual-report/

All previous methods of interaction have one common thread - they require humans to adapt from their natural method of communication to an arcane set of commands or gestures. These are not efficient for humans. Although many people have become expert at them (think of a teenager's fingers zipping around their smartphone at dizzying speed), they require a disproportionate amount of cognitive and mechanical loads. Although we may think it's fast, it's far from as efficient as it could be. It's just as fast as we could make it so far. When seen for what they truly are, these old ways are inefficient and ineffective for many of the common things we do with devices and computers. The fundamental reason humans have been reduced to tapping on keyboards is simply because the computer was not powerful enough to understand our words let alone even begin to decode our intent.

As we move into a more voice-first world, many things will change. A less visual paradigm will particularly challenge our assumptions around for example advertising. While advertising can be somewhat intrusive in a visual world, it can usually be tolerated as we can (sometimes) ignore it on a web page and focus on the content we want. But in a narrow channel like voice, where there is only bandwidth for one message, we will not tolerate commercial intrusions and interruptions in our dialogs.

Ambient Computing

"I expect that one end result of all this work will be that the technology, the computer inside all these things, will fade into the background. In some cases, it may entirely disappear, waiting to be activated by a voice command, a person entering the room, a change in blood chemistry, a shift in temperature, a motion. Maybe even just a thought."

Walt Mossberg[130]

Some of the most significant technological advancements have been nearly invisible, while still happening right before our eyes. The emphasis is on the experience delivered to the end user, not on the

---

[130] https://www.recode.net/2017/5/25/15689094/mossberg-final-column

mechanics of what it takes to deliver that experience. And that makes sense, as end users rarely care about the hidden infrastructure and advances required to enable their clicks, touches and utterances to cater to their every whim.

Technology has now found its way into even the most common place objects - companies are rapidly embedding technology within familiar objects to enhance, simplify, automate or bring entirely new functionality to existing categories of devices. Author Ray Bradbury envisioned a world in which human needs are anticipated by the surrounding environment. He envisaged an era of true ambient computing, where technology is no longer an explicit choice but an integral, invisible actor, part of what we do.

Ambient computing describes an invisible computer interaction facilitated by the many sensors that surround us, enabled by UI-less voice control. The early stages of ambient computing are already taking root in connected homes where basic features such as turning the lights or heating controls on or off are either programmed or respond to a voice command. The combination of more sensors (including cameras) and artificial intelligence will allow connected and smart machines to be much more proactive in satisfying our needs and wants. This will signal a change from our current reliance on screens for inputting commands and receiving information. Graphical interfaces will become more an adjunct to our technology experience rather than the entirety of it. Voice interfaces will mean we are less likely to get distracted from our purpose, unlike all the times we pick up our phones intending to quickly check something only to emerge half an hour later from a fog of social media updates.

Ambient computing—in the broadest sense—is the promise of computing that is not limited to the 100 times a day you check your phone. It is the promise of continuous, multimodal, computing-enhanced interaction with the real world. Increasingly-intelligent listening devices in your home or your ears are a step toward that. Voice is the gateway to ambient computing that will lead eventually to pervasive predictive computing.

Baby Steps

This change in how we interact with computers will take some time to become familiar. It requires user to adapt and unlearn ingrained habits. Despite the advantages of voice over other forms of UI, the evidence suggests that early users are sticking to simple tasks. The graph below shows how early adopters are using their smart speakers. This is to be expected as people test the boundaries of what actually works, and as they get used to the previously impossible and implausible ability to talk to invisible digital assistants. But people will get used to it. Asking for a song is so much easier than searching in an app, knowing how to spell etc. I had honestly never realised that opening an app and typing the song name was a hassle. But compared to telling Alexa to play my music, it's a chore!

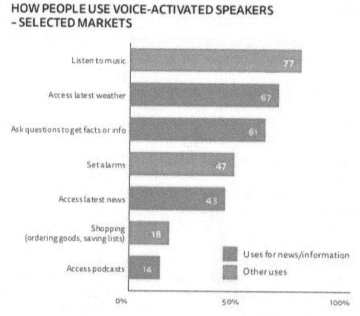

Figure 89: Usage of Smart Speakers

Ironically, the lack of a visual interface can sometimes slow us down. We're so used to seeing what a computer is doing or has found for us, we are slow to let go of control, lacking the trust to delegate to an unseen force. And as businesses react at different speeds, there is still no guarantee that your provider of choice has embraced the technology yet. You may be able to transfer money by voice with one bank but not another. The same was true at the start of the web - while now it's unthinkable for a business not to have a website, the same will be true in a few years for any company unable to conduct its business via voice. For businesses watching the emergence of this new channel of communication, it represents a challenge to decide how and when to engage with their customers. Even the UK Government web site[131], which gets about 3 million visits per day, is looking at developing voice support so that citizens can interact more naturally with the State's services.

The Uncanny Valley

Designing for voice interactions is still in its early days. On the one hand, there are no natural limits to what users can say, and challengingly for developers, users naturally tend to attribute human characteristics to voice systems. On the other hand, for the next few years at least, voice systems simply will not yet be able to react to many queries correctly. The ability for Alexa to answer many queries lulls us into thinking she can answer all queries, and leads us to a heightened sense of disappointment with the technology when it fails us. This will still be common even as the number of queries she can answer continues to expand, although limited by syntax right now. Commentator Ben Evans captures this well in his article[132]:

"I suspect that the ideal number of functions for a voice UI actually follows a U-shaped curve: one command is great and is ten probably OK, but 50 or 100 is terrible, because you still can't ask anything but can't remember what you can ask. The other end of the curve comes as you get closer and closer to a system that really can answer anything, but, again, that would be 'general AI'.

As I circle around this question of awareness, it seems to me that it's useful to compare Alexa with the Apple Watch. Neither of them do anything that you couldn't do on your phone, but they move it to a different context and they do it with less friction - so long as you

---

[131] https://gds.blog.gov.uk/2018/06/27/building-the-gov-uk-of-the-future/

[132] http://ben-evans.com/benedictevans/2017/2/22/voice-and-the-uncanny-valley-of-ai

remember. It's less friction to, say, set a timer or do a weight conversion with Alexa or a smart watch, as you stand in the kitchen, but more friction to remember that you can do it. You have to make a change in your mental model of how you'd achieve something, and that something is a simple, almost reflexive task where you already have the muscle memory to pull out your phone, so can this new device break the habit and form a new one?

There's a set of contradictions here, I think. Voice UIs look, conceptually, like much more unrestricted and general purpose interfaces than a smartphone, but they're actually narrower and more single-purpose. They look like less friction than pulling out your phone, unlocking it, loading an app and so on, and they are - but only if you've shifted your mental model. They look like the future beyond smartphones, but in their (necessarily) closed, locked-down nature they also look a lot like feature phones. And they're a platform, but one that might get worse the bigger the developer ecosystem. This is captured pretty well by the 'uncanny valley' concept from computer animation: as a rendering of a person goes from 'cartoon' to 'real person' there's a point where increased realism makes it look less rather than more real - making the tech better produces a worse user experience at first.

Summary

Historically, each improvement in the way we interact with computers brought about long-term effects nearly impossible to calculate. Just like the printing press before them, the PC, the smartphone and the internet each democratised access to vast storehouses of information and potentially, knowledge. Effective voice interfaces change how we use computers and who can use them. But they will also change the dynamic between consumers and businesses.

Why are big companies rushing to offer voice-powered experiences? Given the cost of the research and development, the hardware and even the servers to run these systems for hundreds of millions of users, why are they selling the gateway devices for $30? Getting more devices running their software into more hands is a loss-leader. What they want is to tie you in to their ecosystem so that, slowly but surely, they can influence (monetise) more aspects of your life. While that can sound slightly sinister, it can also be perceived as efficient and convenient for you - a win-win outcome. A move to voice interfaces can offer control, or at least influence, over three important markets: home automation/utilities, home entertainment/media, and shopping.

The moment you ask an AIssistant to complete a task, you're disintermediated - ask Alexa for a movie and she may choose to serve it to you via one service over another. Amazon may be paid for that. As a consumer, you may not care as long as you get the product you want at a price you're happy with. The supply chain doesn't matter to you. But it makes Amazon the middleman in a way it doesn't get to be when you simply open Netflix via a touch interface or a mouse click. Even if you command Alexa to open Netflix, Amazon now knows you're watching Netflix.

Taken together, the Computer Vision advances from chapter 5 and the Voice technologies in this chapter represent the largest shift in technology in decades as computers gain senses. How will this new generation of technology impact us? In the coming chapters, we'll look at how the AI technologies of Machine Learning, with the Computer Vision and Voice features it enables, are making their way into the real world. We have never thought of computers in terms of senses. Now, what were merely cameras and microphones are their eyes and ears. But the real change is the 'brain' - the ability to process and understand the inputs and then turn them into actions at speeds only computers can achieve.

Chapter 7: Speed Shopping

"One thing I love about customers is that they are divinely discontent. Their expectations are never static – they go up. It's human nature. We didn't ascend from our hunter-gatherer days by being satisfied. People have a voracious appetite for a better way, and yesterday's 'wow' quickly becomes today's 'ordinary'. I see that cycle of improvement happening at a faster rate than ever before. It may be because customers have such easy access to more information than ever before – in only a few seconds and with a couple taps on their phones, customers can read reviews, compare prices from multiple retailers, see whether something's in stock, find out how fast it will ship or be available for pick-up, and more."

Jeff Bezos, Amazon CEO, Shareholder Letter 2018

In this chapter, we'll examine how technology is changing the area of retail. Why single out retail? Isn't the impact of AI in areas such as healthcare important to consider? Absolutely, but retail is undergoing such big change already that it's an excellent precursor of the scale of change coming to other sectors. It's very relatable for most people - it's visible, it touches on society, jobs, property, leisure, basic needs, transport/logistics, discovery, payments and more. It provides good examples of early applications of AI, CV, Voice and more. It's also a confluence point for both online and offline examples of high tech deployments. It raises several ethical questions as well, especially relating to jobs and privacy. It's an area of intense interest to all the major movers in the AI field and has already been a proving ground for many of the recent innovations.

Retail is also a very public battleground for the world's leading companies. Alphabet offers its Google Express online shopping service, and in 2018 spun out Wing (delivery drones) into a separate company just as it did Waymo in 2016 (autonomous cars and trucks). Any shift away from web-based shopping to voice-led or subscriptions could severely impact its bottom line, given its dependence on advertising, so you can be sure it is closely watching developments. Amazon, the world's 2nd largest company, as you'll see in this Chapter, is fiercely innovating and experimenting. And wherever it's not offering consumer solutions itself, even its competitors are using its fulfilment or its cloud services with large AI components involved.

Perhaps it's no surprise that commerce is one of the most active areas of technology. It's largely unregulated, has low barriers to entry and is something that touches consumers most days of their lives. Compared to a sector like healthcare, it's easier to innovate. But will speed be the end of retail as we know it?

The End of Retail?

"I don't think retail is dead. Mediocre retail experiences are dead"

Neil Blumenthal, co-CEO Warby Parker, January 2017

Commerce has been a central activity and economic driver for centuries, evolving through artisan, mass distribution, retail, high streets, catalogues, malls, out of town. How we buy things, when and where are all changing. In many cases, we may no longer make many of the routine purchase decisions ourselves.

First, we had e-commerce, then m-commerce and then the predicted end of retail. Prefixes come and then go as they become business-as-usual. Now that e-commerce and mobile commerce are no longer noteworthy, the next phase may be called Predictive Commerce (P-Commerce) or Speed Commerce (S-Commerce). Even for sceptics, e-commerce was easy to understand, if not to implement. Often more about logistics, channel conflict and experience than pure technology, there wasn't usually any comprehension gap. But with the next wave, understanding the technologies at play and what they enable, is a challenge.

Around half of all US households are now reckoned to have signed up for Amazon's $119-a-year Prime service, which offers free delivery on millions of products. According to estimates,[133] these consumers

---

[133] Wedbush Securities

then spend 10 percent less in physical stores. Figures[134] also show that, compared with a decade ago, Americans now spend 13 fewer hours a year travelling to stores or browsing the shelves.

These changing shopping patterns which have emerged rapidly over the last few years are posing a huge challenge for traditional retailers of all sizes and locations - from shopping malls to high streets to corner stores. The employment implications are clear from the graph below, with as many as 8,640 stores with 147 million square feet of retailing space expected to close down in 2017.

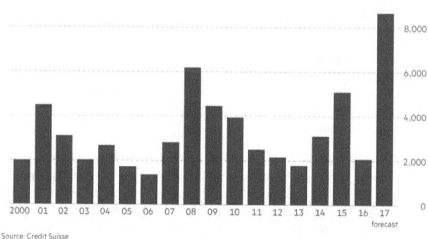

US store closures expected to surpass 8,000 in 2017

Retail store closings by unit

Source: Credit Suisse
© FT

Figure 90: US Retail Closures - Source: FT[135]

Speed Shopping

Shopping is increasingly about speed. People are spending less time in shops, expecting faster delivery and ever-increasing convenience.

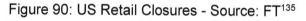

[134] https://www.ft.com/content/cf98680c-738f-11e7-aca6-c6bd07df1a3c
[135] https://www.ft.com/content/d34ad3a6-5fd3-11e7-91a7-502f7ee26895

What has changed, and to what extent is it driven by AI and other technologies?

Online

Just 20 years ago, there was no such thing as online shopping. The only real alternative to going to a shop was choosing products from a catalogue, phoning or mailing in your order and waiting for delivery, sometimes for weeks. But the last decade has seen a dramatic rise in online shopping, just as many smaller retailers had suffered an onslaught of competition from clubs and superstores.

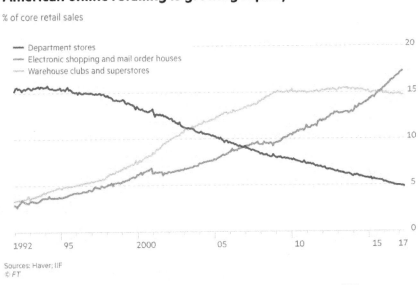

American online retailing is growing rapidly

% of core retail sales

— Department stores
— Electronic shopping and mail order houses
— Warehouse clubs and superstores

Sources: Haver; IIF
© FT

Figure 91: Growth of Online Retail. Source: FT

The early years of e-commerce were marked by a fairly unsophisticated user experience. The sector relied on its inherent benefits of anytime, anywhere shopping and convenience to find its feet. It then expanded from books and CDs to more categories and traditional retailers were forced to build their own online stores, which only larger traders could do. The UI of early e-commerce was fairly slow. Filling in details was cumbersome - the patented Amazon one click was a revolution in online shopping. As user comfort with the experience has grown, it now reaches into categories previously thought immune from online purchases due to a perception that physical contact with the goods was required before purchase; Amazon is now the second largest apparel retailer in the US.

Although Amazon or eBay may be the first to spring to mind when you think of online shopping, it's also worth remembering how many other products and services we buy digitally. The growth of iTunes and Netflix has made physical retailing of music and movies pretty unsustainable, where once they were the staple of the high street, along with banks.

As sector after sector has moved online, so far only groceries have been very resilient to digitisation and remain one of the primary reasons people still go to shopping centres. Even apparel, once thought of as unsuited to online shopping, has seen ⅓ of its volume move to the Internet. If consumer behaviour continues to move towards online shopping for apparel and even for groceries, the outlook for many malls is very bleak. PwC estimates that there is about 24 sq. ft of retailing floor space per person in the US, compared with 11 sq. ft in Australia — the only other developed country that comes close to the US — and between 2 and 5 sq. ft in Europe.

Online for All

Recent years have seen a democratisation or at least proliferation of online technology. After an early stage where only large players could afford their own e-commerce tech, now even sole traders can have access to sophisticated online sales tools. Some have turned to selling via Amazon, eBay or Etsy, but those who want their own virtual storefronts have powerful options available. There's a choice of platforms on which to setup an online shop in minutes. These offer advanced features to ensure a speedy shopping service on a par with the leaders. Commerce platforms like Shopify, combined with advanced payment systems, enable merchants to combine offline and online experiences. Shopify's menu of features for retailers of all sizes includes even Virtual Reality and automated virtual assistants (bots) for customer service. The long tail of commerce is increasingly made up of small brands that can easily nurture a deep, direct, real-time relationship with customers using these technologies, without developing anything themselves or even requiring substantial expertise.

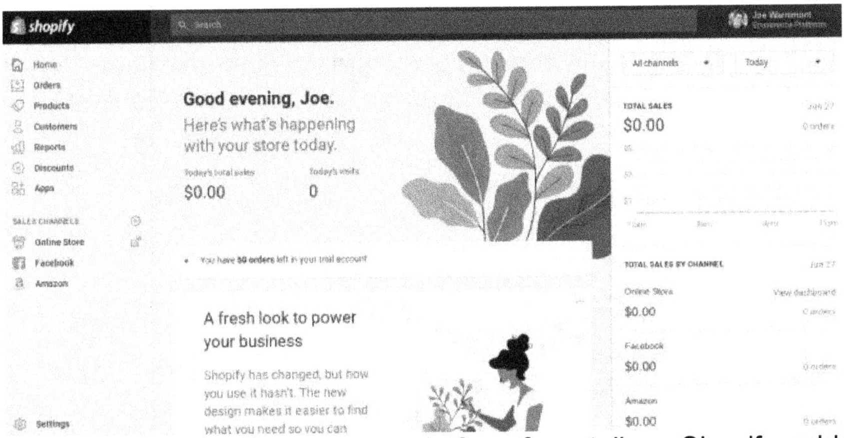

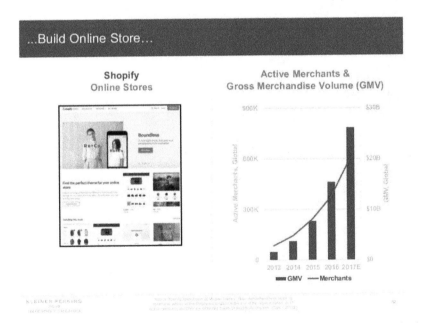

Figure 92: Popular E-commerce platform for retailers, Shopify, adds AI features....

Figure 93: .....as more traditional retailers of all sizes increase their online presence

Social shopping

As the amount of time people spend on social media has grown in recent years, companies (as well as bloggers/influencers) capturing those eyeballs were keen to monetise their free services. Introducing commerce features to supplement ad income has been a key strategy, leading to the addition of features to purchase items directly from within Instagram and Pinterest so you don't have to leave your social flow to purchase.

Figure 94: Social Shopping on Instagram (L) and Pinterest (R)

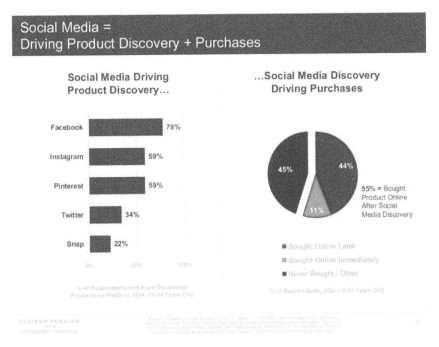

Figure 95: Social Media plays an increasing role in Shopping & Discovery

Replenishment

A lot of what we think of as shopping is actually straight replenishment - no choice involved, just re-purchasing the same item. Retailers like nothing more than a captive customer and every visit to the supermarket is a chance for consumers to be swayed. Producers want it to be easier for you to buy and harder for you to switch.

The Amazon Dash button was introduced to a sceptical audience on April Fool's Day in 2015. A physical, single purpose button that you stick somewhere convenient in your house, pressing it will see a specified item delivered to your home the next day. It's very simple - essentially Amazon are turning the Buy Now one-click button from their website into a physical item in your home. And of course, once it has gained that position, the chances are the consumer is locked into ordering that item and highly unlikely to switch brands or supplier.

Order items that you need to restock on regular basis with the push of a button - you don't even have to fire up your phone or laptop, open Amazon, search for the item and purchase it.

The range of Dash buttons has now expanded to over 300 items and the concept has been so successful that they've even replicated the appearance of the physical button in their app and on their website as a visual cue for shoppers to replenish.

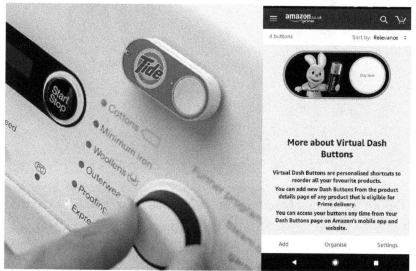

Figure 96: Physical Dash Button (L) and Virtual Dash Button on Mobile (R)

But the genius of the Dash buttons is actually hidden in the technology behind them - the Dash Replenishment Service (DRS) - a service that any product owner can use to offer a replenishment service to their users at the push of a button (or some other defined trigger). All without the requirement for a company to create such a complex logistical platform itself.

Device manufacturers can integrate replenishment services that simply monitor usage and re-order automatically when consumables are running low, without even needing a button press. Examples include printers that can order toner or ink, devices that can order batteries, and water jugs that can order filters.

Order Ink and Toner with

Figure 97: Example of Printer with automated replenishment built-in via DRS

Dash buttons are a great example of how even traditional non-tech companies can embrace technology without having to develop their own, as long as they are happy to cede some control to Amazon. It's in a detergent maker's interest to get their Dash button on your washing machine so that any time you see your supply running out, you'll just push the button rather than go to a supermarket where you may have a choice to change to a competitor. Consumers will pay a premium for the speedy, frictionless transaction. Although a mere button press, the DRS masks a lot of complexity - it places an order for an item and uses your stored payment and address details to complete the transaction. The time from pressing the button to receiving an email confirming your order can be less than 2 seconds. While devices with internet connectivity can connect directly to the DRS, for other devices that lack it, a simple Dash button can make more sense than adding a touchscreen or a Wi-Fi chip.

Amazon Dash Wand
The box of the Amazon Dash wand describes it as "the quick and easy way to shop". It combines a basic barcode scanner with Alexa support in a small device you can magnetically attach to your refrigerator door. The idea is that you scan items in your kitchen to add them to your shopping list, or simply tell Alexa to add them to your list; then open the Amazon app and confirm your order.

Figure 98: The Amazon Dash Wand (L) and Subscription Service (R)

Replenishment is popular with suppliers as it locks consumers into their products. Connected devices can also report usage back to suppliers, helping them to better match supply with demand. But if the act of pressing a button is too hard for you, Amazon also offers one step further - subscription shopping. This lets you put items on recurring order, at an attractive discount - the ultimate in speed for you, and in lock-in for Amazon and the suppliers.

Voice Shopping

Perhaps not surprising given Amazon's position as the "Everything Store"[136], its voice assistant Alexa is another sales channel. As highlighted in this the 2018 KPCB review of Internet Trends, Alexa is growing in importance as a sales channel for Amazon, though it's only believed to have about 1 million users so far, a small percentage of total Echo owners. Google are adding more retail partners to its voice shopping service too for use via Google Home and the Google Assistant.

---

[136]https://www.amazon.co.uk/Everything-Store-Jeff-Bezos-Amazon-ebook/dp/B00DJ3ITKS

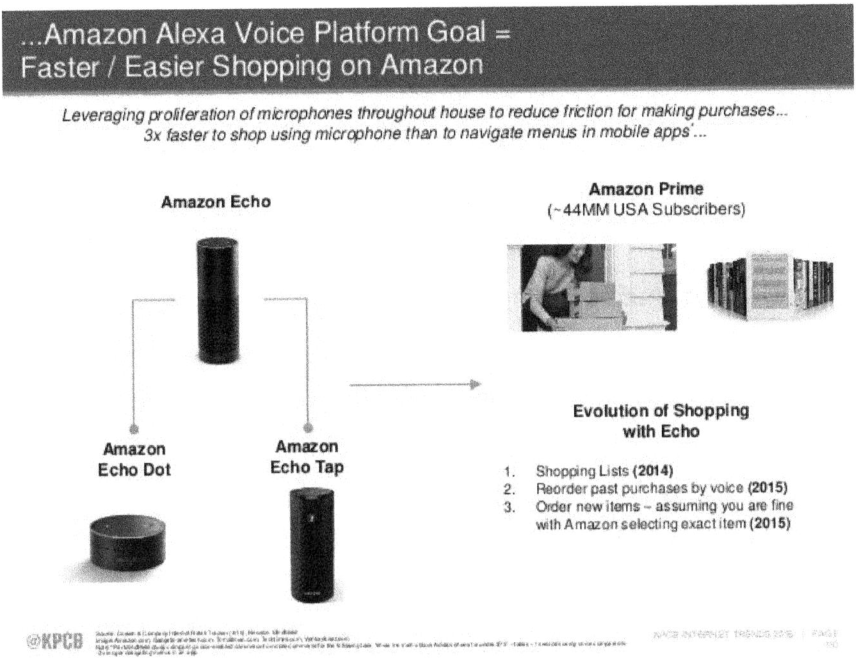
...Amazon Alexa Voice Platform Goal =
Faster / Easier Shopping on Amazon
Leveraging proliferation of microphones throughout house to reduce friction for making purchases...
3x faster to shop using microphone than to navigate menus in mobile apps'...
Amazon Echo
Amazon Echo Dot
Amazon Echo Tap
Amazon Prime
(~44MM USA Subscribers)
Evolution of Shopping with Echo
1. Shopping Lists (2014)
2. Reorder past purchases by voice (2015)
3. Order new items – assuming you are fine with Amazon selecting exact item (2015)
@KPCB
Figure 99: Will shopping by Voice take some getting used to?

So shopping is now as simple as asking the little speaker in the living room to confirm the purchase of whatever you want to be delivered the next day. As we discussed in the previous Chapter, this removes choice - the lack of a UI disintermediates product choice if you aren't specific: "Alexa order 20 AA batteries" will likely result in "Ok, I've ordered batteries - they'll be here tomorrow" as the response and 20 Amazon Basics brand batteries arriving the next day. You might have meant Duracell, but you didn't say that....

62%
of those who regularly use a voice-activated speaker say they are likely to use it to buy something in the next month

58%
of those who regularly use a voice-activated speaker say they use it to create or manage lists

44%
of those who regularly use a voice-activated speaker say they use it to order products

Figure 100: User attitudes to voice purchasing and lists

Self-Service

Away from online and voice shopping, back in the world of physical retail, there's been a huge trend in recent years to install self-checkouts in supermarkets. Although touted as speeding up shopping, there are many who believe it's inspired even more by cost cutting than by a desire for speed. In truth, it's probably a mixture of perceived speed reductions, genuine speed improvements in some situations and staff cost reductions.

Self-serve checkouts became common in the 1990s. There are now over 250,000 in operation worldwide. According to retailer Target, approximately ⅓ of shoppers choose self-checkout. Though frequently frustrating to use due to failures to scan and weigh items correctly, the cost benefits for operators are compelling - at airport check-in, for instance, the cost to process a passenger through an electronic terminal (14 cents[137]) is a fraction of what it costs the airline with a staffed desk ($3). And although some reports note a tendency for otherwise trustworthy shoppers to sometimes steal items, other investigations show that people spend more when they don't feel they and their purchases are being judged by a human cashier - a McDonald's[138] experiment found that people ordering at kiosks spend an average of 30% more than counter-orders.

In terms of speed, an experienced human cashier will outpace a self-checkout, but in reality, it's usually a race between a cashier and multiple self-checkouts, so the overall throughput will be higher. There's also the phenomenon known as "wait warping" - the idea that giving the shopper something to do and/or think about gives the illusion that things are moving faster than they are.

We can soon expect even the self-serve checkout machine to boast new features using the kinds of technologies discussed in the previous chapters. In order to speed their operation and accuracy, the machines will soon have AI enabled visual recognition technology to address pain points such as produce selection. The new versions will use cameras and ML to identify and suggest for example "1 Granny Smith Apple", rather than expecting the consumer to select

---

[137] http://www.itif.org/files/2010-self-service-economy.pdf

[138] http://www.cbc.ca/news/business/marketplace-are-you-being-served-1.3422736

Fruit->Apple->Type->Quantity. This will also benefit retailers in reducing barcode swapping scams and intentional item mis-selection.

Long wait time at checkout is the number one customer complaint in stores. From a merchant point of view, if they add up the transaction times, slow processing is expensive. So, shaving even small amounts off transaction times is attractive to reduce queues. As physical retail battles to survive in many sectors/locations, surveys that show an abandonment rate due to wait lines at 30% make for scary reading.

Another form of self-service that doesn't rely on checkout points is the use of your phone to scan the barcodes of each item as you go. This is better suited to smaller amounts of items than a large shop. An example is Grab+Go from Barclaycard. When you're done picking and scanning your items, you simply checkout inside the app and your purchases are charged to a linked card. It then generates a digital receipt that the merchant also has access to, in case they wish to check your bag for uncounted items.

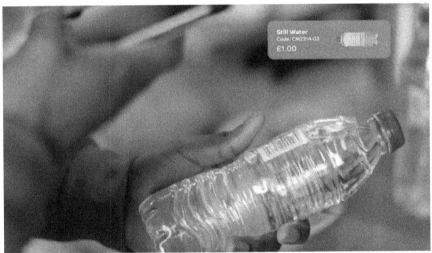

Figure 101: Scan with your phone to checkout with Grab+Go from Barclaycard

No More Checkouts

The next generation of shops may be radically different from what we're used to today. Taking self-serve to its ultimate conclusion, there has been a concerted effort to remove the entire process of checking out and even the need to self-scan.

The concept of a store without checkouts isn't as new as you might think. In 1937, an inventive grocer tried to create an automated store, called Keedoozle[139], that delivered customer orders via a conveyor belt system. Although he never managed to perfect the technology, recent advances in technology have brought the idea back to the table.

In 2006, IBM showed a concept video[140] of someone picking up items and walking out of a store, apparently without paying for them. Using RFID[141] technology, IBM imagined that such a store would be possible. The drawback of RFID is that the store would have had to add a tag to every item - and though inexpensive, it wouldn't be practical to add to every item in every store. Nothing much was heard from the technology sector on the idea for another 10 years.

"We asked ourselves: what if we could create a shopping experience with no lines and no checkout? Could we push the boundaries of computer vision and machine learning to create a store where customers could simply take what they want and go? Our answer to those questions is Amazon Go and Just Walk Out Shopping."

Amazon web site

In December 2016, Amazon unveiled its concept store - Amazon Go[142]. A store without checkouts, you just grab the stuff you want and walk out; with the details of what you bought charged to your Amazon account as you leave. There are no cashiers, no lines, no fumbling for a credit card. You identify yourself to the system by scanning a QR code in your Amazon Go app as you enter the store. From then on, ML-powered cameras in the ceiling track your every move and

---

[139] http://time.com/3880751/keedoozle-americas-first-automated-grocery/

[140] https://www.youtube.com/watch?v=eob532iEpqk

[141] https://en.wikipedia.org/wiki/Radio-frequency_identification

[142] https://youtu.be/NrmMk1Myrxc

note what you pick up (and if you put it back down). The pilot store on the Amazon campus in Seattle is 1,800 square feet in size, stocking perishable grocery goods like bread, milk, and cheese, as well as pre-made snacks and fresh meals.

Figure 102: Amazon Go Checkout-less store - the ceiling is watching...

Around the same time as Amazon unveiled Go, IBM was back with its Instant Checkout[143]. Although not as slick as the Amazon store, it is perhaps more practical for existing stores, requiring little in the way of retrofitting. IBM proudly claimed "it takes only five seconds for the instant checkout to complete a transaction for any number of items – unlike traditional self-checkouts and cashier checkouts that take longer the more items you buy, due to the need for scanning individual barcodes with instant checkout generally performing 15 times faster than a self-checkout, and seven times faster than a cashier."

Walmart is reportedly exploring its own computer vision and ML-

---

[143] https://www.ibm.com/blogs/insights-on-business/ibmix/transforming-customer-experience-with-instant-checkout/

based technologies under Project Kepler[144], while others in the space include AIFI and Bingobox[145] which is already operational with over 12 stores in China offering a less sophisticated than Amazon Go, unmanned checkout-less store that relies on customers scanning items with their phone.

Of course, no more checkouts means no more cashiers. According to the Bureau of Labor Statistics[146] in the US there are 3.4 million people employed as cashiers. Aside from the concern of people who miss the human interaction of a staffed checkout, the employment implications of a threat to what is traditionally a low-entry barrier occupation (i.e. doesn't require a degree) is a major potential downside of AI being deployed on a large scale in the retail sector.

The New Shoppers - Delegated Shopping

Around 70% of all stock trading is now carried out not by humans but by algorithms. Likewise, in day to day shopping, humans are increasingly either not placing orders, or not placing orders for themselves. For those that choose to delegate the chore of shopping to a service such as Instacart, they are unwittingly embracing ML too, as Instacart makes extensive use of Deep Learning to speed shopping[147]. By observing how shoppers have picked millions of customer orders through the Instacart app, they have built models that predict the sequences the fastest shoppers will follow. Instacart shoppers use this predicted fastest sequence to guide their route around the store. The deep learning model offers an increase in picking speed over humans of 50% at large batch sizes. This approach has reduced shopping times by minutes per trip. At scale, every minute saved will translate into 618 years of shopping time per year for Instacart.

Consider also services like Earny.co[148] which will scan your email for

---

[144] https://www.recode.net/2017/12/20/16693406/walmart-personal-styling-jet-black-amazon-go-prime-no-checkout-store

[145] https://www.techinasia.com/china-version-amazon-go-bingobox-funding

[146] https://www.bls.gov/ooh/sales/cashiers.htm

[147] https://tech.instacart.com/deep-learning-with-emojis-not-math-660ba1ad6cdc

[148] https://www.earny.co/home

receipts and monitor opportunities to claim money back on price drops. While many stores offer refunds for shoppers if prices change after purchase, they rely on consumers being too busy to actually follow up. Automated services like this as well as subscription-cancelling apps and price comparison sites will continue to place pricing pressure on retailers without human involvement. Businesses that depend on consumer inertia will be hit hard.

Your Home Fitting Room

"[Our customers] come to us because they don't want to go shopping.5 years from now, people will say, 'Remember when we had to wander malls and find our own things? That's crazy!'"

Eric Colson, Chief Algorithm Officer, Stitch Fix[149]

It's not often a retailer uses AI more than Amazon (though the service is hosted on AWS), but Stitch Fix may be among the most advanced users of AI in the apparel sector. Stitch Fix is an online-only styling service that delivers a personalised shopping experience. You fill out your Style Profile and a Personal Stylist will then pick pieces to fit your tastes, needs and budget. Each box they send you contains a curated selection of clothing, shoes and accessories for you to try on at home. Simply keep the items you want and send back the rest in a prepaid USPS envelope. Shipping and returns are free. Stitch Fix offers an on-demand or subscription service for people who need their wardrobe refreshed with new items on a regular basis. It charges a $20 styling fee, credited if you keep the items - you have 3 days to decide what to keep.

---

[149] https://www.fastcompany.com/90128248/how-stitch-fix-is-using-algorithmic-design-to-become-the-netflix-of-fashion

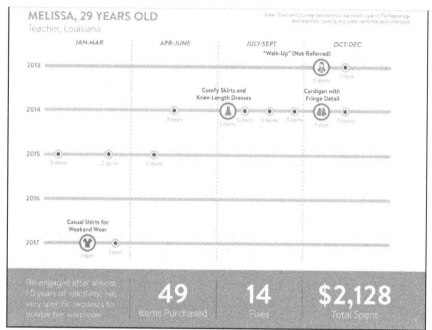

Figure 103: A Stitch Fix User Profile

Stitch Fix employs a team of about 80 data analysts[150] who develop algorithms to match inventory to customer preferences. Some 46% of clients provide their Pinterest profile as input for the stylist. Human stylists finalise the selection before dispatch to the customer. Stitch Fix tracks what the person likes and doesn't like and uses those data points to inform the next batch of items the customer receives. Stitch Fix also uses algorithms not only to pick clothes for its customers but to actually design new pieces. So far, the initiative, called Hybrid Design, has used machine learning to develop over 30 pieces using this methodology. If you're interested in more detail on how Stitch Fix uses algorithms throughout its business, the company has posted a detailed and very accessible animated overview here: https://algorithms-tour.stitchfix.com/

Although the number of people purchasing apparel online has risen in recent years it's an area that has attracted a lot of interest as a

---

[150] https://www.slideshare.net/StefanKrawczyk/data-day-texas-2017-scaling-data-science-at-stitch-fix

category that still offers substantial growth prospects. Amazon itself has recently rolled out its Prime Wardrobe service that lets shoppers select clothing items to try on at home, with a return box for unwanted items. I suppose the ultimate Amazon customer will ask their Echo Look for style advice on the items too, with Amazon undoubtedly exploring what additional services they could offer via the camera-enabled Echo device.

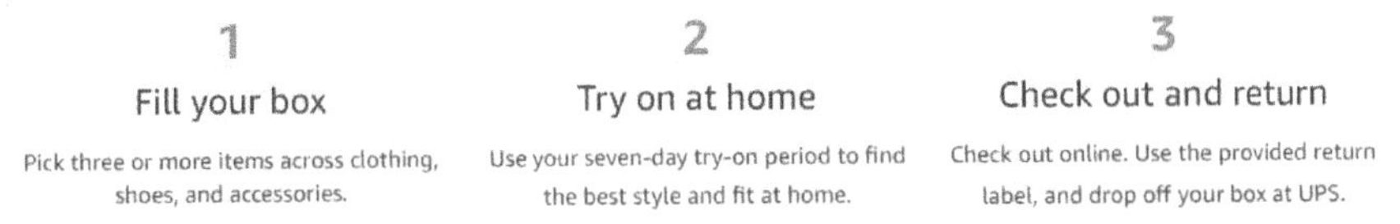

1	2	3
Fill your box	Try on at home	Check out and return
Pick three or more items across clothing, shoes, and accessories.	Use your seven-day try-on period to find the best style and fit at home.	Check out online. Use the provided return label, and drop off your box at UPS.

Figure 104: Amazon Prime Wardrobe User Experience

Payments

Whether it's groceries or clothing, an important part of any transaction is of course the exchange of payment. After centuries of cash being the dominant mechanism for the transfer of value, the payments world has seen large amounts of innovation in recent years as retailers seek to make it easier for us to buy things and financial institutions try to capture as much transaction value as they can.

Paying for things has gotten a lot easier and faster over the years. From the rather imprecise mechanics of barter and the attendant problem of coincidence of wants, we moved to coins and notes with stored value, to credit/debit cards and mobile payments. Cash was relatively quick - though we've all seen the look of a cashier when tendering a note they consider too large for the transaction and then they calculate and gather the requisite change. Credit cards are the globally accepted spiritual successor to the tabs once run by individual stores. 2016 saw card use finally overtake cash in the UK[151], with debit cards leading the way. The popularity of contactless payments for small transactions has bolstered the switch from cash in recent years. Standing orders and direct debits are popular for

---

[151] https://www.theguardian.com/money/2017/jul/12/cash-contactless-payments-uk-stores-cards-british-retail-consortium

recurring payments due to the reduced cash handling and increased certainty of payment over cash.

Faster Cards

If you ask anyone under the age of 30, they probably couldn't explain why some numbers on the front of a credit card are embossed and may not recognise this slip of carbon paper and machine in Figure 103. They'll likely never have endured the delay of a cashier filling in the details by hand and then handing over the multi-layer slip for them to sign.

Figure 105: A credit card imprint machine and a Chip/Swipe/Contactless Terminal

The ability to swipe a card through a POS terminal for the electronic transfer of the card details was a huge time saver compared to the manual transfer process. The introduction of chip and pin in 2004 was intended to reduce card fraud but for many people it was slower than swiping a card. Upgrades to the terminals can reduce the chip reading time from about 10 seconds to about 2 seconds, but that depends on merchants updating their terminals.

Contactless

Not long after chip and pin, the first contactless cards were issued. These allow for payments to be made simply by tapping the contactless payment method on a terminal. The contactless chip can be embedded in a debit/credit/transit card, a phone, a watch, a sticker or a key fob. In contrast to chip and pin transactions, Contactless specifications require a Contactless tap to execute in under 500 milliseconds using a technology called NFC. Ten years after the introduction of contactless to the UK, more than half of all transactions today - up to the £30 spending limit - are made using the 'touch and go' technology.[152]

Phone Payments

In late 2014, Apple announced the launch of Apple Pay with the iPhone 6 - contactless payments built into the iPhone. Google followed with Android Pay (now rebranded as Google Pay) less than a year later and it's now common for most mid and upper tier Android handsets to include the NFC chip required.

Not all phone-based payments are contactless. In China for example, the dominant form of payment is scanning a QR code with either the WeChat or Alipay apps. Developing markets are also embracing the convenience of digital payments. In Kenya and Tanzania, M-Pesa is an SMS-based system for storing and transferring money. Google has launched a payments app called Tez in India that enables payments to businesses or between people (e.g. to split a bill) direct from a bank current account. It also allows digital payment of utility bills and purchases from selected web sites.

HandsFree

In 2016, Google announced a trial of a new payments system called HandsFree. Run in a very limited number of stores around Silicon Valley, the app operated via a combination of Bluetooth, Wi-Fi, and location services to identify if your phone was in a store. When paying, you simply told the cashier your initials and they would be presented with a photo on their till, that the user had previously set up in an app to confirm the transaction. Although it was discontinued after the limited trial, it was the most friction-free payment experience I've ever had - I was able to have dinner, tell the cashier I wanted to "Pay with Google", my initials were DK and the phone in my pocket buzzed with the transaction complete before I could sit down to eat. No card reader, no contactless tap - just totally frictionless payment.

---

[152] http://www.bbc.co.uk/news/amp/business-40802807

We'll likely see continued innovation in this space, with Facial Recognition already being used for payments by Chinese Internet giant Alibaba[153].

Barclaycard Dine and Dash

Over ⅓ of diners in restaurants find waiting for the bill the most frustrating part of eating out, and one solution is to enable them to pay for their meal when they're finished, without waiting for the bill to arrive and then for the server to go get the card machine, and then return to take payment. A small device from Barclaycard on each table is being trialled as a solution to this. The diners use an app to check in to their table and to make their payment. The device colour alerts restaurant staff that payment has been made.

Figure 106: Dine and Dash table top terminal from Barclaycard

[153] https://techcrunch.com/2017/09/03/alibaba-debuts-smile-to-pay/

Subscription

We mentioned earlier that Amazon offers subscription services on several consumables and consumer goods. Subscription services are big business and an increasingly common way of shopping and paying for products and services. Historically quite rare outside of newspapers and magazines, you can now find subscription services for everything from Coffee (Nespresso) to Razor Blades (Dollar Shave Club), Clothes (Stitch Fix), and Meal Kits (Blue Apron). McKinsey research[154] shows that 15 percent of online shoppers have signed up for one or more subscriptions to receive products on a recurring basis, frequently through monthly boxes.

Entertainment services are now among the most common subscription offerings, with the speed and convenience, offered by the likes of Netflix and Spotify for streamed access to a vast library of content, appealing more to people than owning individual items. The following table shows the subscriber base of some leading services:

Subscription Service Growth = Driven by...
Access / Selection / Price / Experience / Personalization

Online Subscription Services Representative Companies		Subscribers 2017	Growth Y/Y
Netflix	Video	118MM	+25%
Amazon	Commerce / Media	100MM	--
Spotify	Music / Audio	71MM	+48%
Sony PlayStation Plus	Gaming	34MM	+30%
Dropbox	File Storage	11MM	+25%
The New York Times	News / Media	3MM	+43%
Stitch Fix	Fashion / Clothing	3MM	+31%
LegalZoom	Legal Services	550K	+16%
Peloton	Fitness	172K	+173%

Figure 107: The Growth of Subscriptions

---

[154] https://www.mckinsey.com/industries/high-tech/our-insights/thinking-inside-the-subscription-box-new-research-on-ecommerce-consumers

Invisible

Perhaps the most notable thing about payments is how much effort goes into making them invisible. Just as you now get out of an Uber or Lyft without the old process of fumbling with cash to pay a taxi, many payments even outside seamless in-app transactions have been reduced to the tap of a phone or card with no physical exchange and no concept of change being given back.

We saw earlier how Amazon DRS-enabled devices will order consumables as needed, while subscriptions will ensure that we have access to the goods and services we want without the effort of making obvious per transaction payments. There is a very real danger in such a world that we will spend more money than we intend to. Researchers coined a name for this: It's called the credit card premium[155]. In short, when you don't have cash, you spend more money. It makes perfect sense — parting with a crisp $20 bill is a little more painful than a thoughtless swipe of a card, even if you tacked on a few more items to raise your total to $25. The majority of consumers behave in this way, and businesses are foaming at the pocketbook to get in line. We are clearly in the middle of the culture of convenience at any (reasonable) cost.

Cashless?

In our quest for speed, could physical cash actually go away entirely? A move to a cashless world is not a purely technical question. While most businesses see significant upside in going cashless, not all consumers are in favour.

Cash free operations have many positives for business - no expensive cash handling, no cash errors, no slow till queues with change issues, no cash robberies, no pilfering. At a macro level, it could also perhaps bring an end to tax evasion and money laundering,[156] as all transactions would be logged. However,

---

[155] http://www.huffingtonpost.com/2014/10/20/apple-pay-will-make-you-s_n_6014870.html
[156] https://www.bloomberg.com/news/articles/2016-09-07/harvard-economist-kenneth-rogoff-is-trying-to-kill-cash

opponents and critics see an end to the privacy that anonymous cash transactions offer, sweeping new powers for government revenue departments, as well as a disproportionate impact on some demographics and especially the poor. For example, Sweden is the most cashless society so far on the planet, with banknotes and coins accounting for just 1.7 percent of its GDP but, while one can even donate to the church electronically, there have been concerns about exclusion of the elderly. An app created by the Swedish banks, Swish, moves money instantaneously between users' bank accounts - all you need is someone's phone number. Since its launch, nearly half the population has started using the app; in December of 2017, Swedes (population 10 million) Swished some 10 million times. Even small businesses now accept Swish payments, as do some homeless people selling magazines on the streets of Stockholm.

Time is Money and Money Takes Time

The cost-benefit is obvious: cards, with their hidden costs and fees, make money for banks, whereas vaults of bills and coins do not. In fact, cash costs banks money. It must be handled, counted, transported, guarded, and counted again. As Niklas Arvidsson, an economist at Stockholm's Royal Institute of Technology, puts it: "It's clear the banks have a business incentive to reduce the use of cash." [157]

According to the Federal Reserve, Americans use cash for 46 percent of their transactions, preferring for the rest the convenience of plastic, check, or the mobile payment apps on their smartphones. The explosion of digital finance platforms, from Square card readers to services like Venmo, Apple Pay, Google Pay, and PayPal, has made spending as easy, fast, and pleasant as sending a text. However, the criminal economy depends on the anonymous, untraceable nature of cash. Indeed, much of the cash in the world, maybe most of it, is simply unaccounted for. The World Bank estimates that about a third of the cash in most countries circulates underground, in black markets and through illegal employment. Take it away and thieves have no fool proof way to sell their stolen goods, drug dealers no way to hide their deals, and eventually the whole shadow economy

---

[157] https://www.wired.com/2016/05/sweden-cashless-economy/?mbid=nl_5916

collapses. It's probably far too simplistic to assume that would be an unconditionally good thing.

But it seems that, for a growing number of people, cashless will become a large part of their daily transactions, even if they choose to make some payments in cash. As financial institutions push their agenda of reducing cash with varying degrees of subtlety, it is reminiscent of the Marxist theory of cultural hegemony, associated particularly with Antonio Gramsci, that the ruling class can manipulate the norms of a society, so that their view becomes the world view. It is also an example of interpellation[158], as described by Louis Althusser, which is a constitutive process where individuals acknowledge and respond to ideologies, recognising themselves as subjects - the basic idea is that you can get people to adopt beliefs by addressing them as if they already had those beliefs. So, even if you never thought that cash was inconvenient, if you see adverts that make it seem like an obvious condition, you will come around to that belief.

Predictive Retail (Pretail)

The future coming into view is an acceleration of what we see today. We're heading toward an age of assistance where, for marketers, friction will mean failure. We'll all be expected to stay a step ahead of consumers—to know their needs even better than they do.

Sridhar Ramaswamy, Google Senior Vice President of Ads & Commerce [159]

As consumer desire for ever-faster shopping shows no sign of abating, how can retailers continue to accelerate? Everything you look at or buy online leaves a trail of data. Combine that with everything people like you buy, and ML can figure out with increasing accuracy what you'll buy before you even realise it.

---

[158] https://en.wikipedia.org/wiki/Interpellation_(philosophy)

[159] https://www.thinkwithgoogle.com/marketing-resources/micro-moments/future-of-marketing-machine-learning-micro-moments/

In August 2012 Amazon filed a patent (granted December 2013) for what it termed "anticipatory shipping". This involves *shipping the package to the destination geographical area without completely specifying the delivery address at the time of shipment, and while the package is in transit, completely specifying the delivery address for the package. In some embodiments, speculative shipping of a package may occur in anticipation of a customer ordering items in that package, but before such an order has actually occurred* - in other words shipping an item Amazon thinks you might order in your general direction and then adding the final details of your address once you confirm your order. The Patent application (which of course may never be implemented) also covers the concept of making speculatively-shipped items available to other consumers based on proximity at a discount, instead of incurring return shipping costs. In reality, although Amazon operates a massive network of regional warehouses to try to ensure the items you want are within easy reach of you for fast delivery (Amazon has over 150 million square feet of fulfilment capacity worldwide), even that may not be enough. This patent if implemented, represents using the parcel carrier network as an extended and more local warehouse.

Thinking back to the cameras we talked about earlier, alongside actual shopping data collected about our retail habits, which provide fuel for ML models to turn into predictions, the emergence of Computer Vision technologies adds a further dimension. Any of the multitude of cameras that watch us, whether in our smartphone, our laptop webcam or an Amazon Echo Look, could potentially scan for opportunities to pitch more items to us. Merchants will have to be careful not to cross a line into privacy-invasion territory but it's quite easy to imagine a feasible future where an unsolicited email arrives offering us a new coat, in our size and preferred colour, because the camera "noticed" that our current coat has signs of wear.

What you're willing to pay

Along with the speed of delivery and the availability/suitability of the product itself, the other major variable in our commercial decisions is usually price. Again here, AI is hard at work analysing data and implementing changes. Retailers traditionally change their prices in response to a number of factors like promotions, competitors, external influences and availability. Large retailers like Walmart and Best Buy change prices maybe 50,000 times over a month but Amazon's algorithms change prices 2.5 million times a day, on about 20% of their inventory. They can test price elasticity with astonishing speed. Amazon pushes new code live every 12 seconds and can test a feature on 5,000 users by turning it on for just 45 seconds.

While I've yet to see any examples of dynamic pricing implementation in retail based on CV data, imagine if the price of a cold drink or ice cream automatically increases if the camera detects you're hot as you enter the store!

Logistics

Nowadays, much of shopping is about logistics, providing people with unprecedented choice and delivering it with unheard of scale and speed. The global supply chain powers the modern life experience with an unappreciated complexity. And technology is revolutionising this field too in both visible and invisible ways, to speed up virtually all links in the chain. To complicate matters further, speed is not always the only parameter - there is increasing consumer expectation that elements of the supply chain will minimise carbon emissions without sacrificing convenience.

Containers

Despite my focus in this book on high tech advances speeding up our lives, a seemingly simple, technology-free innovation has underpinned much of the last few decades of international logistics - the standardised container. Not to be confused with the software use of the term containers (such as Docker or Kubernetes), the metal shipping container transformed global trade as documented in Mark Levinson's 2006 book, The Box[160]. Although now tracked by GPS and potentially soon moved across the seas on autonomous ships[161], the

---

[160] https://www.amazon.com/Box-Shipping-Container-Smaller-Economy/dp/0691170819/ref=dp_ob_title_bk

[161] https://www.ship-technology.com/projects/yara-birkeland-autonomous-container-vessel/

humble origins of the shipping container were crucial to the development of today's mass consumers technologies.

Figure 108: Containers have helped speed up logistics

Warehouses

Warehouses typically look very dull from the outside - slab-sided buildings with no distinguishing features beyond a lack of windows and multiple docking bays for large trucks. Inside though, they are increasingly extremely high-tech enclaves of robots and powerful algorithms managing the flow of goods in and out.

For some variety from all the Amazon-based examples in this book, let's also talk about Ocado in this section. The UK-based firm is the world's largest online-only grocer and recently became a supplier to Kroger, the second-biggest food retailer in the US. A modern Ocado fulfilment centre is home to over 1,000 robots, which fetch food from crates, delivering them to workers at a rate of 3 items per minute for packing. Operating 23 hours a day, 7 days a week, each robot is capable of carrying 340kg and has a forward-facing laser and camera that detect obstacles, such as fallen items, as they travel at up to 9 mph (14 kph). The time to complete a typical 50-item order is now just a few minutes, compared with around two hours in Ocado's first-generation warehouses - a more than 500% speed increase.

Figure 109: Ocado warehouse robots travel across boxes of products

Over time, Ocado plans to streamline the ordering process as far as it possibly can. CTO Paul Clarke suggests that the company could acquire consumption data from your smart fridge, listen to what recipes you're talking about via a smart assistant like Amazon's Alexa, and even mine your calendar for data so it knows you'll be cooking for friends next weekend. Ultimately, he says, it would like for *"the right groceries to turn up, at the right time, as if by magic, without you even having to ask for them."* Supposedly, therefore, if customers can stomach the loss of privacy, Ocado offers something valuable in return. *"We can free people up so that they have more time to experiment and experience the delight of food."*[162]

Once the orders are ready to leave the warehouse, the influence of technology still isn't finished. Ocado's delivery planning and routing algorithms[163] assess 4 million moves per second to determine the optimal route for each van.

---

[162] https://www.technologyreview.com/s/603229/the-robotic-grocery-store-of-the-future-is-here/

[163] https://ocadotechnology.com/blog/ocado-internet-of-vans/

Picking

A major area of focus for engineers working on speeding up warehouse operations is on picking - the process of retrieving and transferring individual items into a customer order fulfilment. Humans are good pickers - we're dextrous and able to grip a large variety of different shaped items without even thinking about how to pick them up or how much force to apply so as not to drop or crush them. Robotic pickers struggle with this - few configurations have proven as adept as the human hand, and replicating the hand is very difficult. But the potential benefits of being able to operate faster than humans are incentive enough to keep working on solving this challenge. Some robotics companies believe that, thanks to machine learning, their machines will soon be able to pick many categories of goods 50% faster than human workers - with both the speed and ability to work 24/7 offering major cost savings.

In an Amazon warehouse, humans already spend less than a minute working on a typical order[164]. In that time, they will take an item off the shelf, then box and send it for shipping. With the customer's goods arriving to a worker station in a yellow bin, a computer screen prescribes to the employee which size box to use. The employee then inserts bubble wrap, seals the package with tape (a machine provides the perfect length of tape for the package automatically) and then applies the labels. Apart from that final packing, the rest of the work is done by robots and automated systems. Amazon's addition of robots in 2014 allowed it to store 50% more inventory, according to the company. With the robots, Amazon can more tightly pack the shelves that hold items.

Stock Taking

Keeping track of stock is of vital importance at every stage of distribution. Again, technology is being employed to speed up this usually onerous oversight function. Lost or misplaced items in a warehouse cost industry billions of dollars per year. Some are now turning to drones to solve the problem - the flying robots can quickly

---

[164] http://money.cnn.com/2016/10/06/technology/amazon-warehouse-robots/?iid=EL

and accurately scan inventory without interrupting activities.

Figure 110: A drone flies around a warehouse scanning inventory

Outside the warehouse, further along in the chain, retailers are also automating stock checks. For example, Bossa Nova Robotics devices can analyse what's on the shelves with computer vision rather than requiring barcodes to scan (which are not usually front-facing on shelves in retail, unlike they are in larger packaging in warehouses). The robots drive autonomously through store aisles figuring out what has sold and then sends back data. The machines will not only evaluate which items are in stock, but also help locate misplaced items. In just two minutes, one robot can image 25 meters (80 feet) of aisle.

Figure 111: A BossaNova autonomous robot checks the shelves

Delivery

"Ten years ago, people thought two-day shipping seemed really fast; now we think two-hour shipping and one-hour shipping will be the standard."

Stephenie Landry, Head of Amazon Prime Now

"Customers don't want to shop, they want things that help them live a better life to magically appear."

Dan Makoski, VP of Design, Walmart

Getting the item to the customer from the nearest warehouse is an area where the is no one-size-fits-all solution. Traditional parcel delivery services (Post Office and Private operators such as DHL, UPS and FedEx) have seen huge growth but face increasingly demanding customers as well as the challenge of conveying everything from single item orders to hot food to groceries.

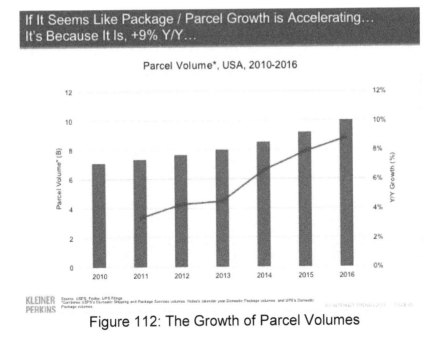

Figure 112: The Growth of Parcel Volumes

And people expect their packages to come sooner:

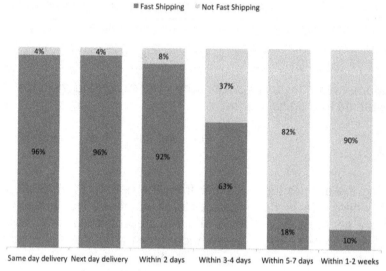

What US Consumers Consider "Fast Shipping" *2015*

Fast Shipping Not Fast Shipping

Source: Deloitte, n=4,009

BI INTELLIGENCE

Figure 113: Consumer expectations for order deliveries

but also to come in a convenient and affordable manner:

Relative importance of features[2]
Percent of constant sum

Which delivery features matter most to you?

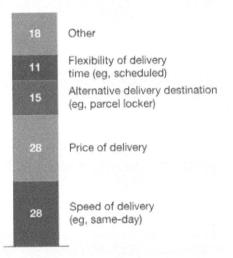

18	Other
11	Flexibility of delivery time (eg, scheduled)
15	Alternative delivery destination (eg, parcel locker)
28	Price of delivery
28	Speed of delivery (eg, same-day)

Figure 114: Speed vs Price of Delivery relative importance from McKinsey Report[165]

This may mean a mix of delivery to domestic addresses, business addresses, lockers, pickup locations or click and collect in store. The "last mile problem", as logistics professionals refer to the challenge of getting the goods from the transportation hub to the end customer, is ferociously complex. E-commerce is growing so fast that delivery infrastructure can't keep up. Otherwise profitable transactions can tip into a loss due to delivery delays, repeat delivery attempts or stolen packages.

---

[165] https://www.mckinsey.com/industries/travel-transport-and-logistics/our-insights/same-day-delivery-the-next-evolutionary-step-in-parcel-logistics

Last mile delivery models

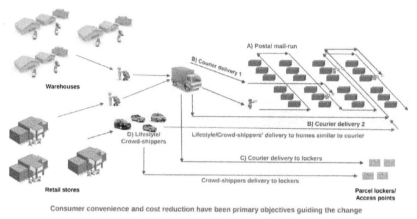

Figure 115: Last Mile Delivery challenges - McKinsey report[166]

As well as using traditional carriers, Amazon has invested in its own delivery solutions, including leasing a fleet of 27 Boeing 767 Freighters and creating Amazon Flex, a solution where anyone with a car and a smartphone can apply to deliver packages at times that suit them, earning between $18 and $25 per hour. It's now competing with Uber and Lyft as a source of employment for on-demand drivers

Figure 116: Amazon now operates a freight airline and an ad-hoc driver service

---

[166] http://www.mckinsey.com/business-functions/sustainability-and-resource-productivity/our-insights/urban-commercial-transport-and-the-future-of-mobility

Accenture[167] has summarised this new world of parcel delivery in the following flow:

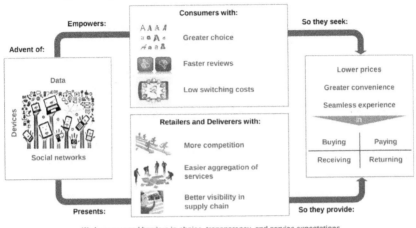

Figure 117: The circular nature of Online Commerce and Logistics

---

[167] https://www.accenture.com/t20170227T024657Z__w__/ie-en/_acnmedia/Accenture/Conversion-Assets/DotCom/Documents/Global/PDF/Dualpub_23/Accenture-Adding-Value-to-Parcel-Delivery.pdf#zoom=50

Figure 117 above also shows the complex interplay of the last mile delivery chain as multiple solutions are required to meet the consumer's speed expectations - expectations clearly shown in the following report:

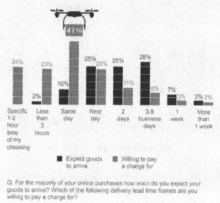

Our research also looked at what delivery services shoppers would pay for. The survey seems to uncover a sweet spot for retailers and their delivery partners: consumers' willingness to pay more for same-day or faster delivery. A quarter of online shoppers said they would dip into their wallets to be sure of getting their packages within a one- or two-hour window of their choosing (see Figure 3). Older shoppers may place an even greater premium on narrow delivery time slots; according to the survey, shoppers ages 65 or over were 8% more likely (52% versus 44%) to choose "delivery at a specific time slot." Observes PwC director Kauschke: "I think it shows that people acknowledge that delivery on the same-day or even faster is a special logistics effort."

And effort it is. Fresh from an exhausting holiday delivery season, many leading consumer companies and their shippers are re-evaluating everything from caps on the numbers of packages shipped to pricing schemes. Having helped raise consumers' expectations, the pressure is now on to find ways to manage those expectations—profitably.

Figure 3: Consumers expect their purchases to arrive promptly and are willing to pay extra for same day delivery

Q: For the majority of your online purchases how soon do you expect your goods to arrive? Which of the following delivery lead time frames are you willing to pay a charge for?
Base: 22,480 (Chart represents percentage of daily and weekly usage combined)
Source: PwC, Global Consumer Insights Survey, 2018

Figure 118: Many consumers are willing to pay for faster delivery

Lock(er)s and Keys

Lockers have proven a popular secure drop off point for deliveries to consumers not at home during the day but willing to stop by a local convenience store on their way home, where of course the store owner hopes they'll impulse purchase something. Amazon operates a network of over 2,000 lockers and has announced plans to enable apartment block owners to locate a locker in their premises. A more advanced solution to reducing package delivery problems is Amazon Key. This works in one of two ways - you can fit a smart lock to your home's front door, as well as a camera, and the delivery person can unlock the door, placing the package in your hallway, under the watchful eye of your camera. Or, with select compatible car models, delivery people can place your package in your car as long as it's parked in an accessible location.

Worry-free delivery at no extra cost, backed by
the Amazon Key
Happiness Guarantee

Figure 119: Amazon Lockers, Amazon Key Home Delivery and
Amazon Key Car Delivery

Pick up

While click-and-collect has been a favourite cross-channel solution offered by many retailers enabling you to order online and pick up from your local store, some are trialling more dedicated pick-up solutions, primarily for grocery shopping, where the typical order is made up of 50 or more different items that are likely too bulky to carry.

The Amazon Fresh Pickup locations in Seattle require as little as 15 minutes advance notice to have your order ready before you drive to the location, pull into a parking space, and watch as your groceries are loaded directly into your car by an Amazon staff member. In a slightly different approach, Walmart is also testing a kiosk in Oklahoma City that lets you pick up your online groceries at any time. Instead of parking and waiting for a staff member to bring out your food, you enter a pickup code and the kiosk to automatically fetches the order for you to load it into your car.

Figure 120: Amazon Fresh Pickup (L) and Walmart Pickup (R)

If lockers, wi-fi enabled locks and remote access to cars aren't high-tech enough, there are other examples of cutting edge technology being trialled to solve last mile challenges and cut delivery costs. Two active areas are delivery robots and delivery drones.

Delivery Robots

The next time you're walking down a sidewalk and think you spot a robot rolling towards you, you might not be imagining things. As of June 2018, Starship Robots had travelled more than 100,000 miles in 20 countries, across 100 cities, in extensive trials of local delivery. These 6-wheeled autonomous robots travel at up to 4pmh, have a capacity of up to 10kg and a range of approx. 2 miles, guided by 9 cameras, 8 ultrasonic detectors and a radar. The Nuro R-1 is larger than the Starship Robot and travels on roads rather than sidewalks. At 25mph, it's not suitable for highways but is designed primarily for urban/residential areas. It is fully autonomous and can carry about 20 grocery bags (110kg). US retailer Kroger has announced a pilot scheme to use the Nuro for grocery delivery. Both of these robots may solve the last mile problem, but you still have to walk the last few metres to retrieve your order from them once they notify you of their arrival by text.

Figure 121: Starship sidewalk delivery robot (L) and Nuro autonomous delivery car (R)

Drones

Drone use in most countries is currently limited to line of sight operations - you can only operate a drone as long as the operator can see it. This rules out delivery use in most situations but that hasn't stopped 1 million consumers (88%) and businesses (12%) registering drones with the US FAA. Both Alphabet and Amazon are at the forefront of developing drones capable of delivering packages, as well as working on the infrastructure that would be required for their widespread use, such as an air traffic control system.

While drones would offer very attractive economics to firms compared to staffed delivery vans, a number of practical issues remain before we'll see commonplace drone deliveries for packages:

- Where will drones land - if the recipient has a clear lawn or yard, it might be ok, but what about apartment blocks?

- Drones may have limited capabilities in anything other than excellent weather conditions

- Drones will likely have limited range and capacity, making them less attractive as substitutes for the costly practice of sending delivery vans to remote properties. Although, 86% of Amazon deliveries meet the size and weight criteria to be delivered in this manner.

- Will there be privacy objections from people who don't want drones (possibly equipped with cameras) flying near or over their property?

I'm sure that many of these challenges will be resolved, and drones will before long become another option for deliveries. And while delivery drones may seem to some to be a first world indulgence of the worst kind, People frequently make the mistake of assessing technology against their own needs or based on its initial use. Their use for blood deliveries in rural Africa by a firm called Zipline already shows a positive benefit.

Figure 122: Wing drone, Prime Air (Top) and Zipline Blood Delivery (Bottom)

However futuristic it may seem today as you take a parcel in from the UPS driver, in less than a decade, it's quite possible that many household purchases will move from their supplier to your hall without a single human touch. Imagine your water jug orders a replacement filter for itself. The signal travels to the Amazon DRS, where it's relayed to a robotic picker in the warehouse. From there, it's loaded by robot onto a drone that brings it to your home. Or, it's loaded onto a courier truck from where a robot approaches your door. Authorised by Amazon, your smart lock opens the hall door and the robot places the item just inside the door, watched by your in-home surveillance camera to provide you with peace of mind.

While drones can be used to speed up deliveries, and also to speed up activities such as scanning stock in a warehouse, these categories of flying robots have many other applications, almost all with an emphasis on speed. One of my personal favourites is the additional speed drones can bring to life-threatening situations. Ranging from use by firefighters to rapidly assess locations from an aerial view[168], to flying lifeguard drones that drop inflatable devices[169], to the delivery of a defibrillator[170] to a cardiac patient faster than any road-based ambulance can reach them, these are speed boosts that have very obvious benefits. Although some regulatory changes may be required, such uses should be possible in the very near term.

The Fightback?

I started this chapter with a look at the pressures physical retailers are facing in the modern world. It seems unavoidable that the shift to more convenient channels for many purchases and replenishments will continue to expose the over-building of retail space in many countries. Of course, retail isn't going to go quietly into the night and despite widespread closures and layoffs, the sector remains a highly

---

[168] https://thenextweb.com/tech/2018/04/25/dji-launches-a-new-emergency-drone-program-in-europe/

[169] https://www.theverge.com/2018/1/18/16904802/drone-rescue-australia-video-ocean

[170] http://www.bbc.com/news/av/technology-40360164/the-defibrillator-drone-that-can-beat-ambulance-times

visible and, in most cases, defining part of our urban landscape. A high street without retail would be a contradiction in terms.

Physical shopping has a lot of drawbacks - getting to the store may not be easy, there's no guarantee it'll have what you want (or that you can find it if it does) and there may be a queue for fitting rooms or just to pay. Then you may well discover that another store had it cheaper than you paid for it. But physical shopping also has a lot in its favour. There's nothing quite like touching a product before you buy it - people do still like to see products. There's always the chance of a serendipitous discovery of something you'd no intention of buying. The opportunity (in some stores) of a conversation with a knowledgeable associate who will help you make an informed personal purchase decision. And there's the instant gratification of leaving the store clutching your purchases. Shopping can also be a social experience and often mixes with coffee or food. Physical retail isn't going to disappear. Closures and consolidations may continue but it will persevere and survive.

The New High Street

Both city authorities and companies need to think carefully about what the new retail experience could become in the digital age, and about how to shape it for the good of the urban environment. They may need to let go of long held notions that long-term leases and upscale shops are preferable for shopping precincts. For smaller brands, pop-up stores may become much more normal, as might spaces that change use based on time of the day; for example, using flexible furniture to transform stores into social spaces in the evening, allowing smaller retailers to pay only partial rents. Larger brands will continue to invest in flagship stores that offer experiences and statements of the brand as much as sales - note Apple's preference to refer to its stores now as Town Squares, not stores.

Technological changes will be employed to keep traditional stores afloat and store experiences will continue to evolve. Initiatives like scan and walk, click and collect and checkout-free stores will make shopping faster, but still a physical experience. Perhaps just as important as identifying and embracing the right technology for their sector will be an organisation's ability to change. Most retailers are not set up internally for the modern world of omni-channel selling. I've personally witnessed protectionist behaviour from senior executives more intent on preserving their channel budget line than growing overall company performance. Stores who resist showrooming products for subsequent online purchase that is attributed to their web team are doomed.

The complexity that comes with this new retail world, in which every screen and every home is a storefront, requires an increased level of sophistication in backend operations. Stores or brands that don't think strategically about collecting and using data, shipping options and last-mile delivery will pay the price. An efficient, communicative delivery model creates the same effect a smiling store associate does when wrapping a customer's package at the till — a pleasant experience that drives loyalty and benefits the brand. It's a whole new way of selling and needs to be treated as such by the highest levels of the business.

To survive, even innovative retailers will need to constantly refine their solutions. Take clothing giant Zara for example - one-third of its global online sales are now picked up in the store[171], but that has created long lines in some cities and waits for attendants to retrieve packages. To speed up the process, Zara said earlier this year it would roll out a robot-run version of click and collect, automating the service so that the collection points in brick-and-mortar stores will allow shoppers who have ordered items online to scan or enter a code; a robot will search for the customer's package, and then deliver it quickly to a drop box. Other retailers are struggling with the impact of online returns being made via stores which drives up footfall but not revenues - this is a problem in malls where their rent is partially determined by footfall, a vestigial measure.

But on the other hand, ask any retailer and they'll tell you they've been offered a bewildering array of technology options, all promised to be the silver bullet required to save retail. There has been much more promised than delivered over the years, as tech suppliers over promise and retailers struggle to execute change effectively.

---

[171] https://www.wsj.com/articles/how-zara-is-defying-a-broad-retail-slump-1497467742

The New Consumer

"In a way, the idea of the old bazaar has gone full circle: rather than visit somewhere where you can be surrounded by every merchant, you are now constantly visited (through your phone's location awareness and notifications – and, increasingly, domestic internet of things devices) by every merchant surrounding you".

Tom Goodwin[172]

For a retailer, consumers have changed beyond imagination in recent years. Everything is shoppable, all the time, from anywhere, with near-perfect knowledge about price, competitive products and availability. The new consumer is more demanding, experiential and discerning, yet price oriented. They expect total convenience and personal service at discount prices.

The upside for retailers is that people do still place a value on curation and many value convenience over ultimate price. So retailers who embrace channels and use technology to deliver the customer experience appropriate to their target market can prosper. Eyewear specialist, Warby Parker, for example, has expanded from its online-only roots to physical showrooms while promoting an ethical image, growing to a value of over $1.8n in just 8 years[173]. The other thing for retailers struggling is to consider - if you can't beat 'em, join 'em....

Embracing the Beast

Blaming Amazon is easy but retailers need to look for solutions to survive, rather than hoping the giant will stumble. Even if Amazon were to fade, there may be an inexorable trend away from retail as we know it for many types of products: a "natural" removal of inefficiencies, duplication and tradition from a sector that no longer serves the needs of its customers.

---

[172] https://www.marketingweek.com/2017/08/07/tom-goodwin-future-retail/

[173] https://www.recode.net/2018/3/14/17115230/warby-parker-75-million-funding-t-rowe-price-ipo

As Amazon's dominance grows - standing at just a touch below 50% of the online shopping market at time of writing (September 2018), many retailers are embracing Amazon as a supplement to their own stores. Amazon offers comprehensive fulfilment services, easing logistical headaches for retailers - in fact more than half of the goods sold on the Amazon platform are from marketplace sellers rather than the Seattle giant itself. But those choosing to use the Amazon platform need to be aware of the visibility it gives Amazon - it uses sales data to plan the Amazon Basics range. Amazon knows about demand and trends via search quicker than you do. They know about returns before you do.

AI Shopping

The end-to-end impact of AI is already happening in retail. Much of the technology speeding up commerce isn't consumer visible but it's vital to the experience. From predicting what you want to buy, to checking your payment for signs of fraud, to packing the order, to routing the delivery to you most efficiently, AI is already omnipresent. The learnings of the retail world will be replicated in other industries. I've already referenced the lifesaving work of delivery drones in healthcare in Africa and guess who, Amazon, have signalled a move into healthcare with the acquisition of PillPack[174]. Even within Amazon, AI is replacing head office staff as well as warehouse personnel. Bloomberg[175] reports that purchasing managers are being replaced by algorithms trained on customer data.

As the online shopping experience has improved over the years, making purchases has become an algorithm-driven frictionless experience of terrifying efficiency. It's easy, it's fast and it's addictive. We live in a time of efficiency, where everything is faster, smoother and more goal-oriented. Online retailers cater to this utilitarian drive, and we in turn forgo the experience of shopping.

---

[174]http://phx.corporate-ir.net/phoenix.zhtml?c=176060&p=irol-newsArticle&ID=2356401
[175] https://medium.com/bloomberg/amazons-clever-machines-are-moving-from-the-warehouse-to-headquarters-e821582a9549

Intention Economy

Another potential outcome is the emergence of the Intention Economy. As described by Doc Serles in his 2012 book of the same name, imagine a world in which the shopper simply advertised their requirements and any supplier could offer to meet it. So, for example, instead of browsing various airline websites to find a flight, you simply say that you want to fly from New York to San Francisco on a particular date and airlines bid for your business. Until now, this would have been very difficult to accomplish as suppliers would not have been able to keep up with consumer demands. But AI suddenly makes this approach to commerce plausible, as suppliers and your AIssistant can mediate and reach a conclusion, presenting you with a purchased item that best meets your needs.

So What Else?

Hopefully by now, you gave a good idea of how the interplay of speed and AI technologies is transforming the world of retail. Let's continue in the next chapter to look at some more sectors where AI is taking root, including ones more sensitive than Retail.

Chapter 8: AI Everywhere

"We have entered a new age of embedded, intuitive computing in which our homes, cars, stores, farms, and factories have the ability to think, sense, understand, and respond to our needs. It's not science fiction, but the dawn of a new era."

Fortune, October 3, 2013[176]

In the previous chapter, we saw how Retail offers a useful case study, given the relatively advanced nature and visibility of much of its use of technology, even though significant amounts of the technology remain behind the scenes or, at least, users are unaware of it. But I believe these technologies will touch *all* Industries, Government and individuals. If there's one point I'd like each reader to take away from this book, it's that nobody will continue to exist untouched by AI in one form or another.

In this chapter, I want to look briefly at some sector-specific uses of AI, and explore more about our changing relationship with technology by taking a look at one of the most hotly debated impacts of AI and next generation automation technologies - the impact on jobs.

Finding AI

"On a day to day basis our lives are being, to some extent, manipulated by AI solutions"

Sir Mark Walport, Chief Executive, UK Research and Innovation Council[177]

Unless you're very familiar with technology, it isn't always obvious when the technologies loosely grouped as AI are in play. While many companies tout their use of AI, others are less explicit about their

---

[176] http://fortune.com/2013/10/03/the-third-wave-of-computing/

[177] https://www.theguardian.com/science/2017/nov/01/artificial-intelligence-risks-gm-style-public-backlash-experts-warn

collection, processing and mining of data. It's also important to remember that it will come in many shapes and sizes, and be exposed through any number of interfaces. AI will take many forms - invisible new user interfaces like voice or bots; as well as automation, drones, smart domestic appliances and in the not too distant future, humanoid robots. Finally - a reminder that as we become more familiar with technology, we tend to stop classifying it as AI, reserving that term for the science-fiction feats we haven't yet conquered. But just because something ceases to be labelled as AI, it may still suffer from the same problems we'll consider in chapter 9.

As you read this book, I'm sure you'll also become aware of the ever-increasing level of coverage of AI by the media. Some publicity-conscious companies are motivated by a desire to look current, others to seem like an attractive place to work amidst a shortage of AI talent. But much of the coverage is focused on the potential negative implications of AI. Before we examine some of these, let's get some more context by reviewing some more of the uses for AI. In discussing aspects of AI, I often get a response of "that's decades away". It may well be if by AI you mean Artificial General Intelligence. But if you mean narrow AI, it's already here and will accelerate dramatically in the next ten years. Here's some of the areas it'll have the biggest impact on in the near term.

The Business of AI

Office work has long been regarded as relatively safe from the advances of automation. The knowledge/information workers created by the PC revolution haven't been as replaceable as other professions. And while it may take many more years for AI to replace some specialties, virtually everyone will see AI being introduced alongside them in the coming years, possibly dramatically changing their work. In an ideal scenario, our new AI helpers will make our jobs far more rewarding by taking over or at least speeding up much of the repetitive work.

Using Machine Learning, you can now ask your Google Spreadsheet in plain English to create graphs and formulas instead of knowing how to create them the normal way[178]. For example, you can ask "what is the distribution of products sold?" or "what are average sales on Sundays". Or, instead of manually building charts, ask Google Sheets to do it by typing in "histogram of 2017 customer ratings" or "bar chart for ice cream sales." Will we use this faster way of creating charts simply to create more charts or free up time for other tasks?

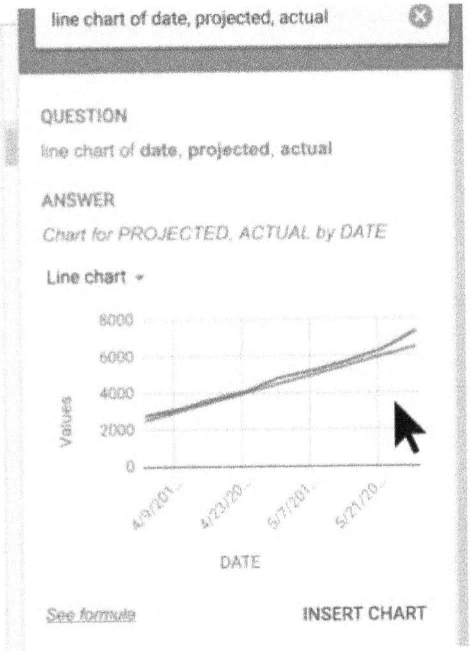

Figure 123: Tell Google Sheets what Chart to draw

Pharmaceuticals giant Novartis[179] is trialling an artificial-intelligence program that will soon tell the company how best to organize its employees' time based on analysis of prescribing patterns, to help sales employees determine when to visit physicians.

---

[178] https://www.blog.google/products/g-suite/visualize-data-instantly-machine-learning-google-sheets/

[179] https://www.bloomberg.com/amp/news/articles/2018-07-24/novartis-s-cultural-revolution-will-be-ai-enabled-and-desk-free

Intelligent Meetings

Given how much time is spent in meetings (with varying degrees of productivity), it's not surprising that AI enthusiasts have identified this as a target area. For anyone who has wasted hours merely trying to agree suitable meeting times with colleagues, salvation may already be here in the form of services like X.Ai[180]. You may find your next meeting invite coming from an AI assistant who will work to find an optimum calendar slot. With this service, you just cc your virtual AI assistant in the email and it will find slots in your calendar.

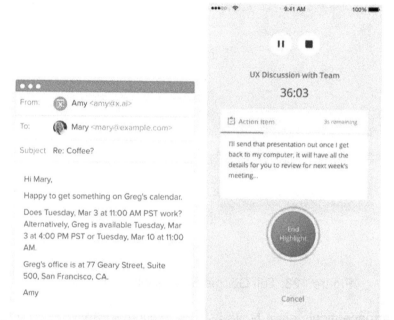

Figure 124: X.ai can schedule meetings on your behalf (L) while Voicera will listen in on the meeting and extract action points automatically (R)

Once the meeting is setup and agreed, AI solutions are emerging to make the meeting itself as efficient as the new process for setting it up. Google's Hangout Meets hardware now supports simple voice commands to start video conference meetings. Solutions like

---

[180] https://x.ai

Voicera[181] listens in to business meetings to take notes, processes the meeting and sends a summary of it to participants. It could also be instructed to complete action items, such as sending a copy of a presentation to everyone in the meeting.

A New Colleague

Aside from more efficient meetings, you may also find AI encroaching into the office in the form of a task-specific worker. Advances in AI mean that some complex cognitive or creative tasks can be completed by AI. Both Associated Press and The Washington Post have been using Natural Language Generation advances to write simple reports. For stories such as corporate earnings data or summaries of sports events AI systems, using the NLG technologies we discussed in Chapter 6, can write thousands of reports in seconds, in multiple languages, each customised to channels such as websites, mobile apps, emails or notifications. AP[182] now produces about 3,500 stories per quarter automatically. A summary item with commentary describing an earnings report can be outputted just seconds after the financial data are released, which frees up 20% of the business desk's resources. Likewise, for the Rio Olympics, The Washington Post used its AI system, Heliograf[183], to create about 300 reports on a variety of events.

---

181 https://www.voicera.com

182 http://niemanreports.org/articles/automation-in-the-newsroom/

183 https://digiday.com/media/washington-posts-robot-reporter-published-500-articles-last-year/

Automated Story Process

Heliograf

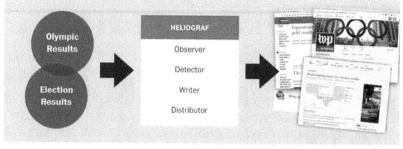

Figure 125: The Washington Post's Heliograf can write stories based on data inputs

JPMorgan Chase introduced a system called Contract Intelligence, or COIN, for reviewing commercial loan contracts; work that used to take legal aides 360,000 hours can now be done in a few seconds.

The suitability of AI to low level, mundane tasks may at first glance seem like a welcome innovation to free up resources for more valuable work. However, such entry-level positions are frequently vital training grounds for junior staff seeking to learn their trade. If we instead train AI for these tasks, we will be changing the career ladder with unknown future consequences.

Law & Order

The emerging capabilities of AI have some obvious potential applications in the field of law and order. Whether real or imagined, premature or imminent, these capabilities will be the subject of much speculation, experimentation and consternation in the coming years. For example, as we touched on in Chapter 5, facial recognition has long been a sought-after solution for security/surveillance.

Technology-based surveillance as a notion isn't new however. In the late 18th century, the philosopher Jeremy Bentham posited the Panopticon—a system of penal institutional design that placed a single watchtower in the centre of a circular structure. From the watchtower, every inmate could be observed. The inmates, however, couldn't see into the tower and couldn't tell when they were being observed. The Panopticon was intended to exert as much control over the inmates as possible, with minimal expenditure and effort. The growth of cheap cameras and computer vision means that the entire public and even private realms could be turned into a true panopticon.

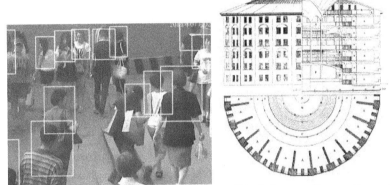

Figure 126: Will Surveillance cameras (L) deliver a Panopticon (R)

Speed and the wheels of justice

The extension of AI technologies into sensitive public domains such as policing will raise many questions. We're facing a new front for crime (cybercrime) and a new emphasis on crime detection in the physical world with many new tools for police forces: tools that will challenge law abiding citizens to decide on questions of privacy vs security. But it is unlikely that we can expect to operate with 19th century policing techniques and policies in an increasingly 21st century world. If crime moves faster, surely police must move faster too?

Technologies intended for one purpose often have multiple unintended side effects. Consider the potential implications of autonomous cars driving everywhere and simultaneously recording everything - a near total coverage of video surveillance. While self-driving cars only care about object detection and avoidance to function, there's now the added layer that facial recognition AI could be applied to the footage enabling its use for purposes other than the safe navigation of streets.

Beyond surveillance, the rest of the criminal justice system is starting to see the challenges and opportunities posed by AI. There may be good reason to progress with caution - algorithms will make mistakes. Or at least they'll make decisions that not everyone agrees with. After all, justice is subjective and intersubjective.

Policing

"While we now may be coming to the realization that the Cyber Age is a revolution of historic proportions, we cannot appreciate yet its full dimensions and vast potential to alter how we think, express ourselves, and define who we want to be. The forces and directions of the Internet are so new, so protean, and so far reaching that courts must be conscious that what they say today might be obsolete tomorrow"
Justice Kennedy, US Supreme Court, 2017[184]

The use of technology by police is already a contentious area due to the potential for what many see as over-reach, as well as uncertainty about how fit for purpose the newest innovations are. In June 2018[185], the US Supreme Court decided a case regarding police access to mobile phone location information, mandating probable cause and a warrant. While most people accept that their phone location is, of course, required by their service provider to connect to the network, the next wave of developments may see its use in the area of surveillance and prediction.

Advanced policing technologies may bring major benefits. The ability to predict and prevent crime, apprehend offenders and find missing persons more quickly is likely to win widespread public backing. But citizens can't make intelligent decisions about policing technology

---

[184] https://www.supremecourt.gov/opinions/16pdf/15-1194_08l1.pdf
[185] https://www.supremecourt.gov/opinions/17pdf/16-402_h315.pdf

unless they understand what the technology does. Naturally though, both police forces and their suppliers may not want to reveal all of their tools.

Predictive Policing

When you hear of projects looking to predict crime, it's hard not to be reminded of the 2002 film Minority Report, which showed a crime-free future where police arrested criminals before they committed crimes. While its premise was based on psychics, the combination of advanced surveillance and predictive algorithms now being tested in some jurisdictions has seemingly done away with the movie's need for the supernatural.

Algorithms process data on the location, time and date of previously committed crimes and this data is superimposed to create hotspots on a map for police officers to patrol. Critics of these analytics argue that from the moment a police officer, with the pre-crime mindset that you are a criminal, steps out of their patrol car to confront you, the presumption of innocence is no longer primary and your fate has been sealed. In new data-based surveillance, the target often emerges from the data. The targeting comes after the data collection, not before. Also of concern are findings that the systems developed so far are not yet reliable. We'll talk more in the next chapter about the very human biases that can be magnified, rather than eliminated, by AI.

A recent FT article quoted the ACLU: *"They said the system posed a particularly "grave threat to communities, including people of colour and immigrants", in a nod to studies that have shown that facial recognition software regularly misidentifies people of colour." This is ironic, given that big data policing was first pushed in the US several years ago as a response to racism and bias. The idea was that it would help circumvent human cognitive biases, such as the conflation of blackness and criminality.*[186]

---

[186] https://www.ft.com/content/279f4d80-5f77-11e8-ad91-e01af256df68

Legal AI

Although not usually thought of as technologically progressive, the legal profession may be one of the earliest to benefit from AI. As a profession heavily dependent on documents that increasingly can be interpreted by NLP, there are opportunities to speed up lengthy procedures. Algorithms can process much more paperwork than humans, in a fraction of the time. Due diligence reviews can be so time-consuming as to typically account for as much as half of the fees that lawyers charge for advising on deals. Lex Machina, a Silicon Valley start-up, uses court documents from previous cases to make predictions about a particular case, such as its time to trial, its likelihood of success in various jurisdictions, and the damages it could win. Other tech firms are aiming at full disintermediation, developing "robot lawyers" to deal with certain narrow tasks, such as appealing parking tickets or seeking flight refunds[187].

Sentencing

The attraction of unbiased, uncompromised, consistent judgements and fairer sentencing is obvious but early attempts at achieving this are mired in controversy. With little public awareness, algorithms already being used in the US justice system in some States to calculate recidivism rates, a person's chances of reoffending, in order to deliver an appropriate sentence. This has been shown to exhibit algorithmic bias where an individual's economic, social or ethnic background has influenced calculations. Take the example of a computer program called COMPAS, a risk assessment algorithm used by the state of Wisconsin. No one knows exactly how COMPAS works; its manufacturer refuses to disclose the proprietary algorithm. We only know the final risk assessment score it spits out, which judges may consider at sentencing. But shifting the sentencing calculation responsibility to a computer does not necessarily eliminate bias; it delegates and often compounds it.[188]

AI can be presented under a cloak of evidence-based objectivity and

---

[187] https://www.donotpay.com/

[188] https://mobile.nytimes.com/2017/10/26/opinion/algorithm-compas-sentencing-bias.html

(algorithmic) infallibility but machine learning algorithms often work on a feedback loop. If they are not constantly retrained, they "lean in" to the assumed correctness of their initial determinations, drifting away from both reality and fairness. Algorithms also thus far lack the human ability to individualise. A computer cannot look a defendant in the eye, account for a troubled childhood or disability, and recommend a rehabilitative sentence. This is precisely the argument against mandatory minimum sentences — they rob judges of the discretion to deliver individualised justice — and it is equally applicable against machine sentencing. Computers may be intelligent, but they are not wise. Everything they know, we taught them, including our biases. They are not going to un-learn them without transparency and corrective action by humans.

Healthcare AI

Along with the legal profession, medicine isn't usually seen as a profession eager to embrace new technology. With good reason, health professionals tend to be cautious about optimistic claims and prefer caution in circumstances where lives are so directly at risk. But given the vast quantities of complex data involved, healthcare is an area that could stand to benefit more than many others; speedier or more accurate identification of issues from patient data might be the difference between life and death. The American Medical Association[189] likes to refer to *augmented intelligence* to reassure people that technology will be used to support rather than replace clinicians. *"To reap the benefits for patient care, physicians must have the skills to work comfortably with health care augmented intelligence".*

Given the opportunities presented by the imperative to provide healthcare at a reasonable cost, many firms are focused on putting AI to work in this space - whether it's trawling through massive amounts of patient data to uncover unseen patterns that can point the way toward better treatments, identifying compounds for use in new drugs or developing personalised medicine, AI offers vast potential to improve how we understand disease and promote health. Machine

---

[189] https://www.mobihealthnews.com/content/ama-creates-regulations-around-augmented-intelligence

learning can, for example, help doctors stay up to date by summarising research they don't have time to read in detail.

All the better to see you with

While advances in imaging technology have enabled breakthroughs in medical diagnosis and treatment, the sheer volume of scans requiring analysis by highly trained professionals is a healthcare challenge. Some of the most promising applications of AI, together with advances in image processing discussed earlier, are being explored for medical application. While a radiologist might see thousands of images in their working life, a computer can be shown millions, including the rarest cases ever and, be trained on them.

Google's AI Team has published results of two early AI trials conducted to examine deep learning algorithms in the areas of cancer pathology[190] and detecting diabetic retinopathy[191] (DR).

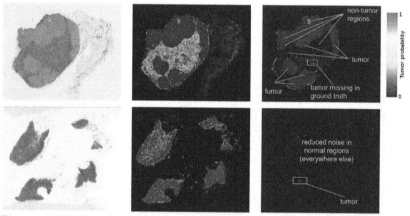

Figure 127: Google's Cancer Detection with Deep Learning (see website for colour version)

In the cancer study, the prediction heat maps produced by the algorithm had improved so much that the localisation score for the algorithm reached 89%, which significantly exceeded the score of

---

[190] https://ai.googleblog.com/2017/03/assisting-pathologists-in-detecting.html
[191] https://ai.googleblog.com/2016/11/deep-learning-for-detection-of-diabetic.html

73% for a pathologist with no time constraint. The authors of the report are cautious and point out the need for further research and the benefits of reviews by experienced pathologists (for example the algorithm is so narrow, it will focus only on what it's trained to find and ignore obvious other issues a human pathologist wouldn't). But there is optimism that, for example, an algorithmic assistant could be used to triage images or provide a second opinion.

In the DR study, the results show the algorithm's performance as on-par with that of a panel of board-certified ophthalmologists. Just as with the cancer study, the hope is that automated DR screening methods with high accuracy have strong potential to assist doctors in evaluating more patients and quickly routing those who need help to a specialist. Following on from the DR study that focused on interpretation of a 2D fundus photograph, Google's DeepMind[192] division is leading work to expand evaluation to more complex 3D images known as optical coherence tomography (OCT) which are also used in diagnosis. Working with famed London eye hospital, Moorfields, DeepMind is analysing one million de-personalised eye scans using machine learning, to explore the impact it can have on our understanding and treatment of eye diseases such as Age-related macular degeneration (AMD) and DR. Currently, Moorfields carries out more than 3,000 OCT scans every week. These scans require highly trained, expert analysis in order to interpret the result, which can cause delays in getting to diagnosis and treatment. The aim of the study is to determine if AI and machine learning technology could reduce the time required for experts to go through all aspects of the scan by spotting patterns and categorising results for faster diagnosis. In order to develop the algorithm, DeepMind will work with the eye images, split by the known diagnoses, using machine learning techniques such as: supervised and semi-supervised convolutional neural networks, recurrent neural networks, unsupervised clustering and reinforcement learning.

DeepMind is also working with head and neck scans at University College London Hospitals NHS Foundation Trust where the purpose of the research is to develop technology which can automatically

---

[192]https://deepmind.com/applied/deepmind-health/working-partners/health-research-tomorrow/

identify and differentiate between cancerous and healthy tissues on CT and MRI scans, to help target radiotherapy treatment. At present, this process, known as segmentation, can take clinicians up to four hours to complete manually. The research aims to develop artificial intelligence technology to assist clinicians in the segmentation process so that it can be done more rapidly but just as accurately - it is hoped that the segmentation process could be reduced from up to four hours to just one hour.

Faster Answers

Medical image registration is a common technique that involves overlaying two images, such as magnetic resonance imaging (MRI) scans, to compare and analyse anatomical differences in great detail. If a patient has a brain tumour, for instance, doctors can overlap a brain scan from several months ago onto a more recent scan to analyse small changes in the tumour's progress.

This process, however, can often take two hours or more, as traditional systems meticulously align each of potentially a million pixels in the combined scans. A team at MIT[193] has been developing an algorithm that can register brain scans and other 3-D images more than 1,000 times faster using machine learning techniques, in this case a convolutional neural network (CNN). This reduces registration time to a minute or two using a normal computer, or less than a second using a GPU, with comparable accuracy to existing state-of-the-art systems.

Finally, for this section, a further example is a Google study published in Nature's Digital Medicine Journal[194] that looks at deep learning models in order to make a broad set of predictions relevant to patients—such as whether patients will be hospitalised, how long they will stay, and whether their health is deteriorating despite treatment. Using de-identified electronic health records and thousands of data points, the project used recurrent neural networks (RNNs) and feedforward neural networks to outperform traditional methods: a score of 0.86 in predicting if patients will stay

---

[193] http://news.mit.edu/2018/faster-analysis-of-medical-images-0618
[194] https://www.nature.com/articles/s41746-018-0029-1.pdf

longer in the hospital (traditional logistic regression scored 0.76); they scored 0.95 in predicting inpatient mortality (traditional methods gave 0.86), and they scored 0.77 in predicting unexpected readmissions after patients are discharged (traditional methods gave 0.70). These gains were statistically significant. A particularly distinguishing feature of the project is the inclusion of hand-written clinicians free-text notes thanks to handwriting recognition and sentiment analysis - an example of ML being used to create data inputs for more ML.

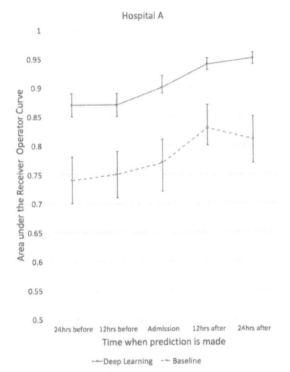

Figure 128: The Deep Learning approach (top line) outperforms baseline methods in the study of hospital records

But despite all the promise of AI in medical advances, it will take time to develop the methods and ensure that they are rigorously tested before we dare to put the lives of patients in the hands of AI. I'm sure that the FDA and other regulators will have toughened their stance on Silicon Valley following the Theranos[195] scandal.

In a useful note of caution, eminent medical technology writer, Dr, Eric Topol in the table below reminds people that *for all the talk of AI matching or exceeding doctor performance, there's a very short list of peer-reviewed publications. And they are all in silico, not prospective, in a clinical, real-world setting*[196].

Specialty	Images	Publication
Radiology	CT head for brain hemorrhage	Arbabshirani, Nature Digital Medicine, 2018
Pathology	Breast cancer	Bejnordi, JAMA,2017
	Brain tumors	Capper, Nature 2018
Dermatology	Skin cancers	Esteva, Nature 2017
	Melanoma	Haenssle, Annals of Oncology, 2018
Ophthalmology	Diabetic retinopathy	Gulshan, JAMA 2016
	Congenital cataracts	Long, Nature Biomedical Engineering 2017
	Macular degeneration	Burlina, JAMA Ophthalmology, 2018
	Retinopathy of Prematurity	Brown, JAMA Ophthalmology, 2018
	AMD and diabetic retinopathy	Kermany, Cell, 2018
Cardiology	Echocardiography	Madani, Nature Digital Medicine, 2018

Agriculture & AI

While we could spend several book lengths looking at all the examples of AI in action, for the sake of brevity, I want to look at one last example where a non-obvious application will have an impact on a large number of daily lives. The agricultural revolution may have begun about 12,000 years ago as humans moved from hunter gatherers to farmers, with another revolution in the 18th century but as global food demand increases, modern farmers are turning to AI to solve their problems.

Some large-scale farms are using AI to process inputs from soil sensors, weather data and satellites to predict a range of outcomes that increase the chances of a successful harvest. On a smaller scale with just mobile phones available in the field, researchers at PlantVillage and the International Institute of Tropical Agriculture

---

[195] https://en.wikipedia.org/wiki/Theranos
[196] https://twitter.com/EricTopol/status/1021149372258533379

(IITA) developed a solution using machine learning that could help farmers better identify and manage diseases quickly using a smartphone app that they just point at the leaves of their crop[197]. In another example, a farmer in the Netherlands is using machine learning to process data from activity sensors on dairy cows to spot early signs of illness among the herd[198].

Figure 129: ML-powered mobile app (Nuru[199]) checks a Cassava leaf for disease

[197] https://www.blog.google/technology/ai/ai-takes-root-helping-farmers-identity-diseased-plants/
[198] https://www.blog.google/technology/ai/using-tensorflow-keep-farmers-happy-and-cows-healthy/
[199]
https://play.google.com/store/apps/details?id=plantvillage.nuru&rdid=plantvillage.nuru (Download Nuru)

Figure 130: ML-powered Robot from Root.ai[200] can identify and pick ripe fruit

Automation

"In times of change, the greatest danger is to act with yesterday's logic"

Peter Drucker

A key recurring theme in any discussion of the impact of technology tends to be its impact on jobs. Predictions vary, some believe that AI will advance to the point where much human labour is no longer needed, causing mass unemployment and requiring a solution such as universal basic income instead of wages; others believe that, just as with the industrial revolution which led to the creation of unimagined new jobs to replace the ones made obsolete by technologies, we will continue to create unforeseen jobs. This is summarised neatly here:

---

[200] https://www.root-ai.com/

There are two poles of thought on how machine learning will affect the labour market:

→ **"Don't worry" - Historically technology has been a net job creator and it won't be different this time.** Machine learning will create more jobs than it destroys and like previous industrial revolutions, most of those jobs will be new ones that we can't imagine today. Yes, we got Automated Teller Machines at banks, but we also got many new jobs that replaced the bank teller jobs that were lost.

→ **"Worry" - This time it's different.** In previous industrial revolutions we automated human muscular power and somewhat routine cognitive skills. With increasingly advanced machine learning we will replicate more and more of human intelligence, reducing the number of well paid jobs and adding fewer jobs than are destroyed.

stateof.ai 2018

And similarly by PWC:

Will this just have the same effects as past technological leaps – short term disruption more than offset by long term economic gains – or is this something more fundamental in terms of taking humans out of the loop not just in manufacturing and routine service sector jobs, but more broadly across the economy?[201]

If we optimistically assume that new types of jobs will be created, regardless of the volume of new jobs, there is a very real risk of a skills gap. Those displaced from service or retail jobs may not be qualified for new types of tasks. *"Work saves a man from three great evils: boredom, vice and need,"* postulated the philosopher Voltaire. If we lose our jobs, what else do we lose?

Robots Everywhere

The world 'robot' itself even derives from the Czech word 'robota', meaning 'forced labourer', and early machinery was largely designed to be just that, a tool to perform manual tasks with greater efficiency than human beings.

In the previous chapter, we talked about automation in places like warehouses and fulfilment centres more from a speed perspective than an employment viewpoint. But although Amazon now employs over 560,000 people worldwide, it is also rapidly increasing the

---

[201] https://www.pwc.co.uk/economic-services/ukeo/pwcukeo-section-4-automation-march-2017-v2.pdf

number of robots it uses. Amazon even sponsored a competition[202] to further research into more dexterous robots that will be able to take on more human tasks like picking up a variety of items.

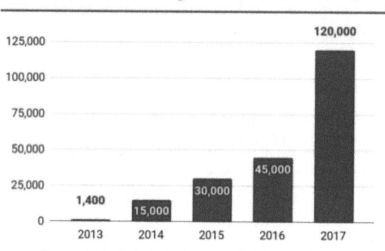

Figure 131: Robots in Amazon Fulfilment Centres

In China, local e-commerce giant JD.com recently unveiled a big new Shanghai fulfilment centre that can organize, pack and ship 200,000 orders a day. It employs four people — all of whom service the robots[203].

For those wondering how many industrial robots they are up against more broadly, there are "only" about 2 million in operation and they are far more common in places like Korea and Singapore than the US and China. But the pace is accelerating: it took 50 years for the world to install the first million industrial robots. The next million will have taken only eight, according to Macquarie University[204]. Consider

202

https://www.amazonrobotics.com/site/binaries/content/assets/amazonrobotics/arc/2017-amazon-robotics-challenge-rules-v3.pdf

[203] https://www.axios.com/in-china-a-picture-of-how-warehouse-jobs-can-vanish-d19f5cf1-f35b-4024-8783-2ba79a573405.html

[204] https://www.bloomberg.com/gadfly/articles/2017-01-09/the-robot-threat-donald-

also that between 2016 and 2017, venture capital investments in industrial robots more than tripled, from $402 million to $1.2 billion. Five years ago, start-ups in this same space raised just $195 million[205].

According to Reuters[206], Boeing is turning out 20 percent more planes, but with one-third fewer workers, than it did in the 1990s. In 2016, it replaced hundreds of employees with 60-ton robots. Boeing says they work twice as fast as people, with two-thirds fewer defects. The impact of automation on the company's workforce has been dramatic. In 1998, the company made 564 planes a year, employing roughly 217 people per plane. In 2015, it made 762 planes, using about 109 workers per plane.

Although for decades, it's been home to an affordable labour force, even Chinese factories have been turning to automation in recent times - with mega manufacturer Foxconn reported to be investing $4bn in robots[207]. When the robots do arrive, just like the famous quote from author William Gibson (*The future is already here — it's just not very evenly distributed*), the robots may not be evenly distributed. In November 2017, the United Nations warned that two-thirds of jobs in developing countries are at risk - many of the jobs done in those countries can be easily automated.

Here's the estimated number of industrial robots active worldwide:

Year	Industrial Robots
2016	1.8 million
2017 (E)	2 million
2018 (E)	2.3 million
2019 (E)	2.6 million
2020 (E)	3 million

Figure 132: There aren't as many robots as you might think...yet

trump-isn-t-talking-abou
[205] https://www.slideshare.net/Tracxn/tracxn-industrial-robotics-startup-landscape
[206] https://www.reuters.com/article/us-boeing-production-robots-insight-idUSKCN0T50E420151116
[207] https://asia.nikkei.com/Business/AC/Foxconn-plots-4bn-automation-push-as-labor-costs-bite

There are fewer robots in U.S. factories compared to other advanced economies

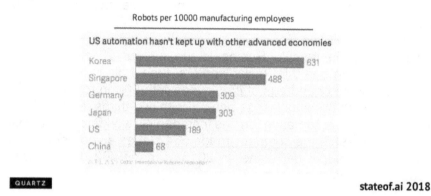

Robots per 10000 manufacturing employees

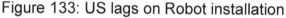

US automation hasn't kept up with other advanced economies

Korea	631
Singapore	488
Germany	309
Japan	303
US	189
China	68

stateof.ai 2018

Figure 133: US lags on Robot installation

Transition to Autonomy

The arrival of new technology will happen gradually, then suddenly. For many workers, they will be unaware of the threat to their position until the exponential progress of technology creeps up and overtakes them. Even for those who see automation as a remote prospect there's an increasing chance that AI may already be determining their shift, route or activities.

Although an example of technology that is speeding up life and replacing or reducing human inputs, robotics is not necessarily using AI. Robots confined to single tasks in factories may not need AI. But for those with ambitions for robots to operate more flexibly and particularly amongst humans, AI is essential. In the case of robots that rely on deep learning, we humans will have to help them learn but with an endgame where they increasingly use the knowledge we transfer to them to replace us. AI will enable a new generation of robots with some of the capabilities we've imagined for decades. Putting AI software in a robot body allows it to use visual recognition, speech, and navigation out in the real world among humans. And because ML gets smarter as it feeds on more data, with every interaction, the software behind these robots will become more and more adept at making sense of the world and how it works.

PwC's economists[208] have identified three overlapping waves of automation: the algorithm wave, the augmentation wave and the autonomy wave.

- *Algorithm wave - to early 2020s*
  Impacting sectors that already use structured data analysis and simple digital tasks, such as credit scoring - financial, professional and technical services, and information and communications sectors are likely to be the most affected.
- *Augmentation wave - to late 2020s*
  Over the next decade, the augmentation wave is focused on automation of repeatable tasks and exchanging information, as well as further developments of aerial drones, robots in warehouses and semi-autonomous vehicles. PwC estimates the share of potential jobs affected could rise to up to 20% by the end of the 2020s, as the use of AI systems becomes much more widespread and robotics technologies advance and mature. Over this period, the effects will be felt across all industry sectors.
- *Autonomy wave - by mid-2030s*
  In the final wave, PwC predicts that AI will be able to analyse data from multiple sources, make decisions and take physical actions with little or no human input. The share of jobs that could be impacted by automation is estimated to rise to 30% by the mid-2030s, as autonomous robots and driverless vehicles roll out more widely across the economy.

While you could debate the specific numbers ad nauseum, the Interactive tool[209] from McKinsey is a useful starting point to see the numbers of people in different categories. You may have a different view than the consultants about what can and will be automated, but it offers useful relative measures. A key concern is a potential polarisation of work, a hollowing out of the middle tier, leaving just extremes of low paid and high paid. As those in the highest paid tier resist the application of AI, and deprioritise its development for their tasks, there may also be some jobs for which it is not seen as worthwhile to invest in AI.

---

[208] https://www.pwc.co.uk/press-room/press-releases/waves-of-automation.html
[209] http://www.visualcapitalist.com/charting-automation-potential-of-u-s-jobs/

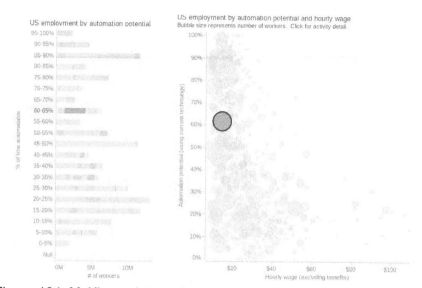

Figure 134: McKinsey Interactive tool on automation risk - explore it online

Lots of commentators, technologists and futurists are convinced that we are on the cusp of a rapid transition, in which automation powered by artificial intelligence and advances in robotics will make a significant portion of today's careers obsolete. As with any future speculations, they might be off the mark either in terms of scope or more likely in terms of timing and detail, but the consequences if they're even partially correct would be huge—potentially a defining challenge of the decades ahead, and one that would demand our social and political attention and action.

It's easy to be sceptical or even ignore those worried about the impact - the technology is still nascent, so of course we're not obviously losing jobs to it. For now, only those that are looking for it are seeing initial glimmers of smarter automation, but nothing beyond narrow AI. And the tendency for a lot of research to be within a narrow domain exacerbates the difficulty of seeing a cohesive big picture.

As one writer puts it: *Remember that artificial intelligence progresses in exponential time. This means that even as computer power doubles from a trillionth of a human brain's power to a billionth and then a millionth, it has little effect on the level of employment. Then, in the relative blink of an eye, the final few doublings take place and robots go from having a thousandth of human brain power to full human-level intelligence. Don't get fooled by the fact that nothing much has happened yet. In another 10 years or so, it will.*[210]

Redesigning Work

As AI and robots change our relationship with technology, it may be wrong to focus on the doomsday scenario of entire professions being replaced. Leading writer on the topic, Eric Brynolfsson[211], believes that "*specific tasks within jobs, rather than entire occupations themselves, will be replaced by automation in the near future, with some jobs more heavily impacted than others, suggesting that a shift is needed in the debate about the effects of AI: away from the common focus on full automation of entire jobs and pervasive occupational replacement toward the redesign of jobs and reengineering of business practices. The analysis suggests that machine learning will affect very different parts of the workforce than earlier waves of automation ... Machine learning technology can transform many jobs in the economy, but full automation will be less significant than the reengineering of processes and the reorganization of tasks.*" The researchers recommended looking at the tasks within each occupation that have high potential to be automated by machine learning, separating them from the tasks that do not, and reorganizing the job to match those developments.

---

[210] http://www.motherjones.com/politics/2017/10/you-will-lose-your-job-to-a-robot-and-sooner-than-you-think/

[211] http://mitsloan.mit.edu/newsroom/articles/machine-learning-will-redesign-not-replace-work/

Fast Food

In an earlier section, we talked about the changes in how we order food (voice ordering), and how it's delivered (robots). But the changes in this vital sector aren't limited to those developments. Our time relationship with food is accelerating - the average amount of time people spend cooking or preparing food per day has come down from 90 minutes in 1970 to 30 minutes now as we move to fast food. It seems likely to come down further.

Food delivery is already a $43 billion business[212]. You can order virtually any imaginable type of food and companies such as DoorDash, GrubHub and Caviar will whisk it from the restaurant to you, making increasing use of AI along the way. Speed is vital - not just because customers are impatient but for the quality of the food - DoorDash's delivery time for Baskin-Robbins's carefully insulated ice cream products averages 12 to 13 minutes. Restaurants are turning to delivery services rather than having to invest in creating the systems required to compete in today's market: algorithms designed to improve the timing of delivery pickups and minimize how long it takes a driver to get from point A to B; cutting-edge mapping tech to match drivers with orders based on traffic, travel time and distance. Caviar — a subsidiary of the business tech start-up Square — even tracks how long its restaurants take to prepare each menu item, to better time drivers' arrivals.

Fast food restaurants have long been a significant source of employment, with over 2.3 million Americans in the sector. The sector, which is particularly important among young people and those without qualifications for other jobs, is now facing automation of even the food preparation tasks. Both Creator[213] and Flippy[214] offer robots to create burgers, while Zume[215] offers Pizza automation. And it's not just fast food: Robotic kitchen provider, Spyce[216], automates the production of healthy salad bowls.

---

[212] https://www.washingtonpost.com/news/wonk/wp/2017/08/08/the-insane-43-billion-system-that-gets-food-delivered-to-your-door/

[213] http://creator.rest/

[214] https://misorobotics.com/

[215] https://zumepizza.com/

[216] https://medium.com/neodotlife/spyce-robotic-kitchen-984779cb5930

Figure 135: Flippy the burger robot

Figure 136: Zume Robot for pizzas

Automation of restaurants with new robots and AI systems to operate them isn't just about reducing cost of staff. Robotic systems not only need no breaks or holidays, they also require less space to operate than kitchen staff, freeing up more space for customer tables.

Away from restaurants, even home appliances are of course not exempt from more technology. General Electric has added Alexa support to their microwave to save you pushing buttons, or you can just use their app to scan a barcode on the packaging with a mobile app and it'll choose the appropriate time and power levels and send them to the microwave. And thankfully, if you spill some of your dinner on your clothes, you can summon a laundry service, Laundrapp, via Alexa too[217].

Taking Stock

"I cannot help fearing that men may reach a point where the look on every new theory as a danger, every innovation as a toilsome trouble, every social advance as a first step toward revolution, and that they absolutely refuse to move at all."

Alexis de Tocqueville

I hope that by now you've a sense that AI is going to have an incredibly broad impact and challenge a lot of norms and assumptions. The scale of change and challenge present by AI is daunting. As in the quote above, many people may come to resist the inexorable march of AI. We will no doubt welcome many of the conveniences it'll afford, but in the next Chapter, we'll examine some of the questions I believe we need to deal with, sooner rather than later, to minimise the negative impacts.

---

[217] https://blog.aboutamazon.co.uk/supporting-small-businesses/small-british-businesses-use-alexa-to-innovate

Chapter 9: Controlling AI

"There is a canyon dividing people who understand technology and people charged with addressing the world's toughest geopolitical issues, and no one has built a bridge"

Schmidt & Coen, The New Digital Age

Even at this early stage in the use of AI, there are very important questions emerging. The key issues are around how effective the algorithms are, and the purposes we employ them for. And in order to know how effective they are, we need a means to measure and quantify that. There's already been a lot of good research highlighting the risks in these early systems and the area of AI ethics is the subject of many detailed studies, so this chapter will focus on just a few examples of the issues raised. While discussions of AI frequently reference dystopian movies such as Terminator or Minority Report, let's for a moment change the cinematic metaphor to Spiderman: "With great power comes great responsibility". As we employ the most powerful computing capabilities yet devised, who is in control?

In this section, I'm not going to talk about controlling a prospective AGI threat to humanity - but rather controlling the technology that's already here or that to which we can see a clear path in the near future. That's not to say we shouldn't be considering options like an AI kill switch (the ability to disconnect an AI system that gets too powerful), but the focus should be on more immediate challenges, we should progress mindful that reaping the benefits of AI will take time, and the systems we have now, though impressive, are not ready to be deployed without debate, controls, supervision and further refinement.

There's a fine line between beneficial applications of AI and some of the more dystopian futures beloved of Science Fiction. For example, a report from OpenAI[218], laying out the potential dangers warns: *"Surveillance tools can be used to catch terrorists or oppress ordinary*

---

[218] https://blog.openai.com/preparing-for-malicious-uses-of-ai/

citizens. Information content filters could be used to bury fake news or manipulate public opinion. Governments and powerful private actors will have access to many of these AI tools and could use them for public good or harm".

It's worth remembering that we're talking about a technology with unprecedented reach - AI deployed via today's leading platforms can reach billions of people all over the world, whether they know it or not. As smartphone use and connectivity expand globally, the next billion people to come online will encounter very different technology than the first billion. Just as mobile led to many developing countries skipping implementation of landlines, smartphones and new interfaces like voice will lead to many more experiencing AI without "computers".

Kids today who grow up talking to Alexa won't have our somewhat atavistic response to new technologies. They won't assume there are as many areas computers aren't suited to as their parents who grew up with computers that came with floppy disks, user manuals and no Internet. Might the familiarity and acceptance of technology among "digital natives" lead to unbridled application of AI? As the human relationship with computers changes, how and where we choose to harness AI will be a defining influence on future generations.

Choosing Where to Use AI

"The problem in working out what ML might enable is that it's a little like reading the spec for SQL and then trying to predict just-in-time supply chains. There's a huge jump between understanding fundamental tech and knowing what it will make possible"

Ben Evans[219]

---

[219] https://twitter.com/BenedictEvans/status/1003551025230434305

Who decides if and when artificial intelligence is ready to be used? Is there a demonstrable threshold of performance we should require of a system before it's allowed to be used on real people? What are the criteria that should be applied? Who will have the final say - will it be regulators or will public opinion prevail? As the researchers battle to resolve the technological challenges, they will do so against a backdrop of increasing regulation and public scrutiny.

Deciding where to first apply our scarce AI resources will be a difficult problem. You could argue that the amount of technical brilliance funnelled into the application of AI to something like advertising — as opposed to medical research — is shocking and a poor choice. As commentator Vinod Khosla[220] noted, *"A single ad shown to you on Facebook has way more computing power applied to it than a $10,000 medical decision you have to make."* But to look at the big picture, many of the companies at the forefront of AI are funding their research through advertising revenues, and are developing solutions what will have broad applicability.

In principle, the idea of a large number of stakeholders coming together and deciding the direction AI development should take seems sensible. AI development has sufficiently global implications that, like genetics or climate change, it's a matter of global concern rather than something that can be left entirely to academia and profit-motivated organisations to determine.

So far in this book, we've looked at some of the areas where AI has already been deployed, and some of the areas that seem to be attracting a lot of either research, Government or commercial attention. It should be obvious that not all areas are equal in terms of reach or potential for impact, positive or negative. Just because AI isn't ready for all areas now doesn't mean we should dismiss it and assume it never can or will be ready. But as part of the hard wave, there will be challenges, disagreements and failures along the way.

---

[220] https://www.medscape.com/viewarticle/892034

Various forms of statistical models for predictive analysis, expert systems and decisions support systems have been in use in the private sector for years (for example, to assist with analysis for granting loans). As their sophistication and availability increase and datasets grow, many Government departments and agencies are exploring and experimenting with their use to support decisions regarding urban planning; benefit fraud detection; policing, social services and criminal sentencing. Although proponents of the systems in Government are pushing them forward, it's far from clear that the public at large is supportive of these methods or even aware of them.

In a UK survey by the RSA[221], most people aren't aware that automated decision systems are being used in these various ways, let alone involved in the process of rolling out or scrutinising these systems.

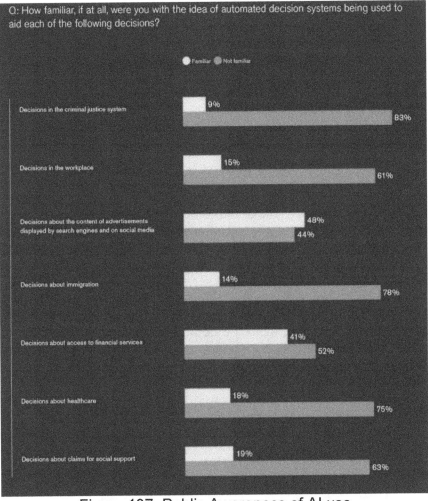

Q: How familiar, if at all, were you with the idea of automated decision systems being used to aid each of the following decisions?

Familiar ● Not familiar

Decision	Familiar	Not familiar
Decisions in the criminal justice system	9%	83%
Decisions in the workplace	15%	61%
Decisions about the content of advertisements displayed by search engines and on social media	48%	44%
Decisions about immigration	14%	78%
Decisions about access to financial services	41%	52%
Decisions about healthcare	18%	75%
Decisions about claims for social support	19%	63%

Figure 137: Public Awareness of AI use

221 https://www.thersa.org/discover/publications-and-articles/rsa-blogs/2018/05/the-ethics-of-ceding-more-power-to-machines

Mission Critical Applications

"These technologies are not neutral facilitators: they embody our politics and biases, they extend beyond the boundaries of nations and legal jurisdictions and increasingly exceed the understanding of even their creators. As a result, we understand less and less about the world as these powerful technologies assume more control over our everyday lives. If we do not understand how complex technologies function then their potential is more easily captured by selfish elites and corporations."

James Bridle[222]

Given that AI is intended to be good at solving big, hard problems, it's not surprising that some of the areas it's being applied in are particularly difficult. But it's increasingly finding its way into some very sensitive areas where flaws could have serious consequences. If we're going to use AI in these areas, we need to be very aware of the risks and have a clear plan to manage them or at least be very confident that an explicit fact-based decision (rather than a hopeful expectation) has been taken that the rewards of its use outweigh the risks.

For most of human history, the major decisions that we don't make for ourselves that determine the course of our lives - decisions like bank loans, eligibility for social housing or benefits or admission to a school or job - were made by other humans. Even if they were following defined processes or using standardised tests, in most cases, even where we disagreed with the outcome, we knew it boiled down to a person making a judgement and hoped that they'd display a degree of empathy, common sense or outright generosity when we needed it.

In today's world, more and more of these types of decisions are being made by machines. Algorithms can assess hundreds of applications and produce results faster than a human assessor can open the first file for consideration. The rationale for widespread use of tech may be driven by cost reductions, efficiency, belief in mass personalisation

[222] https://www.theguardian.com/books/2018/jun/15/rise-of-the-machines-has-technology-evolved-beyond-our-control-

or an attempt to systematise to reduce or remove bias. Or it may be a rush to use the latest shiny things.

Particularly in the public sector, we're starting to see trials of AI. Due to its ability to handle large amounts of data, public servants are considering or trialling AI to help them manage welfare payments and immigration decisions, detect fraud, plan new infrastructure projects, answer citizen queries, adjudicate bail hearings, triage health care cases, and more. The decisions regarding AI that we are making now will shape the impact of artificial intelligence on these and other government functions. Which tasks will be handed over to machines? And how should governments spend the labour time saved by artificial intelligence? In some of the most sensitive areas, AI systems are increasingly being used to steer potentially life-changing decisions, including which people may be eligible for bail after they have been arrested; which families to investigate for potential child abuse, and as we talked about in the previous chapter, predictive policing to assign resources.

Impact Assessment

"The saddest aspect of life now is that science gathers knowledge faster than society gathers wisdom."

Isaac Asimov

For public agencies and those potentially affected who are seeking a framework to assess the likely impact of any AI projects they are considering, the AI Now Institute[223] has proposed a 5-point plan - an Algorithmic Impact Assessment (AIA) - designed to support affected communities and stakeholders as they seek to assess the claims made about these systems, and to determine where – or if – their use is acceptable.

1. Agencies should conduct a self-assessment of existing and proposed automated decision systems, evaluating potential impacts on fairness, justice, bias, or other concerns across affected communities;

---

[223] https://ainowinstitute.org/aiareport2018.pdf

2. Agencies should develop meaningful external researcher review processes to discover, measure, or track impacts over time;

3. Agencies should provide notice to the public disclosing their definition of "automated decision system," existing and proposed systems, and any related self-assessments and researcher review processes before the system has been acquired;

4. Agencies should solicit public comments to clarify concerns and answer outstanding questions; and

5. Governments should provide enhanced due process mechanisms for affected individuals or communities to challenge inadequate assessments or unfair, biased, or otherwise harmful system uses that agencies have failed to mitigate or correct.

AIAs are designed to achieve four key policy goals:

1. Respect the public's right to know which systems impact their lives by publicly listing and describing automated decision systems that significantly affect individuals and communities;

2. Increase public agencies' internal expertise and capacity to evaluate the systems they build or procure, so they can anticipate issues that might raise concerns, such as disparate impacts or due process violations;

3. Ensure greater accountability of automated decision systems by providing a meaningful and ongoing opportunity for external researchers to review, audit, and assess these systems using methods that allow them to identify and detect problems; and

4. Ensure that the public has a meaningful opportunity to respond to and, if necessary, dispute the use of a given system or an agency's approach to algorithmic accountability.

Of course, the rationale for using these tools is a promise that they can help to make decisions more consistent, accurate and rigorous, not to mention faster and at a lower cost than humans. If we can develop AI systems that can improve public services, adding efficiency and objectivity to crucial social and justice programmes, then we could truly see technology-led progress. If these technologies are applied poorly however, they may exacerbate inequalities rather than alleviate them. Core to their application are questions of data, so let's examine that in more detail.

Data Quality

Computers offer a sense of objectivity and impartiality. Because they are machines, we tend to ascribe a neutrality to their actions, assuming they follow programmed logic, and although prone to the odd bug, are generally reliable at executing their instructions without ulterior motives. This has been true until they started learning to do things, rather than simply being told what exactly to do. Now that they can discern patterns in data and infer from it, we've lost the certainty about what exactly they are doing.

An AI project designed without an understanding of how to create fairness in ML solutions may result in unjust or prejudicial treatment of people related to race, income, sexual orientation, religion, gender, and other characteristics historically associated with discrimination and marginalisation. Among the examples of negative consequences associated with some ML systems can be representational harm or opportunity denial.

Bias & Fairness

Herein lies a problem: an AI application is only as good as the data it receives. And it is able to interpret that data only within the narrow confines of the supplied context. It doesn't "understand" what it has analysed, so it is unable to apply its analysis to scenarios in other contexts. And it can't distinguish causation from correlation. So, given that data is the "food" of machine learning, it's obvious that the quality of the data used in the training phase is a key factor in determining the quality of the predictions in the inference or deployment phase.

Here's a brief overview (summarised from https://cloud.google.com/inclusive-ml/) of some of the types of bias to be aware of when considering your training data. If you'd like more detailed resources on this topic, I've added some useful links in the Appendix.

Biased **data distribution** can exist if your training data is not representative of the actual user base. For example, if you rely on user-submitted data, you may over-index on the submissions of the more extrovert or those who have the economic means to submit more frequently. To mitigate this bias, you could try to acquire data from multiple/additional sources, or filter data carefully to ensure you only take proportionate examples from overrepresented groups. For example, when we talk about the use of AI in law enforcement, remember that Police databases are not a complete census of all criminal offences, nor do they constitute a representative random sample.

Biased **data representation** refers to situations where some groups are represented less positively than others. As we'll talk more about later, to be truly effective, the algorithms powering facial recognition software require a massive amount of information. The more images of people of colour it sees, the more likely it is to properly identify them. The problem is, existing software has not been exposed to enough images of people of colour to be confidently relied upon to identify them.

Biased **Labels** - ML models built from supervised learning depend on the labels attached to data. It's important to understand potential biases introduced by the labellers. To assess your data quality, you need to know who your labellers are. Where are they located? What languages do they speak natively? What ages and genders are they? Homogeneous rater pools can yield labels that are incorrect or skewed in ways that might not be immediately obvious.

Evaluating your model for fairness requires careful consideration of your particular use case and what impact your model could have on your end users when it gets things wrong. This means understanding the impact of different types of errors for different user groups. For example, do model errors affect all users equally or are they more harmful for certain user groups? Once you've thought this through, you'll be better able to decide what performance metric it makes sense to optimise for (precision vs. recall), evaluate trade-offs between them, and to examine examples of errors to check for bias.

Even with awareness of the data issues and the biases that an AI system may include, it remains incredibly difficult to assess and measure the operation and impact of these systems. These complex systems often function in oblique, invisible ways that are not subject to the accountability or oversight the users might expect - and there's a huge reliance not only on the data, but on the creators of the algorithms. We'll look in the following section at industry- initiatives in this space, and then move on to the bigger question of regulation.

Fairness

AI experts seeking to address the shortcomings of technology, and aware that concerns about the impact of their algorithms could severely retard their acceptance by the public, are building tools to try to bring a greater degree of fairness to AI. Consultancy firm Accenture[224] offers a suite of AI testing services including a fairness tool to assess datasets and identify biases. Facebook has developed an internal tool called "Fairness Flow", which measures how an algorithm interacts with specific groups of people. Likewise, Microsoft has announced a similar tool[225]. Leading AI firm DeepMind[226] has set up a dedicated research unit to explore the impacts of AI and associated ethical questions. In another initiative, over 50 firms have setup the Partnership on AI[227] to study and formulate best practices in AI technologies, to advance the public's understanding of AI, and to serve as an open platform for discussion and engagement about AI and its influences on people and society.

---

[224] https://newsroom.accenture.com/news/accenture-launches-new-artificial-intelligence-testing-services.htm

[225] https://www.technologyreview.com/s/611138/microsoft-is-creating-an-oracle-for-catching-biased-ai-algorithms/

[226] https://deepmind.com/applied/deepmind-ethics-society/

[227] https://www.partnershiponai.org/#

Figure 138: Industry response on Ethics of AI - DeepMind Ethics & Society initiative (Top) Partnership on AI (Bottom)

Of course, not all AI systems are intended to be impartial. While that may be of grave concern in a system determining criminal cases, there will be far more commercially focused systems in operation with unashamed monetary motives. Amazon's recommendation algorithms are far from unbiased. They are firmly biased towards getting you to purchase a product that is as much in Amazon's interest as yours. (One-third of purchases on Amazon come from these recommendations.) So too, Netflix's recommendation engine is calibrated to steer you towards shows they've produced or acquired at favourable rates compared to major-studio produced fare that is expensive for them. The algorithm needs to balance what it thinks you'll like (and therefore stay subscribed) with the content that's more profitable for the algorithm's creators. There's nothing inherently wrong with biased algorithms that are designed to achieve a purpose - as long as users aren't naive enough to think that commercial considerations aren't heavily weighted.

Transparency

Compared to previous generations of technology, one big change with AI is that people may not even know it's being used. In time, there will likely be no need to be explicit that AI is being used - any scenario where data is available will probably utilise it to some extent. But signposting its implementation is useful at least for now so that people can be on the lookout. Unlike other tools such as databases that are routinely used without mention, AI manipulates rather than stores data. Companies should also routinely disclose where and how they got the data they used to fuel their AI systems' decisions.

At the moment, there's a rush in technology circles to boast about the use of AI, believing it makes a company seem smart, current and investable. Outside of technical circles, there's a lack of awareness about what it even means. However, I think there's a need to be upfront with people in cases where ML is being used in reaching conclusions that matter. Even if the person doesn't understand how it works, I think it's fair they at least know that they're dealing with a machine. The issue of automated bots has become a big concern on platforms like Twitter, so companies using AI systems may want to err on the side of caution in revealing what customer-impacting interactions and processes are automated.

This issue came to the fore when Google unveiled Duplex at their Developer Conference. There was a swift public response that the AI needed to identify itself as such. Google acquiesced and in the next public demo of the technology, it clearly now announces itself as the Google Assistant calling on behalf of someone. It may not make a difference to the task or outcome, but for now people will like to know whether they are dealing with a system or a human.

Black Box

"As these black boxes assume responsibility for more and more of our daily digital tasks, they are not only going to change our relationship to technology—they are going to change how we think about ourselves, our world, and our place within it."

Wired Magazine[228]

Adding to concerns about the risk of AI becoming a bias perpetuation engine due to the data they train on, there's a further concern about how AI arrives at its output. Due to their complexity, AI systems can often be treated like a black box - a system that outputs a prediction or a decision that the recipient of the output cannot trace back through a comprehensible set of stages to understand how the system arrived at the end point.

With neural networks, even the engineer who creates and trains them can't say precisely how the computer arrives at its decision - the neural network's machinations are often inscrutable. This makes AI unsuitable for use in some regulated settings - Capital One[229] for example has investigated the use of ML for decisions on granting credit cards but cannot deploy it as the law requires to explain to a prospective customer how any credit decision is reached.

But this does beg the question: which would you prefer? - a fast answer where you can't know how it was arrived at but is statistically like to be correct, or a slow one, with clear provenance? Is it preferable to trust a computer decision you can't retrace or a human one that may be obviously subjective or made while tired?

Towards Explainable AI

Humans are sometimes quite good at explaining how they arrived at a decision, but there are times when they can't rationally explain it. Currently, how deep learning systems reach decisions or predictions

---

[228] https://www.wired.com/2016/05/the-end-of-code/

[229] https://www.technologyreview.com/s/604122/the-financial-world-wants-to-open-ais-black-boxes/amp/

isn't especially clear, leading to worries about their suitability in situations like those just described, where important decisions are being made and those impacted may well want an explanation of how the decision was reached.

Why are AI systems hard to understand? Part of the advantage of deep learning systems is that the model identifies variables and relationships that humans have not identified or articulated. A deep learning neural network may approach a problem very differently than a human would, even if the system reaches the same conclusion after filtering data inputs through numerous layers. An algorithm's accuracy typically scales with its complexity, so the more complex an algorithm is, the more difficult it is to explain. Thus, there is often an inescapable trade-off between explainability and accuracy in AI systems.

In order to allay fears about AI systems that we can't explain, there has been much recent research into methods to make AI more explainable. In a 2016 presentation[230], DARPA (the people who brought you the Internet) outlined their work on explainable AI and efforts to add explainability to some of the techniques in use today without impacting the accuracy of the models.

---

[230] https://www.cc.gatech.edu/~alanwags/DLAI2016/(Gunning)%20IJCAI-16%20DLAI%20WS.pdf

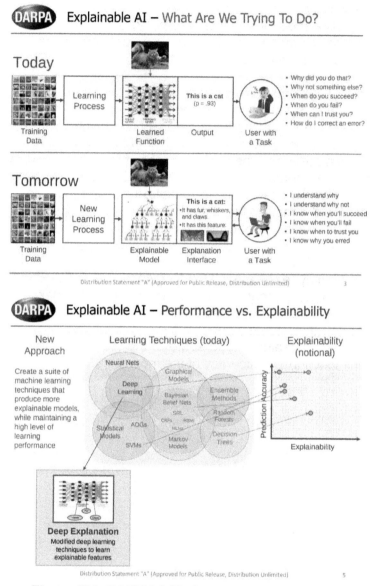

Figure 139: DARPA initiatives on Explainable AI

In the first slide in Figure 139, DARPA outline how an explanation interface could increase user trust in the model. Instead of simply outputting a confidence score that the object in the photo is cat, the envisaged model would also explicitly show contributing factors. The second slide shows the trade-off between performance (accuracy) and explainability for different AI techniques.

In response to transparency concerns, New York City Council passed a Bill to set up a task force that will recommend how to publicly share information about algorithms and investigate them for bias. French President, Emmanuel Macron, has said that the country will make all algorithms used by its government open. However, simply publishing the algorithms underlying AI systems will rarely provide meaningful transparency. With the latest (and often most promising) AI techniques, such as deep neural networks, there typically isn't any algorithmic output that would help people understand how the systems find subtle patterns. And of course, as we've noted before, the training data is crucially important in determining the output.

Ultimately, you may choose to happily or reluctantly treat AI as a blackbox - and think more about what it seems to enable, how well it works and what it means for your business or lifestyle rather than worry about how it works. In that regard, it's not unlike how many IT systems are treated today. The difference is how crucial the decisions it makes are becoming.

What Is Good Enough?

As we rightly consider the ethical dimensions of AI and their potential to cause harm through bias perpetuation, we also need to consider the context in which they operate and the next best alternative. Human systems are not perfect. Humans have biases, make mistakes and do things in a non-transparent way. We generally hope they will use empathy where appropriate. Yet we hold algorithms to a different standard because we want them to offer greater accuracy, otherwise why use them? We face a tricky balance between getting the benefits of the speed and scale at which AI can operate, versus our suspicion of how it operates, and those who operate it.

As the use of AI in sensitive areas such as medical diagnoses and criminal justice grows, there has been a reassuring rise in the number of examinations of their efficacy. The findings so far in books like

Automating Inequality[231] and investigations such as that by ProPublica[232] in 2016 show that we're not ready to hand over agency to these systems. While we may believe that AI can and will improve over the systems in place today, there seems little point in replacing a broken human system, with half-baked AI. But it's also unlikely we'll ever develop AI to the point where it's good enough without large scale trials and research in the field. Knowing how techniques like ML rely on data, without real world use, we can't expect AI to develop and reach its (superhuman) potential.

A 2018 article in Harvard Business Review[233] cites a large body of evidence that, while not perfect, algorithms are less biased and more accurate than the humans they are replacing - the algorithms do exhibit bias, but less than humans. The article concludes: *"If anything should alarm you, it should be the fact that so many important decisions are being made by human beings who we know are inconsistent, biased, and phenomenally bad decision makers. Even if technology can't fully solve the social ills of institutional bias and prejudicial discrimination, the evidence reviewed here suggests that, in practice, it can play a small but measurable part in improving the status quo".*

The Blame Game

I'm always somewhat sceptical of surveys purporting to ask the public their views on emerging technologies. While I absolutely believe that public debate is crucial, in the hard wave, the issues are beyond the simplicity of a survey and until the debate is had, most people aren't in a position to make an informed judgement.

Also, what standard do we judge to be good enough? Drawing from the evolving world of self-driving cars, do we wait for perfection or simply when it's better than the average human? Do we accept that there may be a period of learning during which there is no

---

[231] https://www.amazon.co.uk/Automating-Inequality-High-Tech-Profile-Police-ebook/dp/B0739MF8VF
[232] https://www.propublica.org/article/machine-bias-risk-assessments-in-criminal-sentencing
[233] https://hbr.org/2018/07/want-less-biased-decisions-use-algorithms

improvement, but that without such a period, we can never get to the standard of being better? What is an acceptable margin of error and does it vary by use case? An AI system that over cooks a burger may matter less than one that influences Child Services interventions or removals. My preference is to operate AI systems in parallel where possible in such tricky situations. They can undoubtedly spot patterns that humans miss and make predictions based on myriad parameters that we cannot always weigh. But until we can be more sure, it's not clear that letting them loose on sensitive social services without close supervision is a good idea.

A defining part of our changing relationship with technology may be how we react when it goes badly wrong. Can we learn to forgive an algorithm? Do we even have to forgive it? Because unlike a human, it can definitely be changed. A human can agree to change, can try to change but ultimately may not. Will we seek to assign blame to the humans involved instead? Does responsibility lie with the person who chose the training data or the person who implemented the model? Or the senior engineer who missed something in the code review? With the quality assurance team who, though they tested this thing to death, didn't test that scenario enough times? With the product owner who could have saved lives with a slightly higher standard? Or the regulators who didn't set the legal standard high enough?

Until we're clear about our expectations for AI and the standards to which it will be held, progress may be hard to achieve.

The Giants

"The more data you have, the better your product; the better your product, the more data you can collect; the more data you can collect, the more talent you can attract; the more talent you can attract, the better your product. It's no coincidence that Facebook, Google, and Amazon are intent on gaining as much data as possible and securing some of the brightest AI minds on the planet to work for them"

Kai-Fu Lee[234]

---

[234] https://www.nytimes.com/2017/06/24/opinion/sunday/artificial-intelligence-economic-inequality.html

As a set of advanced technologies that requires massive amounts of computing power as well as expertise and access to huge amounts of data, there's a relatively small number of entities currently developing and determining the future for AI. You can't discuss the impacts of AI without acknowledging the concentration of power in the hands of a few large corporations - Alphabet, Amazon and Apple - the 3 most valuable companies in the world, worth a combined 2.5 trillion dollars (June 2018). Together with academic researchers and the likes of Facebook, Microsoft and Chinese giants, Alibaba and Baidu, these are the firms driving the AI agenda.

Google and Amazon in the US (and Alibaba and Baidu in China) are companies that have grown from nothing in just 20 or so years, and all are desperately keen not to lose their dominance. They are investing aggressively in staving off their potential demise at the hands of a new wave of technology.

Rank	Company	Value (USD - Billions) - Sept 2018
1	Apple	1,100
2	Amazon	978.5
3	Alphabet	820.6

Figure 140: Extract of the most valuable companies in the world as at September 2018

Throughout this book, I've drawn frequently on examples from Apple, Amazon and Alphabet. This is not to say that these three behemoths are the only ones active in the space, but they are leaders, and have unprecedented reach and resources. They are likely to be frequently encountered by consumers and thus may seem especially visible and relevant. Though Apple continues to operate in a relatively closed environment, both Amazon and Alphabet make many of their advanced technologies available to some of the largest businesses in the world, as well as to small businesses and hobbyists, in an usual parity of access. These three corporations are determined to remain at the top of the pile and all 3 have very publicly declared their belief in the importance of AI. Microsoft and Facebook are also investing heavily in AI research, competing for top talent, open sourcing their solutions to gain traction, and deploying AI to their customers where it is reaching billions of people on a daily basis.

Keeping the Midas Touch

"AI has become so central to the operations of companies like ours, that what our leadership has been telling us is: 'Go faster. You're not going fast enough"

Yann LeCun, Chief AI Scientist, Facebook[235]

Last year, the top 15 US companies combined spent over $150 *billion* dollars on R&D. That's an awful lot of money to maintain a competitive edge when the returns are so uncertain. Alphabet (Google's parent company) spends some 15% of its net revenues on R&D, while non-tech consumer companies tend to spend less than 2%. The top 5 spenders (and 10 of the top 16) were all tech companies.

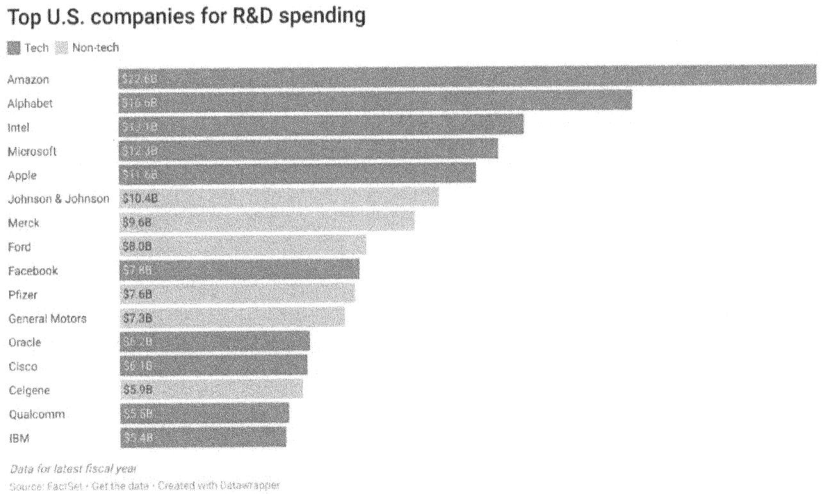

Top U.S. companies for R&D spending

Tech   Non-tech

Amazon	$22.6B
Alphabet	$16.6B
Intel	$13.1B
Microsoft	$12.3B
Apple	$11.6B
Johnson & Johnson	$10.4B
Merck	$9.6B
Ford	$8.0B
Facebook	$7.8B
Pfizer	$7.6B
General Motors	$7.3B
Oracle	$6.2B
Cisco	$6.1B
Celgene	$5.9B
Qualcomm	$5.5B
IBM	$5.4B

Data for latest fiscal year
Source: FactSet · Get the data · Created with Datawrapper

Figure 141: R&D Spending is tech-dominated (and much of that was on AI)

---

[235] https://www.washingtonpost.com/technology/2018/07/17/facebook-boosting-artificial-intelligence-research-says-its-not-going-fast-enough/?noredirect=on&utm_term=.aff5963bb4f1

And they are also busy acquiring companies that boast AI innovators as shown below:

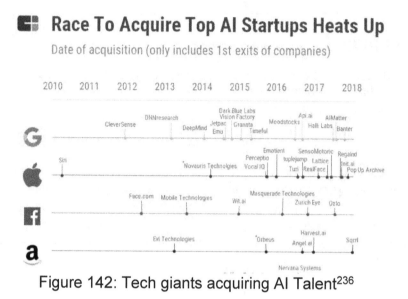

Race To Acquire Top AI Startups Heats Up

Date of acquisition (only includes 1st exits of companies)

Figure 142: Tech giants acquiring AI Talent[236]

AI Principles - A Google perspective

Following criticism of its involvement in a defence project, in mid-2018, Google published a set of principles[237] guiding its AI activities. As arguably the most important player in the space, their thought process is worthy of some examination. Whether you agree with the specific approach or not, whether you believe it's genuine or a PR stunt to deflect criticism or a pre-emptive move against stringent regulation, at least it's a starting point to facilitate a public awareness and discussion:

At its heart, AI is computer programming that learns and adapts. It can't solve every problem, but its potential to improve our lives is profound. We recognize that such powerful technology raises equally powerful questions about its use. How AI is developed and

---

[236] https://www.cbinsights.com/research/top-acquirers-ai-startups-ma-timeline/
[237] https://www.blog.google/topics/ai/ai-principles/

used will have a significant impact on society for many years to come. As a leader in AI, we feel a deep responsibility to get this right. So today, we're announcing seven principles to guide our work going forward. These are not theoretical concepts; they are concrete standards that will actively govern our research and product development and will impact our business decisions. We acknowledge that this area is dynamic and evolving, and we will approach our work with humility, a commitment to internal and external engagement, and a willingness to adapt our approach as we learn over time.

We believe that AI should:

1. Be socially beneficial.

Advances in AI will have transformative impacts in a wide range of fields, including healthcare, security, energy, transportation, manufacturing, and entertainment. As we consider potential development and uses of AI technologies, we will take into account a broad range of social and economic factors, and will proceed where we believe that the overall likely benefits substantially exceed the foreseeable risks and downsides. AI also enhances our ability to understand the meaning of content at scale. We will strive to make high-quality and accurate information readily available using AI, while continuing to respect cultural, social, and legal norms in the countries where we operate. And we will continue to thoughtfully evaluate when to make our technologies available on a non-commercial basis.

2. Avoid creating or reinforcing unfair bias.

AI algorithms and datasets can reflect, reinforce, or reduce unfair biases. We recognize that distinguishing fair from unfair biases is not always simple, and differs across cultures and societies. We will seek to avoid unjust impacts on people, particularly those related to sensitive characteristics such as race, ethnicity, gender, nationality, income, sexual orientation, ability, and political or religious belief.

3. Be built and tested for safety.

We will continue to develop and apply strong safety and security practices to avoid unintended results that create risks of harm. We will design our AI systems to be appropriately cautious, and seek to develop them in accordance with best practices in AI safety research. In appropriate cases, we will test AI technologies in constrained environments and monitor their operation after deployment.

4. Be accountable to people.

We will design AI systems that provide appropriate opportunities for feedback, relevant explanations, and appeal. Our AI technologies will be subject to appropriate human direction and control.

5. Incorporate privacy design principles.
We will incorporate our privacy principles in the development and use of our AI technologies. We will give opportunity for notice and consent, encourage architectures with privacy safeguards, and provide appropriate transparency and control over the use of data.

6. Uphold high standards of scientific excellence.

Technological innovation is rooted in the scientific method and a commitment to open inquiry, intellectual rigor, integrity, and collaboration. AI tools have the potential to unlock new realms of scientific research and knowledge in critical domains like biology, chemistry, medicine, and environmental sciences. We aspire to high standards of scientific excellence as we work to progress AI development. We will work with a range of stakeholders to promote thoughtful leadership in this area, drawing on scientifically rigorous and multidisciplinary approaches. And we will responsibly share AI knowledge by publishing educational materials, best practices, and research that enable more people to develop useful AI applications.

7. Be made available for uses that accord with these principles. Many technologies have multiple uses. We will work to limit potentially harmful or abusive applications. As we develop and deploy AI technologies, we will evaluate likely uses in light of the following factors:

- *Primary purpose and use: the primary purpose and likely use of a technology and application, including how closely the solution is related to or adaptable to a harmful use*
- *Nature and uniqueness: whether we are making available technology that is unique or more generally available*
- *Scale: whether the use of this technology will have significant impact*
- *Nature of Google's involvement: whether we are providing general-purpose tools, integrating tools for customers, or developing custom solutions*

AI applications we will not pursue

In addition to the above objectives, we will not design or deploy AI in the following application areas:

1. *Technologies that cause or are likely to cause overall harm. Where there is a material risk of harm, we will proceed only where we believe that the benefits substantially outweigh the risks, and will incorporate appropriate safety constraints.*
2. *Weapons or other technologies whose principal purpose or implementation is to cause or directly facilitate injury to people.*
3. *Technologies that gather or use information for surveillance violating internationally accepted norms.*
4. *Technologies whose purpose contravenes widely accepted principles of international law and human rights.*

We want to be clear that while we are not developing AI for use in weapons, we will continue our work with governments and the military in many other areas. These include cybersecurity, training, military recruitment, veterans' healthcare, and search and rescue. These collaborations are important and we'll actively look for more ways to augment the critical work of these organizations and keep service members and civilians safe.

AI for the long term

While this is how we're choosing to approach AI, we understand there is room for many voices in this conversation. As AI technologies progress, we'll work with a range of stakeholders to promote thoughtful leadership in this area, drawing on scientifically rigorous and multidisciplinary approaches. And we will continue to share what we've learned to improve AI technologies and practices.

We believe these principles are the right foundation for our company and the future development of AI. This approach is consistent with the values laid out in our original Founders' Letter back in 2004. There we made clear our intention to take a long-term perspective, even if it means making short-term tradeoffs. We said it then, and we believe it now.

While these principles from Google represent the stated position of one of the key players shaping and using AI on a global scale, many questions remain about the best framework for using AI and guiding its development. Even if we accept the principles from a commercial organisation, what about the potential for other actors to subvert the technology? Do we need to consider national or even international regulation, for example at UN level? National regulation is the most likely outcome, as I expect different countries will move at different paces and want different things from. But even at national level, agreeing the shape of regulation will not be easy.

Regulation?

"I am not an advocate for frequent changes in laws and Constitutions. But laws and institutions must go hand in hand with the progress of the human mind. As that becomes more developed, more enlightened, as new discoveries are made, new truths discovered and manners and opinions change, with the change of circumstances, institutions must advance also to keep pace with the times. We might as well require a man to wear still the coat which fitted him when a boy as civilized society to remain ever under the regimen of their barbarous ancestors."

Thomas Jefferson

"The reality is that government, for a long period of time, has for whatever set of reasons become less functional and isn't working at the speed that it once was. And so it does fall, I think, not just on business but on all other areas of society to step up."

Tim Cook[238], CEO, Apple

There isn't a legal system in the world equipped to deal with the wave of technologies enabled by robots and Artificial Intelligence. Few countries have legislation relating to robots. In fact, most legal systems date back closer to the invention of the steam engine than the GPU or TPU. Industries such as aviation and pharmaceuticals are heavily regulated because of the potential for harm but they are more straightforward to regulate due to the physical nature of their products. At present, there is little specific regulation of Internet companies and their intangible or even ephemeral services. Yet politicians and lawmakers are sometimes afraid of clampdowns for fear that the immensely valuable corporations will move to more permissive locations. It's hard to regulate bravely when the companies are bigger than many countries (in terms of population or revenues vs GDP) and location is far less important than it was in the days of worker immobility and physical resource requirements.

While initiatives such as the European Union's GDPR are an answer to some modern challenges, the majority of rules so far are self-enforced by the companies themselves, and much of this work is already done with the help of AI. With the quantities of material being posted, it is very difficult to monitor it in real time without some automation. YouTube, for example, removed 8 million videos in Q4 2017 - 81% were flagged by an algorithm, not a human reporting them, and 75% were removed before first view. However, YouTube plans to employ some 10,000 human content moderators. Facebook removed 21 million pieces of lewd content in Q1 2018, 96% by algorithm.

I hope and expect that we'll soon see attempts to impose additional regulation on the use of AI. This will likely take the form of controls over the use of AI in public sector, as well as requirements in the

---

[238] https://www.fastcompany.com/40460059/tim-cook-since-the-government-isnt-doing-it-apple-has-a-moral-responsibility-to-help-grow-the-economy

areas of transparency, data quality and explainability for companies offering consumer services. Such frameworks will help ensure the responsible evolution of AI, but will be challenging to enshrine in law as regulators struggle to define their reach.

Politics & Tech

"I have a foreboding of an America in my children's or grandchildren's time - when the United States is a service and information economy; when awesome technological powers are in the hands of a very few and no one representing the public interest can even grasp the issues"

Carl Sagan, 1995

One of the key reasons regulators can't keep up is that the politicians to whom the regulators report are frequently out of touch with current developments. While the issues at hand are admittedly technically complex, few administrations seem able to put in place a consultative or advisory framework to include experts and stakeholders. High profile attempts to control technology giants often serve only to expose the lack of understanding among politicians of the big picture: policymakers themselves admit they aren't fully prepared to deal with the issues. At a May 2018 hearing on Quantum Computing, *Rep. Adam Kinzinger thought their highly technical testimony might as well have been delivered in a foreign language. "I can understand about 50 percent of the things you say,"* the Illinois Republican *confessed*[239].

Trouble Ahead?

"This is one of the greatest policy challenges of our generation, and one of the biggest gaps in the prospectus across the political spectrum. Faced with challenges that are so big and complex, it's easy to see why politicians and policymakers often end up

---

[239] https://www.washingtonpost.com/news/the-switch/wp/2018/06/06/i-can-understand-about-50-percent-of-the-things-you-say-how-congress-is-struggling-to-get-smart-on-tech/?noredirect=on&utm_term=.722eda97b200

paralysed, look to the past, or take only the most cautious of steps forward. This is a gross abdication of responsibility: the technologies around us cannot be un-invented and must be responded to confidently and with clarity of purpose. To navigate this world, and ensure that power is wielded responsibly and for the greater good, we will need new ways to think about the relationship between algorithms and the people whose lives are affected by their outputs."

Tony Blair Institute for Global Change[240]

Proclamations of a technology as the next big thing or panacea rarely turn out to be true, at least not at the rate promised by proponents. But eventually, technology tends to cause massive change and we're rapidly reaching a point where the influence wielded by technology companies is attracting a lot of attention - much of it from Governments and regulators. To pre-empt or at least minimize unfavourable legislation, Apple, Amazon, Facebook and Google spent over $12m on political lobbying in the 2nd quarter of 2017 as they sought to influence US policy[241].

Tension between the law and technology is not new. Those in positions of regulatory power can't see the future with any greater certainty than those in the technology companies trying to build it. The involvement of Government in technology is not simple - the Internet itself is an outcome of Government investment in innovation. So who is qualified to draw up the laws for the unclear future? As the 2018 US Senate hearings into Facebook exposed[242], many lawmakers are not sufficiently conversant with day to day technology to be credible in overseeing advanced areas such as Artificial Intelligence.

If the leaders of the top three companies in the world all say that AI is key to the future, should we believe them? Yes, it may be in their interests as the leaders in this field to hype it, but it's also likely that they genuinely see it as a means to continue their dominance. Those

---

[240] https://institute.global/insight/renewing-centre/technology-many-public-policy-platform-better-fairer-future

[241] https://soprweb.senate.gov/index.cfm?event=getFilingDetails&filingID=8CF63BDB-F5A6-4547-8A3B-3E24714DC8FF&filingTypeID=60

[242] https://www.vox.com/policy-and-politics/2018/4/10/17222062/mark-zuckerberg-testimony-graham-facebook-regulations

involved in technology frequently don't help their cause, talking either only in obtuse acronyms to sound clever or using over-hyped marketing that doesn't reflect the reality. As long as tech evolution is driven primarily by profit potential, there'll be a suspicion that, without oversight, technology will struggle to deliver unalloyed benefits for wider humanity without oversight. Pulling back the curtain is hard, as the obtuse acronyms may in fact hide technological complexity little short of magic. And the desire for profits (which are necessary to fund research which is expensive and prone to failure) vies with regulatory regimes that no longer fully grasp what they are regulating.

The original Industrial Revolution produced a vast number of new inventions, which in turn saw new fields of law come into being. From steam boiler regulations to patent law, there was a big effort to provide a normative framework for the opportunities and risks facing a newly industrialized society. With AI, we may see calls for a similar regulatory upheaval to control this "new steam".

There are those who believe that attempts to regulate dominant companies are unnecessary - history tells us that the dominance will come to a natural end. But that is to project the past onto the future as if nothing has changed. The dominance of the current giants and their associated cash, technology and talent resources means they have a better chance than any predecessors to identify and harness the next big thing that might in previous generations have been their undoing. Whether they have the regulatory influence and public support remains to be seen.

Facial Recognition

"Perhaps as much as any advance, facial recognition raises a critical question: what role do we want this type of technology to play in everyday society?"

Brad Smith, President, Microsoft

Delving deeper into the regulatory challenges around one specific area of technology, let's consider facial recognition in more detail. Unlike, say, fingerprints, it requires no close physical contact and you are unlikely to be aware of its being active in many cases. Deep-learning powered improvements to Facial Recognition technology coupled with the prevalence of cameras raises many questions about the potential and acceptable implementations.

Facial recognition tech has been around in some form for decades, but it has been progressing dramatically in recent years due to advances in computing vision powered by AI technologies. Facial recognition is also evolving beyond basic identification to include emotion evaluation and detection of suspicious behaviour. But these advances quickly raise concerns over privacy and civil liberties - when used for finding a missing person or apprehending a criminal or terrorist, facial recognition can seem like a powerful, positive tool. But in order to do that, it can also track any person's location and movements and it can be used to notice associations and patterns.

Facial recognition is advancing quickly but remains far from perfect. As reported widely in mid-2018, biases have been found in the performance of several face recognition technologies, when deployed. The technologies worked more accurately for white men than for white women and were more accurate in identifying persons with lighter complexions than people of colour. Google's Cloud boss Diane Greene told the BBC[243] *"We need to be really careful about how we use this kind of technology. We're thinking really deeply. The humanistic side of AI - it doesn't have the diversity it needs and the data itself will have some inherent biases, so everybody's working to understand that."*

Who are you looking at?

We humans are generally excellent at recognising faces - at a glance being able to identify people we know, even if it's quite some time since we've seen them. We can tell a lot about their state of mind from their expression. But now technology is rapidly catching up with our human ability to recognise and read faces. Except it has greater abilities to store and recall faces. We can't recall every face we see walking down the street or at a football stadium. Yet technology can pick the face of a wanted criminal out of a crowd of 30,000 people.

---

[243] https://www.bbc.co.uk/news/technology-44977366

Our faces are public unlike say our fingerprints which are private - one big difference between faces and other biometric data, such as fingerprints, is that they work at a distance. The EU's GDPR defines a faceprint as personal data that belongs to its owner and that its use requires consent, which may influence how widely it can be used.

In a July 2018 blog[244], Microsoft took the unusual step of calling for Government regulation of this particular area of AI technology:

"It seems especially important to pursue thoughtful government regulation of facial recognition technology, given its broad societal ramifications and potential for abuse. Without a thoughtful approach, public authorities may rely on flawed or biased technological approaches to decide who to track, investigate or even arrest for a crime. Governments may monitor the exercise of political and other public activities in ways that conflict with longstanding expectations in democratic societies, chilling citizens' willingness to turn out for political events and undermining our core freedoms of assembly and expression. Similarly, companies may use facial recognition to make decisions without human intervention that affect our eligibility for credit, jobs or purchases. All these scenarios raise important questions of privacy, free speech, freedom of association and even life and liberty."

We're likely to see a protracted debate over how to balance privacy and security - is a system like SAFR[245] (designed to use facial recognition to control access to school properties in an attempt to prevent school shootings) worth the associated loss of privacy? Is the security argument, which can be persuasive to many, the thin end of the wedge and a step towards a system like the Intelligent Classroom Behaviour Management System[246] being trialled in China, where students in a classroom are monitored for attendance and even attentiveness which can then be highlighted to teachers?

---

[244] https://blogs.microsoft.com/on-the-issues/2018/07/13/facial-recognition-technology-the-need-for-public-regulation-and-corporate-responsibility/

[245] https://www.wired.com/story/realnetworks-facial-recognition-technology-schools/

[246] https://www.techjuice.pk/this-school-scans-classrooms-every-30-seconds-through-facial-recognition-technology/

Figure 143: The Intelligent Classroom

Civil Liberties groups in the US and the UK have challenged the use of facial recognition by police forces. Citing invasion of privacy as well as poor accuracy from current systems, it is likely that we will see frequent court challenges.

Silkie Carlo, director of the civil liberties group Big Brother Watch, said: *"When the police use facial recognition surveillance they subject thousands of people in the area to highly sensitive identity checks without consent. We're hoping the court will intervene, so the lawless use of facial recognition can be stopped. It is crucial our public freedoms are protected"*

Dr Suzanne Shale, who chairs the London Policing Ethics Panel said: *"We have made a series of key recommendations, which we think should be addressed before any further trials are carried out. We believe it is important facial recognition technology remains the subject of ethical scrutiny."*

Beyond the Face

It's also worth noting that recognition technology is continuing to evolve. While some researchers are exploring the potential to even identify covered faces[247], in January 2018, Facebook's AI Research team published a paper[248] describing a method to not only detect humans in pictures, but to also make 3D models of their bodies by estimating the positions of their torsos and limbs. Called DensePose, it's a CNN trained on over 50,000 images of humans that were specifically labelled for the project. Although intended for use in animation or virtual reality, pose estimation could be used to extend surveillance systems to look for certain movements or actions. For example, a group of U.K. and Indian researchers has been developing a drone-mounted system aimed at detecting violence within crowds of people. In small groups of people, it is 94% accurate at identifying violent actions[249].

Figure 144: Facebook DensePose can determine body pose even through clothes

[247] https://arxiv.org/abs/1708.09317

[248] https://research.fb.com/publications/densepose-dense-human-pose-estimation-in-the-wild/

[249] https://spectrum.ieee.org/tech-talk/robotics/artificial-intelligence/ai-drone-learns-to-detect-brawls

Images: University of Cambridge/National Institute of Technology/Indian Institute of Science/IEEE

The Drone Surveillance System highlights violent individuals in red and neutral individuals in cyan.

Figure 145: A drone detecting violent behaviour in a crowd (see website for colour version)

Access to AI

"Technological Progress without an equivalent progress in human institutions can doom us"

Barack Obama

Currently, only a handful of giant businesses in the world have access to the talent and budgets needed to fully appreciate the advancements of ML and other AI solutions. Creating advanced machine learning models is a very specialist skill. But despite its complexity, access to AI is surprisingly easy. Much of the complexity has been successfully abstracted - many useful pretrained models are available on demand, with the barrier to entry being lowered continuously as Google, Amazon and Microsoft expose their services to developers on a pay-as-you-go basis via relatively simple to use APIs.

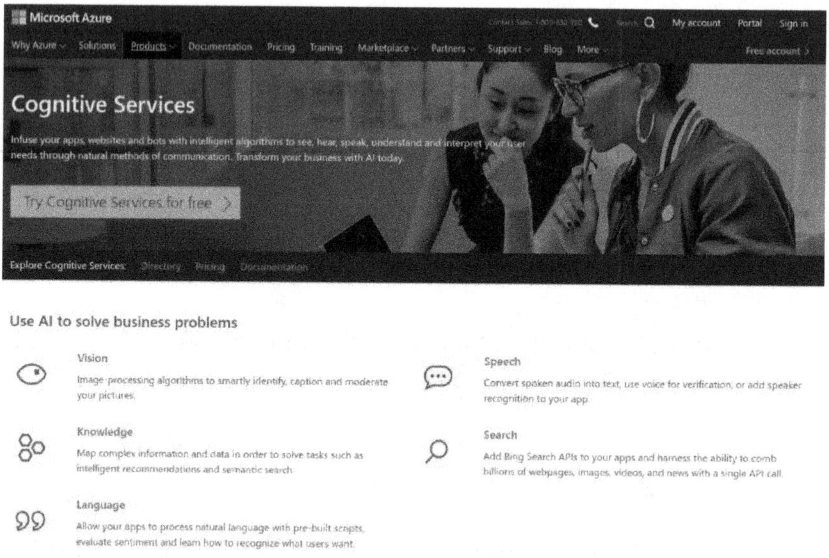

Figure 146: An example of Microsoft's Cognitive Services Website for Developers - AI on Demand

As a powerful enabling technology that will be embedded with varying degrees of visibility, success and speed across virtually all sectors, it's vital to remember that's what it is - a tool. It's not an end-game in itself. Just like, for example, relational databases, it will come to be used by virtually all businesses and Governments. But to be effective, it needs to be part of an overall technology, business and human strategy.

As with Internet solutions before it, there is a low barrier to entry to develop AI solutions, but it requires a high level of technical knowledge. This is an important difference from mobile apps, which also have a low barrier to develop. Where app stores are marred by numerous poor-quality apps, unless you are a serious developer with access to significant data, you won't be able to do much with machine learning in terms of developing and training new models.

It's worth sounding a note of caution though around these alluring efforts to "democratise" AI via these huge datasets, pre-trained models, and readily available cloud APIs. The notion of off-the-shelf AI may lure people into thinking there is no need for business analysis, technical understanding or awareness of issues such as the data bias discussed in this chapter. While it's very encouraging that so much AI technology is broadly available, it also increases the risk of misuse.

Chapter 10: Conclusions

"The future will be moving faster than today. The rate of change that we will experience 5 years from now will be meaningfully higher that the rate of change we experience today. The world is continuing to speed up relative to the rate at which people can adjust"

Astro Teller, Head of Moonshots at X[250]

There's never any shortage of people claiming that some new technology is going to change everything. But just as with the boy who cried wolf, eventually it comes true. Computers that can see, hear, talk and think change everything. It's like we're sharing the planet with a new species. Depending on how the technologies are harnessed, it will rapidly change many of the assumptions that shape our lives. But so far only a small percentage of people understand it, a very small percentage of people have created it and an even smaller percentage are deciding how it will be used.

Around 2007, a number of pre-existing technologies: mobile CPUs, wireless networking, GPS, touch screens, social networks and mobile payments, simultaneously became "good enough" and affordable for a mass audience. In the decade since then we've reached the point of over 3.5 billion people having smartphones and modern life becoming very much dependent on them.

Ten years later, it's happening again. The enabling technologies this time around are massive computing power, sensors, datasets, machine learning, computer vision and speech recognition - collectively giving us AI. These just recently crossed the "good enough" line and will continue to improve exponentially. The twin key ingredients of AI's rise, increased computing speed and increased datasets, will continue to drive AI's march into new realms. Concomitant advances in robotics, genetics and materials will likely both utilise and influence AI's evolution as change accelerates.

---

[250] https://x.company/

Framing AI

The frequent overuse of "AI" when referring to any solution that makes any kind of deduction or prediction has been a major cause of hype that obscures much of the discussion of the topic. Because of frequent overuse, people instinctively associate data science projects with near perfect human-like autonomous solutions. Or, at a minimum, people perceive that data science can easily solve their specific predictive need, without any regard to whether their organisational data will support such a model.

AI isn't a single product or capability. In ways, it is useful to compare it to another enabling technology like relational databases. Corporations don't set out to use SQL, but virtually all do as it is such a flexible tool that is harnessed in different ways to create systems without users being aware. You wouldn't set out to use AI for its own sake, just as you shouldn't set out to use say a database. It's a capability you leverage to solve a problem. It may solve previously insoluble problems. You should set out to use the tools that are most likely to lead to the best results, then you factor in your ability to use those tools and the costs.

AI-powered technologies are an accelerating torrent of disruptions that will shape our future. The era of easy adoption is over, and we now have to prepare for an era of adaptation - ready to adapt to new realities and ready to reconsider previously immutable assumptions. And while these approaching changes are driven by technology, it's not really about technology, but more about how society chooses to harness technology: who makes those decisions, for whose benefit and at whose cost.

So far, we've talked about computers gaining senses in isolation, and even then, the results are proving dramatic. But work has already begun[251] on fusing these senses so that computers can start to see, hear and read in a holistic way, more like humans do. As this work progresses, it will seem like AI is expanding from its current narrow confines, further challenging and changing our relationship with technology.

---

[251] https://arxiv.org/abs/1706.05137

Our Relationship with New Computers

At an Amazon product unveiling, the head of Echo told assembled reporters that *"today's kids won't remember a time when they couldn't speak to their house"*. That's a startling development. The next generation will grow up where talking to computers is perfectly normal and expect that the device will respond instantly and accurately to their every command. We need to redefine our relationship as we reimagine the role of what we've thus far called computers. Though likely still a long way from being fully sentient, the addition of senses changes their role dramatically.

Anthropomorphism

Anthropomorphism is the attribution of human traits, emotions, or intentions to non-human entities. We react differently to computers or robots that display what we consider to be human behaviours - either in how the speak or how they look. After decades of aspirational and sometimes overly enthusiastic anthropomorphism, we are now finally seeing computers that can see, listen, talk and even being to think. Their movements are getting better too, as robots such as those from Boston Dynamics walk, run and even do somersaults[252] while OpenAI uses machine learning to mimic human dexterity[253].

But anthropomorphism is a dangerous if beguiling distraction - it's overly simplistic to equate form and function - their abilities are more significant than their shape. Just because we can't see the technology, we shouldn't underestimate it - hidden behind the tiny form factors of our earphones, smartphones or speakers that contain an Assistant are massive data centres with some of the most powerful computers ever created. Just because Alexa or Google Duplex sound human and can carry on natural conversations with us (albeit in limited domains) does not mean we should treat them like a human. Yet some surveys report that 41% of people speak to Alexa as if she were a person or a friend. This is backed up by 1990s research called the Computers as Social Actors (CASA) paradigm[254]. According to

---

[252] https://www.youtube.com/watch?v=fRj34o4hN4I

[253] https://blog.openai.com/learning-dexterity/

[254] Computers as social actors. In INTERACT'93 and CHI'93 conference

the CASA paradigm, people respond to technologies as though they were human, despite knowing that they are interacting with a machine. Thus, people ascribe personalities to computers and even apply politeness norms to these interactions. Clifford Nass, Associate Professor of Communication at Stanford, has written extensively[255] on how adults logically reject anthropomorphism of personal computers but there is clear evidence that individuals mindlessly apply social rules and expectations to computers.

From Commands to Conversations

"We wanted Alexa to be compassionate and then helpful—to give the customer the kind of information they needed. In the case of depression, it was the depression and suicide hotline number"

Toni Reid, VP of Alexa Experience and Echo Devices[256]

The continued conversation feature discussed earlier is an important step along the way to more natural conversations without the need to say 'Alexa' or 'Hey Google' between each phrase. While we're still quite a long way from being able to have a natural, flowing, meandering conversation on wide ranging topics, Amazon is offering a $3.5m prize fund[257] for the advancement of this technology. Amazon is also tackling sensitive topics, such as depression, finding that in some cases, people are more willing to initially open up to the invisible AI which can then advise they seek help.

---

companion on Human factors in computing systems

[255] http://ldt.stanford.edu/~ejbailey/02_FALL/ED_147X/Readings/nass-JOSI.pdf

[256] https://www.wsj.com/articles/alexa-can-you-prevent-suicide-1508762311

[257] https://developer.amazon.com/alexaprize

The Human Touch

"Life moves pretty fast. If you don't stop and look around once in a while, you could miss it."

Ferris Bueller

A side effect of the growth of technology has been the reduction of direct human interaction. Although it enables free video chats around the world, it also tends to isolate us from the people around us, removing the need for many social moments. If walking in to an Amazon Go store, picking what you want and walking out without stopping at a till is efficient, what will we do with the time we would have spent talking to a cashier? If instead of spending that saved time on another more valuable to us social encounter, we spend it playing a video game, do we risk blunting our social skills? In a world where it often seems tolerance is decreasing, the relentless march towards efficiency at the expense of human interactions may lead to isolation if we don't consciously choose to seek social encounters.

Writer Mark Wilson[258] presents an interesting perspective on the impact of ceding too much control to algorithms: *"These sorts of advancements may seem thrilling—or at least benignly helpful—at first. But what do they all add up to? At what point does Google's power of suggestion grow so strong that it's not about how well its services anticipate what we want, but how much we've internalized their recommendations—and think of them as our own? Most of the conversation around artificial intelligence today is focused on what happens when robots think like humans. Perhaps we should be just as concerned about humans thinking like robots."*

---

[258] https://medium.com/fast-company/google-you-auto-complete-me-7f1836353a55

Negative Technology

"Technological development now outpaces our ability to adapt to it, which has caused a flare in our anxiety about technology and its impact. While the temptation may be to try and slow down technological progress, the best antidote to this anxiety is to remember that society has the power to shape new technologies."

Obi Felten, Head of Getting Moonshots Ready for Contact with the Real World, X[259]

In the previous chapter, we talked about the ethical issues of AI. When it comes to our relationship with technology, we've already demonstrated our inability to use technology in moderation; indeed, both Google and Apple have added features to their dominant mobile phone operating systems to encourage us to spend less time on our devices. Depending on which survey[260] you believe, people either check their phone every 12 minutes or touch, swipe or tap their phone 2,617 times a day. As our dependence on technology grows, it's leading to "continuous partial attention", severely limiting people's ability to focus, and possibly lowering IQ. Doug Tompkins[261], founder of The North Face, claims that rather than adding to our knowledge, computers and smartphones represent *"deskilling devices; they make us dumber"*. Another study[262] showed that the mere presence of smartphones damages cognitive capacity – even when the device is turned off. Will AI make this better or worse?

I suspect it will make it worse, at least initially. As we experiment with delegating tasks to our AI, we will need time to adjust in order to learn to trust the AIssistant and let it get on with saving us time, and freeing us to spend time away from technology. If we can successfully cede agency to our digital helper, we can look forward to less direct interaction with the technology even as we become more dependent

---

[259] https://blog.x.company/living-in-modern-times-why-we-worry-about-new-technology-and-what-we-can-do-about-it-cf584632e549

[260] https://www.theguardian.com/technology/2017/oct/05/smartphone-addiction-silicon-valley-dystopia

[261] https://www.theguardian.com/sustainable-business/technology-stopped-evolution-destroying-world

[262] http://www.journals.uchicago.edu/doi/10.1086/691462

on it. What we may choose to do with any additional time we recoup is another question.

Business Faster Than the Speed of Thought

People running organisations today face a bigger challenge than they did with the emergence of the Internet some twenty years ago. It's harder to get your head around the changes AI technologies will bring on top of a connected world. Embedding AI across any traditional business requires significant investment in talent as well as far-reaching change initiatives. Many businesses will struggle to identify, collect and prepare the data required to train models, then turn inference into actionable insights. So too, they will struggle to reengineer their business to operate at the speed which the ambient computing generation will expect. The speed of change is unprecedented. Generational shifts now happen in months. A single killer app can be on half a billion phones before you can build a single response. If you get disintermediated by an AIssistant, you may never get your customer back. When customers stop making choices, how will you deal with their autonomous agents?

While the Internet changed how many businesses interacted with their customers, AI will change the speed of all their processes. Those who don't adapt will be overrun by the more nimble organisations who see the potential first. AI lets even small business operate on virtually any scale. Most businesses are limited by resources. How often do businesses have to decide on priorities based on whatever assessment they could cobble together with limited resources in limited timeframes? But what if instead of limited resources, an ML model gives you you the equivalent of 10,000 interns to rent by the hour from a distant datacentre? AI provides tools and techniques that every business should be aware of and planning to implement or watch as the consumer world speeds past them. Businesses that can't or won't take part, need to prepare for a life in the shadow of the speedsters. Business at the Speed of Thought is not enough.

Getting Ready

If that seems daunting, it is. But for context, how do you think the people running steam-powered factories felt when electricity arrived? Those who thought they could soldier on with steam engines failed. Those who thought they could simply replace steam engines with electric motors also failed. Those who changed their entire factory layout and processes succeeded. I have no doubt that different industries and different firms within the same industry will adopt AI at varying paces. But if you're not taking steps to understand it, assessing its potential and your readiness for it, then you're placing your business at great risk. AI won't replace managers, but managers who use AI will replace those who don't.

Measure What Matters

"The real danger of machine intelligence is that executives will make bad decisions about what machine intelligence capabilities to build."
O'Reilly State of AI[263]

Successful use of AI in an organisation is not easy - it requires a change in thinking more challenging than any previous technology deployment. And even then, the challenges of having the right data and/or models mean it can't be bought off the shelf like some previous technologies. The processes of appropriately framing a business problem, collecting and cleaning the data, building the model, implementing the result, and then monitoring for changes, are interconnected in many ways that often make it hard to suit traditional organisation structures. For businesses deciding where to apply AI, there's a real risk that they will choose to focus on the wrong metric but be very successful at achieving it.

Take the example of a hospital that tasked an AI with reviewing patient data with the goal of speedier discharges. In keeping with its training, the system duly made recommendations higher than the previous human tally. But in this case, a system that weighted data for readmissions more highly might have had a better overall outcome. Take another example - today most call centres operate

---

[263] https://www.oreilly.com/ideas/the-current-state-of-machine-intelligence-3-0

largely guided by the metric of Average Call Handling Time (ACHT). It's critical for the profitability of the call centre to reduce ACHT, in many cases even if the customer isn't fully satisfied. But in a centre "staffed" by AI, the cost of the operator becomes irrelevant. Now the metric can be customer satisfaction however long the call takes. The moral of the story is to be very careful what metric you're training your AI to achieve.

Pervasive and Predictive

We've exhausted our human ability to keep up with the speed and scale we now operate at, and the speed of computers is self-fuelling - we need ever more capable systems to keep up with the world we've envisaged. In fact, we now move so fast that, without computing embedded in virtually everything we do, life would come to a grinding halt. Such is our demand for instant gratification that computers can no longer even wait for us to signal our intent - they must anticipate what we are likely to want.

The End of Choosing or the End of Choice?

"When we allow complexity to be hidden and handled for us, we should at least notice what we are giving up. We risk becoming users of components. . .[as we] work with mechanisms that we do not understand in crucial ways. This not-knowing is fine while everything works as expected. But when something breaks or goes wrong or needs fundamental change, what will we do except stand helpless in the face of our own creations?"

Ellen Ullman, Life in Code

As technology gains the ability to sense, predict and respond to our needs and is being integrated into our natural behaviours, becoming both more pervasive and less overt, present wherever we are and always accessible, does this signal a step change in our cognitive load? Will we stop making those small decisions we don't even realise we make today? And if we do, are we happy to let go?

Shaving seconds off transactions/interactions that you would never have thought of as inconvenient may not seem important to you until that friction is removed and you realise its value and suddenly don't want to live without the advantage of it. Eventually, inevitably, technology reaches the point where it can't respond to us fast enough - then the only way to be faster is to anticipate.

Figure 147: Do you want your regular?

The shift towards shortcuts and prediction has begun. The first signs of daily or even hourly use of ML are here as our phone and its channelled assistant automate the ordering of your regular coffee. This removal of routine could be seen as an end to spontaneity (will you actually order a different coffee today?) but is balanced by convenience - both for you and for Starbucks.

The firms adding increasingly predictive AI will need to work out what's useful versus what's creepy. A proactive reminder that Mother's Day is coming might be useful if we've forgotten, but if we're in the wrong mood, we may feel it's an intrusive, overly commercial, opportunistic, cynical upsell. Answering questions before we ask may be the holy grail for Google, but many people are likely to resist, at least initially, attempts at being *too* smart for our liking.

Schrodinger's Future

We have a strange relationship with the future. The future will never actually be here, but in many ways, it sort of is. As we anticipate how technology will change the world, we live somewhere between the present and the future. You can never reach the future; it's always, well, the future. Yet what seemed futuristic or impossible until just recently is in many cases now routine. There are glimpses of the future all around us. Well, glimpses of a future anyway. Much writing treats the future as if it's some magical state that will suddenly appear, as if we will one day go to sleep in the present and wake up in a different future - either idyllic or dystopian, depending on your perspective. There are multiple possible futures, on an individual and collective basis, depending on the decisions and developments of today.

A Living Laboratory

Although as it develops, much of today's (and tomorrow's) tech is still quite disjointed; but for those who can piece together a possible or probable integrated outcome, it can be quite instructive as to where things *could* go. In Silicon Valley, two of the world's most valuable and AI-focused companies are headquartered within 10 miles of each other, alongside Stanford University and numerous start-ups. It shows in the surrounding towns, even for those without access to what's going on behind closed doors in their expansive labs - as conspicuous consumption vies with value signalling in a slightly uncomfortable living laboratory. Here, and in places like Seattle, where Amazon and Microsoft race to develop their AI solutions, you can already see autonomous cars, automated restaurants, delivery robots and flying cars (being tested) in a single day. What you can't see are the thousands of engineers working on AI technologies for use in commercial, government, healthcare and countless other areas.

The New Norm

"One of the great liabilities of life is that all too many people find themselves living amid a great period of social change and yet they fail to develop the new attitudes, the new mental responses that the new situation demands. They end up sleeping through a revolution."

Martin Luther King, 1968

Once a technology is launched, it is no longer considered "future" even though it would have seemed (and been) utterly impossible a few years ago - one generation's future is the next's norm. Most of what will constitute change, at least in the short to medium-term, is simply the spread of these niche or minority things to become more pervasive. New technology filters down rapidly - what starts as expensive is guaranteed to become cheap. The immutable law of electronics is that it becomes smaller, faster & cheaper.

Understanding how technologies permeate society is key to understanding and influencing the arrival of the future. Studies such as Everett's seminal Diffusion of Innovations (1962) provide a useful framework but the pattern of dissemination is not always as smooth as the models suggest. As technologies mature and the market decides if and how they should work together, there will be less of a need for patient and forgiving early adopters to stitch together the early building blocks as they emerge. But as technology embeds itself deeper into our lives, it is worth noting that technological developments are getting increasingly complex as the quick wins are largely gone. What we now talk of as the future requires growing levels of investment, access to larger data sets and bigger changes in consumer behaviour and acceptance, as boundaries such as privacy are tested, ostensibly in return for ever-greater convenience.

The future is about piecing together what we have to make what we want, while developing the things we still lack. It is a never-ending process. Much of the focus of technology is largely on solutions to first world problems, as they're what's immediately lucrative. But the technological dividend for the developing world will likely be greater in the next decades than in previous centuries, as access to innovation spreads. I've written here about the challenges and opportunities of integrating large scale technological change into our existing infrastructural constraints, and the Markovian nature of technology means that a fresh start (where it's possible) will accelerate our learnings for broader use. But in most cases, technology must fit into the existing world in a largely incremental, combinatorial manner.

My Future, Your Future, Our Future

"This scope is less about the realization of science-fiction dreams or nightmares of super-human machines, and more about the need for humans to understand and shape technology as it becomes ever more present and influential in their daily lives. Moreover, in this understanding and shaping there is a need for a diverse set of voices from all walks of life, not merely a dialog among the technologically attuned. Focusing narrowly on human-imitative AI prevents an appropriately wide range of voices from being heard."

Prof. Michael Jordan, UC Berkeley[264]

It's important to remember that individuals and societies will embrace the future at very different rates, which will cause tensions. Individual conveniences are not necessarily compatible with the cumulative greater good. Take a look around at the direction technology is heading and don't assume that the future is some distant concept, unrelated to today - the glimpses are there. If we do wake up in a future and don't like it, we may be sorry we didn't pay more attention to defining the future, starting today.

---

[264] https://medium.com/@mijordan3/artificial-intelligence-the-revolution-hasnt-happened-yet-5e1d5812e1e7

What do you want from AI?

"Ultimately the question is not only what computers can do. It's what computers should do"

Microsoft, The Future Computed[265]

The promise of many of our digital gadgets has been to help us achieve more, more quickly. While the advent of the internet and the smartphone has put incredible abilities at our fingertips, it has also brought with it a number of questions about the impact of technology on individuals and on society. Just as we grapple with many of these issues, we face an onslaught of new, perhaps more insidious technologies, which pose even greater challenges to our futures, alongside their alluring promises of massive benefits.

Maybe the simplest question is what do we want from AI?

- To cater to our whim
- To eliminate jobs
- To eliminate car crashes
- To solve medical challenges
- To reduce crime
- All of the above?

Or to look at it the other way, what do we not want from AI?

- To automate away all the jobs
- To enable constant surveillance
- To create autonomous weapons
- To curtail freedom and spontaneity
- All of the above?

---

[265] https://blogs.microsoft.com/blog/2018/01/17/future-computed-artificial-intelligence-role-society/

The speed and scale of innovation mean that we can no longer afford to take a wait-and-see approach. The questions being asked of us by technology are coming faster than we have answers - but opting out is not a solution in the absence of an answer.

Seeking Answers

Digital technology has become critical to the personal and economic well-being of everyone on the planet, but decisions about how it is designed, operated and developed have never been voted on by anyone.

Wall Street Journal[266]

As I've researched this book, it's become clear to me that we are rushing head first into the beginnings of an AI-powered world with surprisingly little awareness and almost no widespread debate about its implications. There is a real risk that the opacity of the technology may lead people to opt out of debates about its implementation. But we are in need of a wider debate about how and when to use this new toolset. The decisions of AI teams at a few large tech companies, with unprecedented reach, are driving the agenda for a largely disinterested populace. We can't expect its creators to have all the answers or domain expertise to oversee its effective deployment in areas as diverse as military, medical, legal and government sectors.

Why It's important to talk about the future

Technology - it's been about getting smaller, faster, cheaper - but now it's about taking on new tasks. The next decade will see a battle between companies expanding the reach of technology and consumers juggling the compromises of convenience and intrusiveness. At what point does it go from friend to foe? From helpful to invasive, from efficient to replacive from support to surveillance.

The technological quick wins are gone, the easy integrations are over. We're now facing existential, fundamental changes. How we

---

[266] https://www.wsj.com/articles/can-the-tech-giants-be-stopped-1500057243

choose to develop and use our new capabilities is one of the biggest challenges facing humanity today and our decisions will shape generations to come. Embracing them, even with regulation and control, is no guarantee of survival. But choosing to ignore them is a guarantee of serious trouble ahead. As I've pointed out earlier in the book, the era of easy adoption is over, and we now should prepare for an era of adaptation; ready to adapt to new realities and ready to reconsider previously immutable assumptions. And while these approaching changes are driven by technology, it's not really about technology - but more about how society chooses to harness technology; who makes those decisions and for whose benefit.

On the surface, computers that predict our whims and cater to them are a good thing. But at what price will such speedy convenience come? New AI advances enable faster and more profound progress across virtually every area of human endeavour, but may be concentrated in the hands of even fewer people than previous revolutions, which augurs poorly for those who aren't involved or at least aware of the changes.

How Soon?

"What I want is to have people understand how urgent it is, when this thing shows up, to have made a plan."

Robin Hanson, Author[267]

---

[267] https://www.theguardian.com/commentisfree/2016/may/24/robots-future-work-humans-jobs-leisure

For those who still believe that AI is not an immediate issue, tech commentator Ben Evans has a useful analogy for emerging technology taken from the building industry:

New tech is like a skyscraper: months messing about in a hole doing 'nothing', then frame shoots up in a week, then months fitting out. The period where dramatic progress is visible is not the only or most important part of innovation around new primary tech.

Ben Evans[268]

Generally, when discussing emerging technologies, we tend to overestimate the effect of a technology in the short run and underestimate the effect in the long run - this is known as Amara's Law.[269] For example, just 10 years ago, an assertion that 3 billion people would have a computer in their pocket with more power than a supercomputer and access to millions of apps would have seemed ludicrous. But it's only taken 10 years for the smartphone to reach this prevalence and now it seems perfectly normal.

While there is much optimism around the future potential benefits of AI technologies, there's a mixture of uncertainty, pessimism and even fear around the timing of the transition. Sceptics compare technology promises with Zeno's Dichotomy paradox:[270] every leap will take us halfway to our destination without ever reaching it. And while it's true that it may take longer than promised or expected to arrive, each step brings its own challenges - should we work with what we have now, or keep waiting for the always-to-come better product? What is good enough?

---

[268] https://twitter.com/BenedictEvans/status/872729507429367808?s=09
[269] https://en.wikipedia.org/wiki/Roy_Amara
[270] https://en.wikipedia.org/wiki/Zeno%27s_paradoxes#Dichotomy_paradox

Progress or Change

"It's vital we understand this new language, and what it's increasingly telling us, for the ramifications are set to alter everything we take for granted about the way our globalized economy functions, and the ways in which we as humans exist within it."

Scott Scantens, Author[271]

We will soon be sharing the world with computers that bear little resemblance to how we've used the term in the past. A world that is built around you, proxied for you by your agent. A world that predicts what you need and what you want. Many will feel that some of the joys will be lost while others will argue that time will be freed up.

For anyone seeking solace in the principles for responsible AI such as those from Google discussed earlier, remember that the Google AI principles refer to norms. And of course, norms change over time. Norms are based on what's technologically been possible up to a given time, and typically lag the actual capabilities of technology.

Most people have no heuristics, rules, or even checklists to assist in deciding what technology to adopt and what to avoid. Many purchase decisions are based on what's cool, popular or affordable more than being a considered choice to acquire something we have assessed as likely to make us happier or more productive. But AI isn't just a personal technology. As we've seen repeatedly, it is a technology increasingly at home in society-level apparatus. Sci-fi author Frederik Pohl once said: *"A good science fiction story should be able to predict not the automobile but the traffic jam."* For AI, any prediction of increasing speed should be accompanied with a clear consideration of any traffic jams it collaterally creates.

The pace of change can be more about human than technical factors. How we assimilate technology - the transition to a future is the issue. It's not a switch that happens overnight. While machine learning won't replace humans, it will change things for humanity. These are the

---

[271] https://medium.com/basic-income/deep-learning-is-going-to-teach-us-all-the-lesson-of-our-lives-jobs-are-for-machines-7c6442e37a49

technologies that will define the major computing projects of the coming decades, across areas as diverse as education, justice, healthcare and transport. But their lack of visibility does not diminish their importance. Just because AI might have started by being able to identify your friends in a Facebook feed, don't be fooled by these simple training grounds. The AI revolution is on the scale of the Industrial Revolution—probably larger and definitely faster.

Technology is now at the heart of everything we do. But as mechanical, electrical and computational systems have become increasingly complex, the control of everyday life is increasingly in the hands of those that build it. Are things complicated now beyond most people's' comprehension? Even their creators can't be sure how an AI will react in many cases.

In the last decade or so, billions if not trillions of dollars have been invested in all manner of technologies, gadgets and infrastructure to make our personal lives more convenient. We've sped up everything from shopping to television to food ordering to transport hailing, even turning on a light by voice instead of by switch. Once we get used to a new faster way of doing something, we rarely look back. But we also rarely stop to consider if faster is necessarily better. Using those terms as synonyms is a false equivalency. Faster almost inevitably comes with a cost - be it financial, social, physical or psychological. And despite our best intentions, we rarely choose to reinvest the time we've saved particularly wisely. I hope we choose at least occasionally to forgo the convenience and enjoy the sense of manual completion and achievement or revel in the serendipity of discovery rather than the convenience of routine.

"The dream of convenience is premised on the nightmare of physical work. But is physical work always a nightmare? Do we really want to be emancipated from all of it? Perhaps our humanity is sometimes expressed in inconvenient actions and time-consuming pursuits. Perhaps this is why, with every advance of convenience, there have always been those who resist it. They resist out of stubbornness, yes (and because they have the luxury to do so), but also because they see a threat to their sense of who they are, to their feeling of control over things that matter to them."

The New York Times[272]

AI: The Water is Boiling

"We are at an inflection point in our relationship with technology. Technology allows us to do amazing things that have immeasurably improved our lives. But at the same time, it's accelerated the pace of our lives beyond our ability to keep up. And it's getting worse."

Arianna Huffington[273]

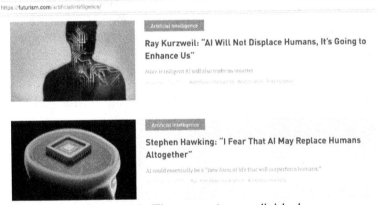

Figure 148: The experts are divided

272 https://www.nytimes.com/2018/02/16/opinion/sunday/tyranny-convenience.html
273 https://www.nbcnews.com/think/amp/ncna810246

AI, after many false dawns, is becoming very real in everyday life, and visible - if you know what to look for. A concerted effort from academics and corporates, the availability of massive quantities of data inputs for machine learning and rapid advances in processing power have brought us to an inflection point. AI and its various subset technologies are now sufficiently advanced to take on high-level decision-making tasks previously the preserve of humans - and to do them faster and more accurately than we can.

Yet, outside of tech circles and some dramatic dystopian headlines, I don't so far see much awareness of just how big a shift AI will cause. This strikes me as akin to the parable describing a frog being slowly boiled alive. The premise is that if a frog is put suddenly into boiling water, it will jump out, but if the frog is put in tepid water which is then brought to a boil slowly, it will not perceive the danger and will be cooked to death. After years of slow burn, where AI failed to deliver on its promise/threat of the science-fiction-style overthrow of humanity, the metaphorical water is getting very hot indeed.

There are those (such as Elon Musk and Stephen Hawking) who argue that we need to hop out of the water before it's too late, or at the very least take steps to control the rising temperature. Others, such as Facebook founder Mark Zuckerberg, believe that the benefits outweigh the risks and we can reap massive advantages in areas such as medicine. Many people may not like living in the predictive world created by AI - yes, there are benefits in waste reduction or efficiency, but people may struggle to cede control and spontaneity. What if people don't like the AI decisions? - not all human decisions are rational or in peoples' best interests or are for the greater good, but sometimes, common sense doesn't prevail and we reach decisions anyway that no well-trained model would.

AI and the debates about it may seem slightly abstract while the sentient artificial general intelligence portrayed in the movies remains firmly in the future. But make no mistake, huge advances in the technology mean it's already in our pockets, even if we don't realise it. AI tends to be used as a buzzword or blanket term. There's no need for most people to become an expert but blithely referring to "AI" is analogous to a CEO saying they know "business" without being able to differentiate between finance, marketing and logistics.

We should start cutting through the hype and trying to promote a conversation based on urgent issues. We've been through a so-called AI winter before, where promised solutions failed to materialise, and I'm sure we'll see the various applications of AI move along the hype curve, with some inevitable casualties along the way. For some, the curve may more resemble a game of snakes and ladders than a straight path. AI is likely neither a panglossian panacea nor a pandemic. The truth lies on a continuum - in some cases, it's already here, in others it may still be many years away. In most, it's coming somewhere between soon and very soon.

Should we hop away from AI? I personally don't think so, but I do believe we each need to give some serious thought to how we want to harness this next generation in computing capabilities. By not asking questions about artificial intelligence and its related fields, we relinquish a massive amount of control of the future. Anyone who ignores it may find themselves living in a world they don't like and wonder how they ended up there. The New Acceleration is happening - what will you do with it?

Note from the Author:
Thank you for reading this book! If you enjoyed it, I'd really appreciate a 5-star review on Amazon. Remember to visit the website to see colour version of all the figures and lease feel free to contact me via http://david-kerrigan.com with any suggestions you have for improvements.

DK, Dublin, September 2018

Glossary of Terms

AI - Artificial Intelligence is a broad term for machines that exhibit human-like levels of intelligence such as the ability to think or reason.

Amara's Law - the tendency for us to overestimate the impact of technology in the short term and underestimate it in the longer term.

ANI - Artificial Narrow Intelligence is a computer system that displays human-like abilities in a single domain - for example the ability to distinguish dog breeds in photographs. But it is narrow in that an AI system trained for that purpose is no good at another task.

AGI - Artificial General Intelligence is the aspirational concept of a computer system that displays human or superhuman abilities across multiple domains.

AMP - Accelerated Mobile Pages is a technology to make mobile web pages load faster

ANPR - Automatic Number Plate Recognition is a computer vision system used by police forces to identify number plates on cars so that cars can be located and identity checks can be run instantly.

API - Application Programming Interface is a way for computers to talk to each other and perform services for each other - for example Google might provide an API to which app developers could upload a photo and the AI system will return an answer to the app via the API.

ASR - Automatic Speech Recognition is the process of a computer recognising human speech either from a person talking or a recording of a person talking.

AR - Augmented Reality is a method of super-imposing computer-generated images so that they appear in the real world either via a Phone screen or glasses.

AV - Autonomous Vehicle is a self-driving car where a computer controls the car based on inputs from a variety of sensors.

Blockchain - is a ledger of records (blocks) linked by cryptography.

CNN - Convolutional Neural Networks are a form of deep learning frequently used for image recognition.

CPU - Central Processing Unit is the "brain" of a computer which does the calculations required to run software.

CTC - Connectionist Temporal Classification is a method of training recurrent neural networks that is popular in speech recognition tasks.

CV - Computer Vision is the field of computers understanding digital images and videos

DARPA - Defense Advanced Research Projects Agency is an agency of the United States Department of Defense responsible for the development of emerging technologies for use by the military. It is best known in civilian/technology circles for its role in the creation of the Internet.

DL - Deep Learning is a type of Machine Learning that uses multiple layers in a neural network to process information.

DRS - Dash Replenishment Service is an Amazon service to capture, process and fulfil automated product orders from hardware devices.

FLOPS - Floating Operations per second - a measure of speed for computers. Gigaflops is a billion flops (10^9)

FPGA - Field Programmable Gate Array is a type of computer chip that can be reprogrammed for different tasks

GAN - Generative Adversarial Networks are a type of machine learning framework where two neural networks contest with each other to produce a desired outcome - One network generates candidates (generative) and the other evaluates them (discriminative)

GPU - Graphics Processing Unit is a type of computer chip designed to complete rapid parallel calculations. Although originally designed for the high-speed creation of graphics, they have been found to be very effective at running machine learning algorithms when compared to traditional CPUs.

IOT - Internet of Things refers to various connected devices with Internet connectivity (beyond standard devices, such as desktops, laptops, smartphones and tablets) These can be any traditionally 'dumb' or non-internet-enabled physical devices and everyday objects. Enhanced with technology, these devices can communicate and interact over the Internet, and they can be remotely monitored and controlled.

LDA - Latent Dirichlet Allocation is a type of statistical topic model used to classify text in a document to a particular topic and is therefore useful in Natural Language Processing.

LSTM - Long Short Term Memory is a type of Recurrent Neural Network that is particularly useful for sequence prediction challenges. LSTM can remember previous inputs for longer than standard RNNs.

ML - Machine Learning is a subset of artificial intelligence which uses statistical techniques to give computers the ability to learn from data, without being explicitly programmed

MLP - Multilayer Perceptron is a basic type of neural network

Moravec's Paradox is the contention by AI and robotics researchers that, contrary to traditional assumptions, high-level reasoning requires very little computation, but low-level sensorimotor skills require enormous computational resources. For example, it's easier to build a computer to win at chess than a robot that can move like a one-year old human.

Moore's Law, which dates from 1965 is the observation that the number of transistors in a dense integrated circuit doubles about every two years.

NLG - Natural Language Generation is the process of computers generating natural language

NLP - Natural Language Processing is the field of computers being able to process and analyse human language text

NLU - Natural Language Understanding is the area of computers being able to understand human language text, such as comprehension of intent

Polanyi's Paradox refers to our ability to acquire knowledge that we can't quite explain - e.g. we can learn to ride a bike but can't really describe how we know how to do it.

PWA - Progressive Web Apps are web applications that are regular web pages or websites, but can appear to the user like native mobile apps, which tend to offer richer user experiences than web pages.

RFID - Radio Frequency Identification - electromagnetic tags usually used to track items.

RL - Reinforcement Learning is a type of machine learning where the software agents are rewarded for correct behaviours

RNN - Recurrent Neural Networks are a type of neural network with internal memory in each layer.

TPU - Tensor Processing Unit is a Google-designed computer chip intended for high speed Machine Learning processing

TTS - Text To Speech is the process of converting text into a synthesized computer voice output

UI - User Interface is the way we interact with computers - for example a common type of UI is a Graphical User Interface where we interact with a computer by pointing and clicking on graphical elements such as icons. Microsoft Windows is a common example of a GUI. Speech is an alternative UI.

VR - Virtual Reality refers to the creation of animated virtual/simulated worlds, visible and navigable by wearing a virtual reality headset. VR offers users an immersive, 360-degree experience,

Zettabyte - A zettabyte is a trillion gigabytes (or a billion terabytes)

Appendix 1: AI Learning Resources

There are amazing resources available to learn about AI technologies. Most of the key breakthroughs are published in scientific journals and there is very open access to the papers of top scientists and educational resources from the best institutions in the world. There are powerful tools you can download for free and get some hands-on experience of running Machine Learning on your own laptop or even your phone if you have a few hours to dedicate to the process.

I've included some links here to mainly free resources, as well as links to some paid online courses. Depending on your level of pre-existing knowledge, you may want to start with some introductory materials, or skip straight to the practical examples. I've also included links to the main AI services offered by the major providers via their APIs - most are free to try or use for small hobbyist projects.

While many courses assume a reasonably advanced knowledge of mathematics and/or familiarity with basic programming, simply following the detailed tutorials will, in many cases, enable you to experience some AI yourself.

Introductions to AI

If you have half an hour and want a good intro to AI from Silicon Valley Venture Capital firm Andressen Horowitz, check out: https://a16z.com/2016/06/10/ai-deep-learning-machines/

Then consider their AI Playbook which offers some useful guidance on using AI:
http://aiplaybook.a16z.com/

Good overview of DL: https://www.zdnet.com/article/what-is-deep-learning-everything-you-need-to-know/

McKinsey overview of AI:
https://www.mckinsey.com/business-functions/mckinsey-analytics/our-insights/an-executives-guide-to-ai

A nice short visual intro to ML Machine Learning:
http://www.r2d3.us/visual-intro-to-machine-learning-part-1/

An excellent AI overview:
https://medium.com/mmc-writes/the-fourth-industrial-revolution-a-primer-on-artificial-intelligence-ai-ff5e7fffcae1

Courses on AI

Machine Learning by Professor Andrew Ng on Coursera ($75 for certificate - 19 Hours)

Google Machine Learning Crash Course (Free - 15 Hours)

Bloomberg Foundations of Machine Learning Course with over 30 YouTube lectures (Free):
https://bloomberg.github.io/foml/#home

Online Services

https://cloud.google.com/products/ai/

https://azure.microsoft.com/en-us/overview/ai-platform/

https://aws.amazon.com/machine-learning/

Downloads to Try

https://www.tensorflow.org/tutorials/

Downloads for Developers Only

You need to be a developer to try this one:

Build a simple Android app for Image Recognition with Tensorflow
https://codelabs.developers.google.com/codelabs/tensorflow-for-poets/index.html#0

Other things to try

If you're not a developer but would like to try to build your own speech recognition or computer vision projects, try these kits from Google:
https://aiyprojects.withgoogle.com/

Interesting Links

A thought-provoking Speculative Design exercise from Google:
https://www.theverge.com/2018/5/17/17344250/google-x-selfish-ledger-video-data-privacy

Video of robot picker in a grocery warehouse:
https://www.bbc.com/news/av/technology-42158043/ocado-robot-picks-up-and-packs-supermarket-goods

An excellent resource on AI vs Human performance across multiple areas: https://www.eff.org/ai/metrics

The challenges of Designing for Voice Interactions:
https://design.google/library/conversation-design-speaking-same-language/

More details on data quality and bias:
https://developers.google.com/machine-learning/fairness-overview/
https://research.google.com/bigpicture/attacking-discrimination-in-ml/
https://cloud.google.com/inclusive-ml/

CPSIA information can be obtained
at www.ICGtesting.com
Printed in the USA
FSHW020953140920
73763FS

9 781727 097863